PELICAN BOOKS

A 578

THE THEORY AND PRACTICE OF COMMUNISM

R. N. Carew Hunt was born in 1890, the eldest son of Canon Carew Hunt of Christ Church, Oxford. He was educated at Bradfield College and Merton College, Oxford, and served as an officer in the Oxfordshire and Buckinghamshire Light Infantry in the First World War. Later he was employed at the War Office and then acted as an authority on international communism at the Foreign Office. He worked in the Civil Service from 1919 until his retirement in 1955, when he was elected a supernumerary fellow of St Antony's College, Oxford. On several occasions he delivered a course of lectures on communism at the School of Advanced International Studies, Johns Hopkins University, and was visiting lecturer during one semester at Indiana University. He was the author of a book on Calvin, and his books on communism, which have been translated into many languages, include *Marxism, Past and Present* and *A Guide to Communist Jargon*. R. N. Carew Hunt was married and had one son; he died in 1959.

R. N. CAREW HUNT

THE
THEORY AND PRACTICE
OF COMMUNISM

AN INTRODUCTION

With a Preface
by Leonard Schapiro

PENGUIN BOOKS

BALTIMORE · MARYLAND

Penguin Books Ltd, Harmondsworth, Middlesex, England
Penguin Books Inc., 3300 Clipper Mill Road, Baltimore 11, Md, U.S.A.
Penguin Books Pty Ltd, Ringwood, Victoria, Australia

—

First published by Geoffrey Bles 1950
Published in Pelican Books 1963
Reprinted 1963, 1964, 1966

—

—

Made and printed in Great Britain
by Hazell Watson & Viney Ltd,
Aylesbury, Bucks
Set in Linotype Times

Contents

CONTENTS

Preface

The Theory and Practice of Communism was first published in January 1950. It won instant acclaim, was reprinted several times, and revised editions appeared in June 1951 and finally in January 1957. The text reproduced for the present Pelican edition is that of the latest revision by the author, carried out in 1956.

It is not difficult to understand the success of Carew Hunt's study, to which generations of university students already owe their first acquaintance with marxism, and which has already become a classic of political exegesis. The subject is of burning topical interest, and is likely to remain so. No political and social doctrine has ever led to such passionate commitment for or against it. No theory of society which has an earthly utopia as its ultimate aim has ever been put into practice, or been claimed to have been put into practice, at what appears to the observer brought up in the liberal tradition an inordinate toll of human life and suffering. The faith in the ultimate attainability of the utopia still dominates many minds throughout the world. It is small wonder that some students of marxism have interpreted it as a religious or quasi-religious phenomenon, with parallels in its effects on the human mind and conduct in Christianity and Islam.

Whole libraries could be filled with books written about Marx and about his avowed followers in the Soviet Union, and now in China and elsewhere. Some of these volumes may have dealt with different aspects of Marx's economic, social, or political thought, or with the practice of his disciples in the Soviet Union, in greater depth, perhaps with greater insight, than Carew Hunt. But the subject is difficult, abstruse, and, except to the enthusiast or expert, often very dull. The facts are often controversial, difficult to establish for lack of evidence and overlaid with political bias from which only the most strictly disciplined and dispassionate analysis has been able to disengage them. Besides, the English reader, I think, recoils instinctively from studies which are partisan, and many of the simpler expositions of Marx and the marxists have suffered from this fault: they either accept on trust what the practical exponents of communism tell them are the facts, or else are so determined to take issue with communism that they do not fairly present the communists' case. Carew Hunt was no communist. It is difficult to think of a writer on politics who was more steeped in the liberal, empirical tradition of Locke and John Stuart Mill. I think it was because this tradition was so strong in him that he was able to expound views, many of which he did not himself accept, so fairly and objectively. He argues with Marx and Lenin, argues with them from the standpoint of one to whom no political dogma is acceptable on trust, or as a faith: it must stand up to the logic of argument, or be rejected. He believed, I think, in the words of Locke, that 'the strength of our persuasions are no evidence at all of their own rectitude: crooked things may be as stiff and inflexible as straight, and men may be as positive and peremptory in error as in truth'. There is nothing positive or peremptory in the exposition of communism which is contained in the pages that follow. Those who are looking for an anti-communist tract had better put this book down straightaway. No man respected other men's ideas more than Carew Hunt. If he criticized the marxists when he believed them to be wrong, he was equally critical of those who condemned them for what they did not do or say. To quote from his Foreword to the first edition, he believed that the strength of marxism 'like that of every system of thought, lies in its power to attract intelligent people; and it is not to be refuted by attributing to its best exponents positions which they have not adopted'.

Not everyone would agree that the strength of marxism in its modern form lies in the realm of thought. For some its main strength seems to lie more in its organizational power, and I shall have something to say about this view a little later. Much has been written about this organizational side of communism in practice, especially in the U.S.S.R., since Carew Hunt first wrote his book. In a sense it is true that his book did much to help to clarify the ideas which underlie, or once underlay, the practice. I think it is also true to say that some of the views expressed incidentally in this work on communism in practice would require modification in the light of subsequent research. But for Carew Hunt communism was primarily a matter of ideas, and this book (in spite of its title) is primarily about ideas. To write about ideas, to transmute the often involved and difficult exposition of a political or social thinker into an intelligible summary, crystal clear, yet undistorted in the process – such was Carew Hunt's rare gift. His paragraphs seem to seize on the essence of the matter in hand, push aside the irrelevant, and emerge with a summary, epigrammatic in its quality, which imprints itself on the mind. Never, so far as I am aware, has the contrast between the liberal and the communist view of society, freedom, the state, and government been better delineated than in the following single sentence:

In the West there has been a tendency to stress the *political* aspect of democracy rather than its *economic* aspect, and although at times this may have been carried too far, the fault is on the right side, seeing that a people which surrenders its political rights in return for promises of economic security will soon discover that it has made a bad bargain, as it is helpless if the promises are not kept.

*

The exposition in this book falls into three parts. The first deals with the basis of communist theory as laid down by Marx and Engels. The second part discusses the development of the European labour movement, both as influenced by Marx in his lifetime, and as shaped by other influences after the Master's death. The third deals with Lenin, and with Leninism and its development in Russia after the revolution. The development is traced up to and including the Twentieth Congress of the Communist Party of the Soviet Union in February 1956.

Had the author lived, I have no doubt that a new edition would have been called for to include the developments which have taken place in the last six years. As it is, it fell to me to consider whether the interests of the many new readers, whom a popular edition of this kind should attract, would be best served by adding a further chapter on more recent developments which the author could not take into account. I decided against this for two reasons. In the first place it would be no easy matter, if indeed it were possible, to find an author for this chapter who could combine Carew Hunt's mastery of the materials with his felicity of expression. And it would be a poor service to readers to have the last chapter sticking out like a sore thumb from the body of this elegant treatise. Secondly, the book has a unity of form and thought, and it would do violence to its originality and freshness to introduce another hand to treat the issues with which it deals, even in the light of new developments. The text reprinted in this edition is therefore identical with the fifth (revised) edition published in 1957. All that I have done is to correct a few slips and misprints which had escaped notice; and to add to the bibliography, but without evaluatory comment, the titles of a few of the books which have been published since 1956 (when the manuscript was completed), and which may prove helpful to those who wish to pursue some aspects of the subject.

What this book offers the reader is an accurate exposition of the theories of Marx and the marxists in their development up to 1956 – a span of over a hundred years. The six years which have passed since 1956 have certainly produced what look like modifications of the doctrine as expounded by its adherents in the Soviet Union and elsewhere. How far a balanced assessment of their importance, or permanence, is already possible now is another matter. But it may none the less be useful to indicate briefly of what these modifications seem to consist, and to point to th literature to which those interested can turn. First, a word about new sources of official Soviet doctrine, which Carew Hunt could not take into account. In 1959 a new official History of the Communist Party of the Soviet Union was published to replace the now discredited *Short Course*, approved if not written by Stalin himself, which was first published in 1938. The new History is not, in truth, very different from the old. Its main interest, from the point of view of doctrine, probably lies in the new emphasis which it places on the importance of the Party as the guiding and controlling element in society. Much more important for the study of doctrine are the *Foundations of Marxism-Leninism*, also published in 1959, and the Programme adopted by the Party at its Twenty-Second Congress in October 1961. All three works are readily available in English translations published in Moscow. *Foundations of Marxism-Leninism* includes sections on Dialectical and Historical Materialism, the philosophical basis of marxism. Carew Hunt, in dealing with the modern form of doctrine, relied on what was at that date the latest official exposition – Stalin's *Dialectical and Historical Materialism*, which dates from 1938. The more recent exposition, which is in some respects different, reflects the slightly more relaxed atmosphere in philosophy of the post-Stalin period. For the time being it can be treated as the officially approved interpretation.

Of more interest, perhaps, are the sections of the *Foundations* dealing with the transition to communism, and the new Programme of the Communist Party of the Soviet Union replacing the Programme adopted as far back as 1919. The 1961 Programme envisages the transition of Soviet society from the present phase, that of socialism, to communism, or at least to the 'threshold' of communism, within the next twenty years, by 1980. For Marx communism was foreseen as a condition of such abundance that each would contribute according to his ability and fairly take according to his needs. Moreover, Marx believed that with the ending of all exploitation and of all class conflict, the state would no longer be necessary, and would 'wither away'. And Engels, echoing Saint-Simon, foresaw that government of men, involving force and compulsion, would be replaced by a rational and voluntary 'administration of things'.

This is not the picture presented by the Programme, at any rate in the foreseeable future. The determination of needs will still remain a function of government; the state, though it will begin to 'wither away' in the sense that its functions will gradually be transferred to 'public organizations' is to remain for a long time to come; above all, the Party, so far from 'withering away' is to play an enhanced role in the transition to communism in guiding and controlling the whole process. Of its fate after the 'threshold' of communism is reached there is no mention.[1] However, the theoretical nature of the Party has undergone a change. The phase of the 'dictatorship of the proletariat', in which the proletariat was said to exercise its dictatorship through its vanguard, the Party is now declared to be over; while the Party, no longer the vanguard of the proletariat, is now described as the 'vanguard of the whole people'.

Such have been the main changes in theory so far as it relates to policy at home. But there have also been important developments in the sphere of the doctrine underlying the relations of the U.S.S.R. with the outer world – with her fellow-communist, or more accurately, 'socialist' states (since no country has yet claimed to have achieved communism); with the developed 'capitalist' powers; and with the 'colonial' or 'ex-colonial' new pre-industrial states. These issues have been highlighted by the emergence into the open in the course of 1960 of a latent disagreement between the Communist parties of the Soviet Union and of China, in which all these questions, and others, were involved. It is perhaps too early to judge to what extent these are genuinely questions of doctrine rather than tactics; or how much the disagreement is due to a divergence of views on the correct interpretation of the marxist canon rather than to rivalry for control over the world communist movement. It would in any case be quite impossible to do justice to this question of Sino-Soviet differences in the space of this Preface. Its importance, however, both practical and theoretical, is such that no study of present-day communism could be regarded as complete without it. It scarcely figures in Carew Hunt's book, because in 1956 the Sino-Soviet differences, if they existed, were not discernible. Even so, the paragraphs which he devoted to the relations between the two parties (*see* p. 259 ff.) contain some very shrewd observations, which subsequent events have borne out. But it must be ob-

1. A volume of studies of the Programme by various scholars (of which I am editor) is due to appear in the course of 1962, under the title *The U.S.S.R. and the Future*.

served that the statement that 'if a nationalist movement leads to the establishment of a non-communist government, that government will be opposed', though still true of China, and though true at the time of writing for Soviet Communist policy, must now be regarded as no longer true so far as the Soviet Communist Party is concerned. Indeed, relations with 'bourgeois nationalist' governments is one of the big issues in dispute between the two countries. The other key issue is the well-worked doctrine of 'peaceful co-existence'. The U.S.S.R. (fully alive as it is to the dangers of a nuclear war) upholds this form of propaganda contest – in the new Programme and elsewhere – as the best form of intensifying the class war in the non-communist world, and therefore of ultimately promoting the universal triumph of communism. China, perhaps for demographic and geographical reasons less afraid of the consequences of nuclear war, maintains (with Lenin on her side) that the defeat of the 'imperialist' powers is ultimately inconceivable without an armed clash; and that to refuse to face this is to risk demoralizing revolutionary ardour. At the time of writing there is little immediate prospect of a real reconciliation of these divergences, which are spreading to other communist parties. The significance of this emergence of two centres, each claiming authority in the world communist movement, can hardly be exaggerated.[1]

*

Carew Hunt would have been the last to claim that in the short compass of some two hundred and fifty pages he had exhausted every aspect of marxism worthy of study. Besides, it is important to remember that at the time when his book was first written, the study of marxism in its Soviet form of marxism-leninism was in its infancy in the English-speaking world. Dozens of important scholarly works, which have thrown much new light on the development of marxism in theory and in practice, have appeared only in the last decade. Works on the

1. A detailed study of the dispute between the two parties, in which all the known evidence is assembled, has recently been published by Princeton University Press. See Donald S. Zagoria, *The Sino-Soviet Conflict 1956–1961*.

Soviet Union, especially, published before the war and for a
few years after the war, often tended to reproduce uncritically
the image which the Soviet Union sought to project, rather than
to search out the reality. *Soviet Communism* by Sidney and
Beatrice Webb is a fair example of this type of study. It is only
necessary to compare what Soviet official sources alone have
since disclosed about the period covered by the Webbs in their
book with what those authors wrote, to realize the value of
this kind of writing about the Soviet Union. Carew Hunt's book
was therefore essentially a pioneering work – which is not the
least of its merits, and in itself a good reason why it has so soon
taken its place as the standard introductory work on the subject. It is thus no disparagement of the book to indicate briefly
a few topics which it does not discuss; and to draw attention to
some recent works in which they have been studied.

There seem to me to be four such topics. The first is Marx's
treatment, in some of his early works, of the 'Asiatic mode of
production', alongside with feudalism and bourgeois capitalism.
By this Marx meant the static form of society found in parts of
Asia where a strong central despotism autocratically controls
the means of production – the land – through landlords completely subordinate to itself. Although the matter is not free
from doubt, it would seem (from his writings on India) that
Marx did not regard a society with this Asiatic mode of production as capable of progressing towards socialism, except
through the intermediate stage of bourgeois capitalism. The
practical importance of this, admittedly fragmentary, part of
Marx's social analysis is that it raises serious doubts about the
relevance of Marx's analysis not only to China, but also to the
Russia of 1917. (In the case of Russia, of course, Marx never
committed himself to the view that his theories were relevant to
it, though Engels did get very near to saying so.) The theory of
the 'Asiatic mode of production' influenced Plekhanov and
some of the earlier theorists after 1917, and discussion of it has
been vigorously suppressed in the Soviet Union (and in China)
for years.[1]

1. For a full discussion of this question *see* Karl A. Wittfogel, *Oriental
Despotism*, 1957, Chapter IX.

This leads to the next of these topics – that of Mao Tse Tung's contribution to the theory of marxism. No one would dispute that Mao is an important theoretical writer as well as revolutionary leader – on such matters as revolutionary guerilla warfare, for example, he is a recognized master. Carew Hunt does recognize his importance, but treats him as an orthodox marxist-leninist. This is not a universally accepted view, though many would agree that he is an orthodox leninist-stalinist. Some go further and see in some of Mao's writings, especially on Contradictions and on what he calls the 'New Democracy', original contributions to marxist-leninist theory. I express no view on this question, which has been the subject of quite spirited controversy.[1]

Thirdly, Carew Hunt scarcely touches on the early Marx, who has been the subject of considerable study in recent years. The primary source of the early views of Marx is the set of writings known as the *Economic and Philosophic Manuscripts of 1844*. These were first published in 1927, and were therefore unknown to Lenin. These writings have revealed Marx in a comprehensive philosophical framework, where much greater emphasis is laid on moral questions than might be supposed from his later works. The main preoccupation in this early work is with man estranged from himself, in an 'alienated' world – a theme which has strong quasi-religious undertones. It may have left little trace on his later work. But its re-discovery has had considerable influence outside the Soviet Union, and the 1844 manuscript has recently been republished in the Soviet Union too.[2]

Finally mention should be made of what is now vaguely known as 'revisionism'. This is a collective and very imprecise term for various degrees of critical approach to marxism-leninism which have developed both inside the countries of the

1. Four volumes of Mao's *Selected Works* have been published in English translation in Peking. For a documented introduction to Chinese communism *see* C. Brandt, B. Schwarz, and J. K. Fairbank. *A Documentary History of Chinese Communism*, 1952. For the controversy on Mao's originality see *China Quarterly* Nos. 1 and 2, 1960.

2. For an admirable discussion of this early Marx *see* Robert C. Tucker, *Philosophy and Myth in Karl Marx*, 1961.

communist bloc and outside it in Western Europe.[1] The subject
is perhaps only on the fringes of a study of modern communism. In its modern form 'revisionism' is part of the aftermath of the Hungarian revolution of 1956 and of Soviet
admissions about Stalin's tyranny – as such, it could not, of
course, have been dealt with by Carew Hunt. But the various
forms of contemporary 'revisionist' thought are of importance
as an attempt to salvage what its advocates believe to be the
real essence of marxism, while jettisoning some of its more dis-
agreeable and discreditable consequences in practice in the
Soviet Union and elsewhere.

*

No one had a keener appetite for intellectual controversy than
Carew Hunt. He welcomed a good contest on the views which
he expressed, where they came into conflict with the judgement
of others. On one such subject, indeed, perhaps the most important of all the debatable views in the book, he did engage in
such public controversy. This was the theme of the relationship
of ideology to political action in the practice of communist
states. Leaders of communist states all claim that their policy is
strictly based on a scientific theory, marxism; and that in determining this policy they are in fact putting this theory into
practice. At the same time the Russian leaders, at any rate, from
Lenin onwards, have always claimed that theory must not be
applied automatically and that marxism has to be interpreted
'creatively'. Opponents of communism, on the other hand, have
argued that the conduct of the Soviet communist leaders has so
often been at plain variance with the theory of Marx, and their
interpretation of the theory has been so different at different
times, that it can no longer be contended that their policy is in
fact dictated by a scientific theory at all, or by any theory.
Those who hold this view would argue that communist leaders,
like all political leaders, are actuated by motives of power, by
consideration of the interests of their own country; and that
they only use theoretical arguments as an additional aid for

1. A useful collection of essays, under the general title of *Revisionism*,
has recently been published, edited by L. Labedz.

what is essentially the pursuit of plain power-politics. Carew
Hunt would have none of this view, and in the public controversy to which I have referred argued vigorously against opponents who held a different opinion.[1] His own view is summed up
in his Foreword to the first edition, and runs like a scarlet thread
through the whole of his book: 'Yet there is no doubt that
communists do believe that they are applying to political situations a theory which they fervently accept and which they hold
to be scientific.'

I am inclined to think that while this may be true sometimes,
it is in general an overstatement. I think communist leaders
certainly act within a framework of beliefs which are never
challenged and which therefore govern their actions. Such are,
for example, the belief that their form of socialism is the one
which is historically destined to supersede all other forms of
social organization; the belief that the advancement of this
'socialism' (if such it be) in other countries is historically progressive and that any attempt to oppose the rule of a communist
party when it is established is retrograde and 'counter-revolutionary'; or the conviction of the superiority of industrial
society over what Marx called the 'idiocy of rural life'. But
perhaps one ought to go further than Carew Hunt did, and
distinguish (as, incidentally, Marx did) between what party
leaders believe or persuade themselves they are doing, and
what, objectively speaking, they actually are doing. In the case
of the leaders of the Soviet Communist Party, for example, I
think many of their actions are to be explained not in terms
of ideology, but in terms of the form of one-party rule which
Lenin created, in other words, as the result of a necessity engendered by the organizational forms of rule which have been
set up. One-party rule entails certain fictions which have varied
at different times – the fiction of 1917, for example, that the
party was the vanguard of the proletariat; or the fiction today
that the Supreme Soviets are the real legislative power in the
country. When once you embark on maintaining such fictions
at all costs and erect them into unchallengeable principles,

1. For this discussion, see *Problems of Communism*, Washington, D.C.,
No. 2, March–April 1958 and No. 3, May–June 1958.

political conduct is bound at every step to be influenced by this factor. Moreover, the importance attached to maintaining party rule in undiminished form (which has never been more apparent in the Soviet Union than today) necessarily affects actions more than any other single factor. In a sense, of course, the doctrine of the 'divine right of the party' is ideology; but that is not, I think, what Carew Hunt meant.

Indeed, his treatment of Lenin's doctrine of the supremacy of the party is perhaps the most controversial side of the whole book. The argument turns on the question whether Lenin's introduction into marxism of the doctrine of the party as the active and indispensable leader of the proletariat is consistent with the revolution visualized by Marx as an inevitable social process, and not as a voluntarist process at all. I need hardly say that Carew Hunt gives full weight to all views which may be held on this rather important question. But he comes down squarely for the opinion that Lenin's doctrine is a legitimate adaptation of Marx to Russian conditions and fully consistent with orthodox marxism. This remained Carew Hunt's considered opinion. In a series of lectures published some years after this book (entitled *Marxism Past and Present*, 1954) he reiterated the view that the doctrine expounded by Marx led logically to the form of dictatorship set up by Lenin. But he also, in my view erroneously, argued that such dictatorship had never been Lenin's conscious intention. In fact I think there is good evidence that Lenin was aware as far back as 1902 that his victory would necessarily lead to a dictatorship. However, the question is a difficult one, and there is no space to discuss it at length here. It has received a good deal of attention from scholars since Carew Hunt wrote his book, and readers may wish to refer particularly to the recent works by Lichtheim and by Ulam, which are to be found in the bibliography.

Lastly, I think Carew Hunt's conclusions on the marxist ethic (Chapter 7) would not today be accepted by all scholars of marxism. What he says is certainly true of the later Marx, of Engels and of the current interpretation of Marx by Soviet marxists. He concludes that 'the basis of the marxist ethic is what present-day marxists often call "the concrete human

situation" in which the conditions of production are the determining factor. It is an ethic which is rooted in demands, not in
intuitions, and which rejects every "transcendent" element'.
(*See* p. 115) Deeper study of the early works of Marx, to which
I have referred, would, I think, incline some scholars to question the truth of this assertion for the thought of Marx as a
whole, or at any rate for its origins. One of the outstanding
French students of Marx concluded recently: 'At the basis of
marxist sociology we find ... an ethical conception of labour, a
value judgement founded on the intuition of a social state where
productive labour, having become a common task and undertaken by all, would occupy the first place in the scale of norms
of existence.'[1] This conclusion by Rubel emerged from the
study of the philosophical roots of Marx's sociological and
economic doctrines, to which, as I have already indicated,
attention has been devoted only very recently.

*

The author of this book, Robert Nigel Carew Hunt, was born
in 1890 and died in February 1959. He was educated at Bradfield and at Merton College, Oxford. In 1914 he volunteered for
the army and, though at first rejected on medical grounds, was
later commissioned in the Oxford and Buckinghamshire Light
Infantry. His active career was spent in the Foreign Office. On
retirement he settled in Oxford, attached to St Antony's College
as a supernumerary Fellow.

I was privileged to enjoy his friendship during the latter part
of his life. Like all who were so privileged – and there are many
of us – we remember him with affection and respect. Affection
first – for the unfailing kindness, the courtesy, the readiness to
go to endless trouble to help, when help was asked. And then
respect – respect for that burning integrity which rejected error,
cant, or falsehood with passion, which would not tolerate, for
any consideration, any deviation from what he believed was

1. See Maximilien Rubel, *Karl Marx: Essai de biographie intellec-*
tuelle, Paris, 1957, p. 138. This important study of Marx has not been
translated into English. So far as I know Carew Hunt was not acquainted
with it.

the truth. He was the perfect scholar of ideas, for which no man had greater respect. He was enormously learned in the history of political thought. Long before he turned his attention to marxism, he had written a number of erudite and eloquent articles – on Luther, on Calvin, on Zwingli, on Machiavelli, on Thomas Müntzer – all, it will be noted, passionate men, in whom the single dominant idea was likely to take hold. The fascination of Marx and Lenin for a man like Carew Hunt is thus easy to understand. If a man be but true to the leanings of his own intellect, he is worthy of honour and respect – such was his doctrine. Such a man might be right or wrong – this was not very relevant in the end, because fundamentally no idea or system of ideas can be pronounced wholly right or wholly wrong.

At the conclusion of a biography of Calvin which Carew Hunt published in 1933 he wrote words which I think he would equally have applied to Lenin : 'To order the people in the ways of that awful and terrifying Deity had been his life's work, and from this task no thought of safety or of personal convenience had ever made him falter. At this point, what we may think of his system becomes of no importance. We are left in the presence of a man who followed what he believed to be the truth, and consecrated his life to its attainment, and for this he will be held in honour as long as courage and singleness of purpose are held as virtues among men.[1]

Carew Hunt did not live long to enjoy his retirement in Oxford, in the university atmosphere to which he at heart belonged. His early death deprived his Oxford colleagues and students alike of a friend and a guide. I like to think that it would have delighted him to know that this book, his chief work, will remain as a memorial to him for many future generations of students of political ideas.

LEONARD SCHAPIRO

London School of Economics and
Political Science,
April 1962

1. R. N. Carew Hunt, *Calvin*, the Centenary Press, London, 1933, pp. 315–16.

Foreword

IN view of the importance of communism at the present time, some acquaintance with the principles which lead people to become communists is desirable. There is indeed no lack of books in which these principles are set out, but not only are many of them out of print, but there is none which covers the whole ground from Marx and his immediate predecessors to Stalin, as is the purpose of this book to do.

As the study of theory is normally uncongenial to our national temperament, it is commonly argued that the present Russian rulers are hard-headed realists who believe in nothing, that they are simply engaged upon 'power politics' and that the communist parties which they direct act likewise. In this event we need only be concerned with their practice, and may regard their theories as no more than *ex post facto* rationalizations. Yet there is no doubt that communists do believe that they are applying to political situations a theory which they fervently accept and which they hold to be scientific. It has been pointed out in an able pamphlet, *The Strategy and Tactics of World Communism*, issued in 1948 by the United States Committee on Foreign Affairs, that they are rather to be compared to engineers than to theorists of the academic type, but that for an engineer to be wholly intent upon the practical aspects of a problem does not mean that he does not believe in the principles of theoretical mechanics. We are apt to forget that there is any theory behind our own institutions. But communists never forget their own theoretical principles. In part this is a question of age, for younger movements are always more conscious of theory than older ones. But it reflects also the belief that marxism is a science, and that communist strategy and tactics derive from it by strictly logical deduction.

The present book falls naturally into three sections. The first deals with the basis of communist theory as laid down by Marx and Engels, which is still the official creed of the movement.

The second covers the development of the European labour movement in the nineteenth century, with special reference to marxist influence upon it, and to the cross-currents of opinion which arose by way of reaction to his doctrines. As many of these cross-currents correspond to certain fundamental human characteristics, they are not simply of academic interest, but are still operative today. The third brings us to the period when the revolutionary movement begins to be shaped by Russia, which has since directed it, and deals with the attempts by Lenin and Stalin to apply marxist principles to the changed conditions of the present century.

The communists have developed propaganda to a fine art, and their brass band is never silent. As they are seeking to reach the masses, much of what they say is so fantastic that the only difficulty in answering it is to know where to begin. This even applies to much propaganda intended for the higher levels, since there is always a temptation to use any argument, however worthless, so long as there is a chance that it will convince someone. At the same time marxism must be taken seriously, and there is a grave danger of under-rating it. In the last resort, its strength, like that of every system of thought, lies in its power to attract intelligent people; and it is not to be refuted by attributing to its best exponents positions which they have not adopted. Every attempt will therefore be made to present it fairly and objectively.

It is obvious that any such sketch as is here attempted is bound to be superficial, but this is true of all brief introductions to difficult subjects. It is also impossible that all readers should agree on the relative emphasis given to the various elements that make up the communist way of thought. All that can be said is that every effort has been made to give due consideration to each of these elements; and to represent marxism as a formidable creed which can only be successfully opposed by those who understand it.

The chapter on the marxist ethic appeared in the *Nineteenth Century and After* of February 1949, and I am grateful for permission to reprint it here.

R. N. CAREW HUNT

Note to the Fifth (Revised) Edition

THIS edition brings the account given of the theory and practice of the communist movement and of the Russian Communist Party which directs it up to the 20th Russian Party Congress of February 1956. Certain changes have been made in the body of the text where it was felt necessary to correct opinions earlier expressed, or where the treatment of the subject-matter called for amplification. Since the book was revised in 1951 a number of important works on various aspects of communism have appeared, and these have been included in the bibliography.

R. N. CAREW HUNT

St Antony's College,
Oxford

PART ONE

THE MARXIST BASIS

*

1. General Introduction

COMMUNISM as an ideal reaches back to the very beginning of western political thought, when Plato conceived the most famous of all Utopias in his *Republic*. As soon as men are capable of serious reflection, the inequalities of human life become apparent and are seen largely to derive from private property. For nearly two thousand years European civilization has rested upon a seeming contradiction – between a philosophy and a religion which teach that all men are brothers, and an economic system which organizes them as masters and servants. In almost every century men sought to resolve this contradiction by demanding a readjustment of the social order; but such schemes as they put forward did not rest on any clear analysis of that order, or upon a just appreciation of the part which man plays in creating it. This applies equally to the social theorists of the eighteenth and early nineteenth centuries, who were largely influenced by the prevailing belief that man was by nature a rational being and had become corrupted only as a result of bad political institutions. Yet as to how these institutions were to be removed they had no clear idea, while those which they intended to replace them were generally impracticable. Marx, it has been well said, took up what was one of the oldest instincts of Europe (*When Adam delved and Eve span, who was then the gentleman?*) and applied it to the new fourth estate of the industrial workers, who were bound, as they grew in political consciousness, to seek a justification of their place in society.[1] He put forward a philosophy which claimed to show how the present order had come about, and how it would be changed in due time into a better one; and he succeeded be-

1. *Marxist Centenary* (*Economist*, 21 February 1948), p. 292.

cause he created a belief that the ultimate salvation of man was guaranteed by science. His system brought into being the largest mass movement since the rise of Christianity; and it is the greatest subversive force in the modern world, though it took a revolution in Russia for the West to become aware of this.

Communism, at least according to classical theory, aims at creating a classless society in which all the means of production, distribution, and exchange will be owned by the community, and from which the State – conceived as an instrument of coercion and oppression – will have disappeared. Between the revolution which abolishes the capitalist order and this communist society there lies, however, a transitional period known as the dictatorship of the proletariat. It is through this stage that Russia claims to be now passing. It is important to recognize that the Russians call it socialism and not communism, and that the group of republics which form the Soviet Union is thus designated as the Union of Soviet *Socialist* (not *Communist*) Republics. Communism is a 'higher phase' which still lies in the future. The criterion of a communist society is that it should be governed by the principle of 'from each according to his ability, to each according to his needs'; whereas, as Marx first taught and Stalin constantly repeated, such equality is impossible in the socialist State, which must therefore be governed by the principle of 'from each according to his ability, to each according to his work'. In his *Critique of the Gotha Programme* (1875), the principal work in which he sought to explain the difference between the two systems, Marx does indeed call this transitional period of planned economy the first phase of communism; but in his other writings he normally refers to it as Socialism. He called the party he formed in 1847 'communist' because of the existence in France of Louis Blanc's Socialist Party; and he called his famous Manifesto 'Communist' only because, as Engels explained in the Introduction to the edition of 1890, the term 'Socialist' was then associated with Utopianism and with 'multifarious social quacks'.[1]

1. John Strachey, *The Theory and Practice of Socialism* (1936), p. 113; H. J. Laski, *The Communist Manifesto. A Socialist Landmark* (1948), Introduction, pp. 115–16.

Lenin and Stalin follow Marx, and consistently define the new order to be established on the ruins of capitalism as Socialism. Thus the Soviet Constitution of 3 December, 1936, does not mention communism at all, save in Article 126, which specifically refers to the Communist Party, and it defines the Soviet Union as 'a socialist State of workers and peasants'. In his Report on the Constitution of December 5th following, Stalin explained that up to the present all that had been achieved was Socialism, and he rejected an amendment to insert a statement that 'the final end of the soviet movement was the creation of a completely communist society' as having no direct connexion with the Constitution, which merely sought to consecrate the gains already won.[1]

Many socialists will indeed deny Stalin's right so to describe the present soviet political and economic system. Yet where the ends they seek are concerned, socialism and communism are virtually interchangeable terms, as anyone who consults the *Oxford English Dictionary* or any standard text-book will discover.[2] The essence of both is that the means of production shall belong to the community. As, however, no one has yet discovered how the community can control them, they are administered on its behalf by the State, or by such bodies as it may appoint for the purpose. Hence public ownership comes in practice to mean State capitalism, of which soviet socialism is simply the most ruthless and consistent version. Before considering the theoretical basis of communism, we should therefore do well to remind ourselves that its final objective is the same as that of socialism, and that whatever differences exist between the two have to do with means rather than ends. The socialists hold that they can both introduce and maintain their system by democratic methods. The communists hold that neither is possible.

The term communist is used, however, to distinguish the Communist Party from the Socialist, or, as it is generally called upon the Continent, the Social Democratic Party; and its members thus call themselves communists to show that they belong

1. *Leninism* (ed. 1940), pp. 569–70.
2. Ivor Thomas, *The Tragedy of Socialism* (1949), pp. 18–19.

to the communist rather than to the social democratic section of the labour movement, which they accuse of temporizing with the bourgeois-capitalist order. Indeed Lenin's party continued to call itself 'Social Democratic' until the 7th Party Congress of March 1918, when it substituted the term 'Bolshevik' as a protest against the non-revolutionary attitude of the socialist parties of the West. But, strictly speaking, there are no such persons as communists, because nowhere, not even in Russia, has communism been achieved. Nor indeed will it ever be. For Russian socialism will never pass beyond State capitalism, and all the talk of the disappearance of the State and of the future communal society in which men will work for the good of all, and coercion will no longer be necessary, is pure mythology.

The creed accepted by all communists is that delivered to the world in the last century by Marx and Engels, and interpreted in accordance with the changed conditions of the present century by Lenin and Stalin. To be exact we should therefore call it marxism-engelism-leninism-stalinism, but it is often referred to as marxism-leninism and more commonly as marxism. This last designation will generally be used in the present survey, while by marxists will be understood those who accept marxism as above defined. What, we may first ask, lies behind it at the present time? It does not spring from poverty and bad social conditions, for it is to the better-paid worker – the skilled artisan – rather than to the very poor that it appeals. Nor has it arisen because the masses have suddenly become aware of the alleged inhumanities of the capitalist system, since in every generation their interests have been increasingly protected by the State. Nor, again, is it due to the monotony of factory labour, as there is little evidence that the workers have any objection to routine tasks provided they have a sense of security and feel that their standard of living is not in danger. It is not, in essence, a 'popular' movement at all, for it was in origin a bourgeois movement and, as Marx and Engels always recognized, its strength has lain in its power to influence, as it certainly now does, large sections of the intelligentsia by whom it is relayed downwards. It is in the last analysis a body of ideas which has filled the vacuum created by the breakdown of organized religion as a result of the increasing secularization of thought during the last three centuries, and it can be combated only by opposing to it a conception of life based upon wholly different principles.

But for its devotees communism has the *value* of a religion in so far as it is felt to provide a complete explanation of reality and of man as part of reality, and at the same time to give to life, as does religion, a sense of purpose. And much as communists resent the analogy, it must be pressed still farther. If reason is to be our *sole* guide, the only intelligible attitude towards the riddle of existence is agnosticism, seeing that all our knowledge is conditioned by the nature and limitations of our human faculties, and that there is nothing outside ourselves and the products of our minds by which its final truth can ever be tested. As neither communism nor religion is content to rest in this position, each is ultimately driven to appeal to certain propositions which have to be accepted by faith, but from which, once accepted, whatever else it is desired to prove logically follows. Only while religion frankly accepts this, communism maintains that its fundamental dogmas are guaranteed by science, which they certainly are not, since one and all are very disputable. Nor indeed would the issue be affected if they were so guaranteed, since a belief in the hypotheses upon which science rests requires an act of faith like any other.

Every creed must of necessity possess a dogmatic basis, and when this begins to be questioned it is a sure sign that the creed itself is losing its hold. There is no sign, however, that this is yet true of communism. The fundamental doctrines on which it rests are held to be of irresistible cogency to any properly instructed mind, and discussion is only permissible within their frame of reference. Every step forward, or it may be backward, must be shown to be in strict accordance with these doctrines or a logical application of them. Communists, and particularly Russian communists, have thus suffered from an excessive tendency to dogmatize which shows no symptoms of decline. Lenin, it is true, insisted that 'Marxism is not a dogma, but a guide to action', that it must not be taken literally and that it was necessary to adapt it to changing conditions, as indeed he himself did; and at the 18th Russian Party Congress of 1939 Stalin again told Party members that they must not expect to find the answer to all their problems in Marx, Engels, or even in Lenin himself, and that it was their duty to work them out for themselves in accordance with general communist principles.[1] Yet even Stalin never ventured to challenge these principles, however startling may have been his interpretation of them.

Communism is thus a *Weltanschauung* based upon a closely articulated body of doctrine – philosophic, economic, political and social – which claims alone to provide the scientific explanation of the world. It has to be studied as a whole, and it is impermissible to abstract from it certain elements which may happen to interest us and to ignore the others. It is impossible to understand communist activity without a knowledge of the system upon which it rests. Every communist who holds any important position has been well instructed in it so that he knows just where he stands, and has an answer to everything, which is far from being the case with the majority of his opponents; and to discuss any problem with an intelligent and politically developed communist is to become aware that he is living in a different climate of opinion from our own and that his values are not ours. For the communist believes that he is living in a doomed world – one which is shot to pieces by internal contradictions. Yet out of it a better world is being born in accordance with laws that are irresistible in their operation and can be scientifically demonstrated. In such a situation there are only two possible courses – to oppose the process which is heralding the new order, or to collaborate with it. The wise man will choose the second of these alternatives. It is this belief that he is allying himself with the forces of progress that gives the communist his assurance and his creed its astringent quality.

We have seen that the four apostles of communism are Marx, Engels, Lenin, and Stalin, whose works alone possess authority, no others having ever been added to the canon of scripture. Chronologically they pair off. Marx and Engels being concerned with laying down the basis of communist theory

1. *Leninism*, p. 659.

and practice in the last century, and Lenin and Stalin with the application of their doctrines to the new conditions which arose at the beginning of the present century. Lenin developed marxism in more than one direction, but broadly speaking it is true to say that his most important contribution was in the field of Party organization and tactics; and that Stalin's contribution was his theory of 'Socialism in one country' with all that this implies. We shall therefore first deal with Marx and Engels, and then with Lenin and Stalin.

2. Marx and Engels [1]

MARX was born in 1818 at Treves in the Rhineland, where French influence had penetrated more deeply than in other parts of Germany. He was descended from a long line of rabbis, but his father was a lawyer. When he was six years old the family became Christian, and he was brought up as a Protestant, though he early abandoned religion altogether. His rabbinical ancestry is important for two reasons. First, he derived from it his peculiar sense of authority; and, secondly, it was responsible for that messianic element which plays so important a part in Jewish thought. For Jewish thought has never been 'other-worldly' and, as Nicolas Berdyaev points out, it has always insisted upon the duty of establishing an era of peace and happiness in this present world.[2] It is no accident that so many of the communist leaders from Marx's day onwards have been Jews.

During the years when Marx was a student, the youth of Germany were passing through a time of intense intellectual activity; and as philosophy played a large part in their education, it was inevitable that they should have been much influenced by Hegel, the philosopher then most in vogue in Berlin. Later we shall be considering Hegel's position. Here we need only note that behind the cosmic process as he conceived it was a directing force which constituted if not a personal God at least some kind of Providence. But the younger generation of neo-hegelians to which Marx belonged resented the intrusion of this abstraction, and in general the conservative conclusions that Hegel drew from it, which appeared to contradict the dynamic nature of the dialectic; and of this school the most prominent representative, and indeed its only philosopher, was

1. The standard biography of Marx is that by Franz Mehring (1920, Eng. trans. 1936, reissued 1948); see also E. H. Carr, *Karl Marx* (1934), and Isaiah Berlin, *Karl Marx* (1939, reissued 1948). On Engels, see Gustav Mayer, *Friedrich Engels* (2 vols., 1920; abridged Eng. trans. 1935).

2. *The Meaning of History* (1936), p. 99.

Ludwig Feuerbach, who had sought to show in his *Essence of Christianity* (1841) that religion was the reflection of man's material conditions which created a contradiction between what he was and what he aspired to be. Yet Feuerbach was not, strictly speaking, a materialist, and it is unfair to judge him by his often-quoted aphorism, *Der Mensch ist was er isst* (Man is what he eats), in which he ascribed the failure of the 1848 revolutions to the fact that the working-class lived on a diet of potatoes instead of more energizing beans.[1] He was, rather, a humanist, concerned to assert the pre-eminence of man as a part of nature. He had nothing in common with the rational scepticism of the eighteenth century, and has been described as a 'pious atheist', since he gave his humanism an almost religious character. He did not deny the values of religion. What he did maintain was that man became estranged from himself by projecting into a supernatural being qualities which belonged to his own nature, and would be realized one day in a 'religion of humanity'. Thus it was from Feuerbach that Marx got the idea that religion – and by extension all the products of the human mind – were derivatives of man's material conditions. Only whereas Feuerbach held that these conditions determined 'being', that is, man in the abstract, Marx held that they determined 'social being', that is, the life of the community.[2]

In 1842 Marx joined the staff of the *Neue Rheinische Zeitung* in Cologne, and was almost immediately appointed its editor. He had been brought in to steer the paper into smoother waters, but in 1843 the Prussian Government introduced a new divorce law which led him to ride off on his atheistic hobby-horse with an article which caused the suppression of the paper. He therefore went to Paris to study socialism at its headquarters. Here he met Proudhon, who was ultimately to exercise a greater influence than any other of the French socialist leaders; and whom, as he told a correspondent many years later, 'in the

1. H. Höffding, *History of Philosophy* (1900, Eng. trans. 1924) II, p. 281.

2. Carr, *Karl Marx*, pp. 71–2. On Feuerbach's influence *see* Sidney Hook, *From Hegel to Marx* (1936), pp. 200 ff.; Gustav A. Wetter, *Der dialektische Materialismus* (Vienna, 1952), pp. 13–14.

course of lengthy debates, often lasting all night, I infected with hegelianism which, owing to his ignorance of German, he could not properly study'.[1] He also met Michael Bakunin – later to become his bitterest enemy – who had arrived in Paris in January 1844 after expulsion from Germany and Switzerland. And here too he renewed his acquaintance with Friedrich Engels. A Rhinelander like himself, Engels was the son of a cotton-spinner with factories in Westphalia and Manchester. He had arrived independently at much the same conclusions as Marx, and had visited him in Cologne, only to be somewhat curtly dismissed. But soon after he reached Paris, Marx came upon an article he had written which greatly interested him; and when the young man introduced himself a second time, he met with a very different reception.

Thus, there was laid the foundation of the most important literary partnership of the nineteenth century, and perhaps of all time. Had it not been for Engels, Marx might have remained a purely academic thinker. But Engels had made a first-hand study of British labour conditions, on which he had published in 1845 his *Condition of the Working-Class in England*; and he was thus able not only to show Marx how the capitalist system really worked, but also to draw his attention to the important role that Great Britain was playing in its development at a time when Marx's thought was still centred upon Germany. He combined generous instincts with an industry and versatility which had made him competent in many fields – 'Engels', said Marx, 'is always one step ahead of me.' And with this went a modesty which led him consistently to underrate his contribution to their joint achievement. All these qualities he placed at Marx's disposal, and he was to be the only friend with whom that most difficult man never quarrelled. Marx, indeed, always recognized his debt to him, and his famous theory was 'our theory'.

In 1845 Marx was expelled from Paris at the request of the Prussian Government, and went to Brussels. Here, with Engels's assistance, he conducted communist propaganda among various

1. Letter to J. von Schweitzer, 21 April, 1865, *Correspondence* (ed. Dona Torr, 1934), p. 171.

bodies, including a group of German exiles, the 'Federation of the Just', which later became the 'Communist League', and for which he drew up at the end of 1847 the *Communist Manifesto*, the most famous of all political pamphlets. He took part in the revolutions of 1848 in France and Germany, but in May 1849 he was expelled from Prussia and never received permission to return. In fact, he made it the more difficult to obtain such permission by most unwisely renouncing his Prussian citizenship, with the result that when Prussia twenty years later became the centre of the first worker's movement, he was only able to influence it indirectly. Henceforth, he lived in London, where he led a Micawberish existence, eked out by remittances from the faithful Engels, until the latter, on his father's death in 1869, was able to settle on him a fixed income of £350 a year. He passed his time in writing, organizing the international revolutionary movement and pursuing the many feuds to which these activities led. He died in 1883, and Engels pronounced over his grave an oration in which he declared that his work in the field of social science was equal to Darwin's in that of natural science. Engels himself died in 1895. Some years earlier he had sold his share of the family business in Manchester and had moved to London, where he lived the life of that bourgeois rentier whose elimination from society he had spent his life in advocating. He left all his property to Marx's children.

3. The Principal Writings of Marx and Engels[1]

THE *Communist Manifesto*, published in February 1848, is the creed of the Communist Party, and *Capital* is its bible. But this is an inversion of the natural order, as creeds are normally subsequent to the scriptures and are based upon them. The *Manifesto* was a brilliant exposition of the view that capitalism was doomed to disappear, but it contained no final proof as to why it should do so, and Marx's followers at once urged him to supply it. Yet although he had developed the main lines of his thesis by the early forties, it was with great difficulty that he could be persuaded to put it on paper. In 1844 he had signed a contract for a work to be entitled *The Critique of Politics and Economics*; but he did not get on with it, and by 1859 he had written only two chapters, which appeared in that year as an instalment with the title of *The Critique of Political Economy*. It caused some disappointment, as it did not contain the long-awaited demonstration of his thesis, but was an exposition of the theory of value; though its preface, a document of the first importance, contains the most complete formulation of his doctrine of historical materialism. Meanwhile, in 1845–6, he had written, in collaboration with Engels, the *Deutsche Ideologie*, in which that same doctrine had been outlined; but it was only in 1932 that it was issued by Moscow. In 1862 he made a fresh start. He decided to produce his exposure of capitalism by combining the two chapters of the *Critique* with the mass of material that he had been intermittently collecting in the British Museum since 1850. But he made slow progress, and it was not until 1867 that there appeared the first volume of *Capital*, 'the task', as he told a correspondent, 'to which I have sacrificed my life, my happiness, and my family'.[2] He had

1. *See* Ch-F. Hubert's *Bibliographie à l'œuvre de Marx et d'Engels* at the end of H. C. Desroches's *Signification du Marxisme* (Paris, 1949).
2. Letter to S. Meyer, Hanover, 2 April 1867, *Correspondence*, p. 219.

wished to dedicate it to Darwin, but the latter declined the honour in a cautious letter, pretexting his ignorance of economics. The book was published in German by the Hamburg firm of Meissner, and did not appear in an English translation (and then only the first volume) until 1886.[1] The later volumes appeared posthumously, the second in 1885, and the third in 1894.

In addition to the above, there are other writings that deserve especial mention. Two of these belong to the second half of the forties, when he was most prolific. The first is the brief *Thesis on Feuerbach* (1845), which Engels discovered in a note-book after Marx's death and published in 1888 as an appendix to his own *Ludwig Feuerbach*. Marx then took leave of philosophy for many years. But the gift from his friend Frieligrath early in 1857 of some volumes of Hegel left behind by Bakunin seems to have revived his interest in it; and may have been responsible for the dialectical method he adopted in the preface to the *Critique* and later in *Capital*.[2] The second is the *Poverty of Philosophy* (1847), written in French with the title *La Misère de la philosophie* by way of reply to Proudhon's *La Philosophie de la misère*. He also wrote a number of extremely important pamphlets, such as the *Class Struggles in France*, the *Eighteenth Brumaire*, and the *Civil War in France*, the first two being inspired by the revolution of 1848, and the third by the Commune of 1871. And, finally, there are a number of works provoked by personal controversies, since Marx was abnormally sensitive to criticism, and thus wasted much time in polemics which neither added to his doctrine nor advanced his reputation.

Yet there is no single book that contains a complete statement of his position, and the best general exposition of it is Engels's *Anti-Dühring* (1877), which Marx approved, and to which he contributed the chapter on political economy. It was to have

1. Mehring, p. 380 ff.
2. *See* Marx to Engels, 14 January 1858 (*Briefwechsel*, II, 235). It is, however, impossible to accept the thesis put forward by H. Lefebre in his *Le Matérialisme dialectique* (Paris, 1940), that Marx's acceptance of the dialectic dates from this incident.

appeared serially in the German Social Democrat newspaper *Vorwärts*; but at the annual Party Congress of May 1877 it was decided that its publication be discontinued as 'it was entirely without interest to the majority of members and, in fact, repellent to them in the highest degree'. With difficulty, a compromise was reached, and it was published as a supplement.[1] None the less, no single work contributed more to the diffusion of Marx's teaching.

1. Mehring, p. 512.

4. The Philosophic Theory of Marxism

MARXISM consists of three elements:

1. A dialectical philosophy borrowed from Hegel but transformed into dialectical materialism, from which in turn historical materialism derives.

2. A system of political economy, of which the dynamic part is the labour theory of value, the theory of surplus value and the conclusions drawn from them.

3. A theory of the State and of revolution.

As Lenin points out, the first of these elements is taken from German classical philosophy, the second from the classical school of British political economy and the third from the French revolutionary tradition; and thus he says that Marx 'continued and completed the main ideological currents of the nineteenth century belonging to the three most advanced countries of mankind'.[1] The above is of interest in view of the tendency that later developed in the Soviet Union to minimize the debt of Communism to western thought.

1. DIALECTICAL MATERIALISM

Hegel's philosophy, to which Marx was so much indebted, is extremely difficult, and it is impossible to do more than indicate its general trend. What must be noticed at the outset is that it abhors the irrational, and holds the whole cosmic process to be directed by a rational principle of which World-Spirit, scarcely distinguishable in Hegel's thought from the will of God, is the personification. It is this that leads him to make his famous statement that 'whatever is rational is real, and whatever is real is rational', which comes very near to saying that whatever is is right, and, indeed, in the opinion of many of his critics must carry this implication. And certainly there is a fatalistic element

1. *The Teaching of Karl Marx* (1914) (Little Lenin Library), p. 17.

in his system. For if the world is sustained by reason, even the most retrograde movement would seem to be a part of reason's plan, so that a hegelian looking back on nazism may reflect that, however apparently irrational, it constituted an inevitable stage in human development.

Hegel develops a system of concepts, or, as he calls them, categories – quantity, quality, substance, causality, essence, existence, and the like – which resemble the Platonic world of forms, save that they are dynamic and not static; and to this dynamic world of forms, he refers collectively as the Idea or the Absolute. This is the ultimate reality, and the source or creator of nature, and through nature of mind. In his *Logic*, he exhibits the operation of these concepts in their purely abstract form, and shows that the connexion between them is dialectical, that is, that it is of such a kind that if any one of them is scrutinized with sufficient attention, it will be found to lead on to another, either as a reaction from its one-sidedness or as a reconciliation of its contradictions. But in Hegel's system the Absolute is the totality not only of thought but of all experience, that is, it includes time and all that has occurred in time. Thus the passage of events which we call history, as well as our comprehension of them, are part of it, and will exhibit that same dialectical interconnexion which has been shown to be a property of the forms of thought. Hence, the dialectic not only governs thought, but also events in the temporal order, since both are conceived as aspects of a single whole. And as nothing possesses complete reality except the Absolute, it is in proportion as a thing is seen in its relation to the Absolute that it possesses a greater or less degree of reality, and thus of reason and truth.[1]

For Hegel therefore history was a process in which the Absolute progressively unfolds itself, revealing more of its true nature in later periods than in earlier, and thus more in the national State than in primitive communities. The dialectic provided the clue to this development. But it should be noted that Hegel confined its operations to the past, if only because he believed that the sole task of philosophy, whether applied to

1. Bertrand Russell, *History of Philosophy* (1947), pp. 757 ff.; R. G. Collingwood, *The Idea of Nature* (1945), pp. 121 ff.

history or to anything else, was to arrive at an understanding of what had happened. 'Philosophy comes too late to teach the world what it should be. . . . The owl of Minerva begins its flight when the shades of twilight have already fallen.' Marx wholly disagreed with this, as he held that the function of philosophy was not to interpret the world, but to change it: and having found, as he believed, a convenient instrument in the dialectic, he went further than Hegel in applying it to the future, and indulged in much pseudo-scientific fortune-telling for which the Hegelian system gave him no warrant.

The same belief that the whole is alone completely real, and that the parts partake of reality only in proportion as they are related to it, led Hegel to the view that 'the State is the Divine Idea as it exists on earth', and that the individual achieves self-realization only as a member of it. Thus, the two most important modern political movements derive from him. Through his dialectic, as revised by Marx, he became the source of the proletarian radicalism which culminated in communism; while through his idealization of the State he became the source of that conservative nationalism which culminated in fascism.[1] The two great wars caused attention to be directed to elements in his thought the true purport of which his transcendentalism had concealed, and which were certainly not apparent in the last quarter of the nineteenth century when hegelianism (in a somewhat emasculated version it is true) was being proclaimed in this country as the supreme oracle of human wisdom. There are those who believe that, although he may have been at times somewhat incautiously patriotic, he never intended his writings to provide text-books for totalitarian dictators. But others hold that he was not the court philosopher of Friedrich Wilhelm III for nothing, and that the whole theory of the absolute State is not only implicitly, but also explicitly set out in his philosophy. Certainly its anti-liberalism was deplored by some of the most distinguished of his contemporaries. But this is a controversy in which we are not called upon to take sides.

1. George H. Sabine, *History of Political Theory* (1937, ed. 1948), p. 523; Henri Sée, *Matérialisme historique et l'interprétation economique de l'histoire* (Paris, 1927), pp. 43-4.

Yet the conclusions which Hegel may have drawn from his system in no way affect the fact that it constitutes a revolution in thought comparable with Newton's law of gravitation and Darwin's theory of evolution; and all historians are indebted to him, whether or not they accept his dialectical interpretation. For his system is, on one side at least, the expression of a new sense of history. He insisted that it is not simply a bare sequence of events, but a gradual process of unfolding; that, as in other empirical spheres, reason is at work in it, which is what he means by his identification of the real and the rational; and that the phenomena which make up history become intelligible in proportion as they are viewed as a whole, so that an understanding of the present requires an understanding of the past, a truth of which many eighteenth-century historians certainly needed to be reminded.

2. THE DIALECTIC

The dialectic may be provisionally defined as 'the theory of the union of opposites'. The term itself comes from a Greek word meaning to discuss or debate, and it originally signified the art of discussion with a view to arriving at the truth by exposing the contradictions contained in the arguments of the disputants. Thus, in the Platonic dialogues Socrates used it to show the inadequacy of popular beliefs, or to expose people who were talking nonsense; and when Plato put out his famous theory that ideas alone are real and phenomena only the reflection of them, he gave the name of the dialectic to the science which arrives at a knowledge of the nature of ideas. But while Plato regarded contradictions simply as obstacles to arriving at the truth, and thus used the dialectic to get rid of them, Hegel maintained that they lay at the root of everything and were of the utmost value, since it was only through their opposition that any progress towards reality and truth was possible. Every proposition has a subject and a predicate, as for example 'Liberty is the right to act as we please'. But every predicate which has not attained to the category of the Absolute proves on examination to be incomplete or self-contradictory. The dialectical process is thus one of thesis, antithesis, and synthesis. The thesis affirms a proposition. The antithesis denies, or in hegelian terminology 'negates', it. The synthesis embraces what is true in both the thesis and the antithesis, and thus brings us one step nearer to reality. But as soon as the synthesis is subjected to a closer inspection, it, too, is found defective; and thus the whole process starts over again with a further thesis, negated in turn by its antithesis and reconciled in a new synthesis. In this triangular manner does thought proceed until at last we reach the Absolute, which we can go on contemplating for ever without discerning in it any contradiction. The term dialectic is thus used for that process of conflict and reconciliation which goes on within reality itself, and within human thought about reality.

Not unnaturally there has been a wide diversity of opinion as to the viability of the dialectic. In a sense, as Arland Ussher has pointed out, Hegel's use of the co-relative terms of thesis, antithesis, and synthesis implies an altogether revolutionary way of thought. The classical philosophers had used words like matter, form, and consciousness. The theologians had spoken of body, soul, and spirit. It was Hegel's originality that he brought down ideas from Olympus and set them in motion. He showed that an abstraction like Being is by itself Nothing, but that the two when combined in thought engender a third idea – Becoming – which again is empty and ambiguous until united with its counterpart, Ceasing-to-Be: and so on in an unending spiral. In one place he likens reality to a 'Bacchic dance in which there is not one of the constituents that is not drunk', perhaps, as Ussher says, the most exciting assertion ever made about the universe.[1] Yet there are those who have felt this triadic movement to be as monotonous as the Prussian goose-step; while to Edmund Wilson it is simply that mythical and magical triangle which from the time of Pythagoras and before has stood as the symbol of certainty and power, and in which some have discerned a phallic origin. Its influence upon marxists has undoubtedly been that of a religious myth; for, as Wilson points out, it concentrates the complexities of society into

1. *Three Aesthetic Philosophers* (*The Listener*, 15 April 1948, pp. 623–4.)

an obvious protagonist and antagonist; and, by giving an assurance of the final upshot of the struggle, it symbolizes the recurrent insurgence of the young and growing forces of life against the old and sterile.[1]

3. THE LAWS OF THE DIALECTIC[2]

In his *Notes on Hegel's Logic* Lenin lays down sixteen points which profess to exhibit the essential unity of the different aspects of the dialectic. We need not concern ourselves with them, as they are simply an attempt to link together the three fundamental laws of the dialectic as formulated by Hegel. These laws, which Marx and Engels found no difficulty in accepting, are the following:

a. *The Law of the Transformation of Quantity into Quality, and vice versa.*

This law professes to explain the appearance of new qualities and the consequence of their emergence. Change takes place by imperceptible quantitative mutations until there arrives a point, which Hegel calls the 'node', beyond which a thing cannot vary while remaining the same. The classical illustration of this is the change of state of a substance, as when water turns to steam at 100° C. and into ice at 0° C. But just as the change occurs abruptly so that water is at one moment water and at the next steam or ice, so the progress of humanity is not affected by a gradual process of growth but by sudden 'jumps'. Marxists call these jumps revolutions, and use the above law to show their inevitability. Thus, the monopoly-capitalism of Imperialism, which they hold to represent the last stage beyond which capitalism can no longer develop, is not something that has gradually evolved out of pre-monopoly capitalism. It is qualitatively different, though the way for it has been prepared by quantitative changes. Having come into existence, it, too, will

1. Edmund Wilson, *To the Finland Station* (1940), p. 195.
2. The latest official marxist exposition of the dialectic and its laws is Stalin's *Dialectical and Historical Materialism* (1938), printed in *Leninism* (ed. 1940), pp. 591 ff.; *see* also M. Shirokov's *Textbook of Marxist Philosophy* (n.d.) for a fuller statement.

develop quantitatively until the point is reached when the 'dialectical leap' occurs, and it passes into socialism. In his *Concerning Marxism in Linguistics* (1950) Stalin laid down, however, that the passage from socialism into the qualitatively different order of communism would be accomplished in the Soviet Union by a gradual transition and without any 'leap' or revolution, as he maintained that antagonistic contradictions no longer existed in Soviet society. To any society which chooses to assert their absence, the above law therefore ceases to apply.

b. *The Law of the Unity of Opposites.*

This asserts the essentially contradictory nature of reality, but also that the contradictions thus revealed exist in unity. Positive and negative, for example, so far from being opposites, express no absolute difference, just as a road to the east is also one to the west. And just as science has proved (at least according to marxists) that every unity contains within itself polar opposites, such as the positive and negative poles of the electron, so these opposites are interdependent. In capitalist society the bourgeoisie and proletariat are thus connected. Neither of these classes can develop without the other, as the bourgeoisie cannot exist without exploiting the labour of the proletariat, and the proletariat cannot exist without selling its labour to the bourgeoisie. Marxists thus use contradiction to explain the evolution of society; and so important a part does it play in their thought that Lenin has called it 'the salt of dialectics'.

c. *The Law of the Negation of the Negation.*

This asserts that thesis, antithesis, and synthesis are forms or stages of development. The thesis breaks down by reason of its internal contradictions and gives way to the antithesis (the negation of the thesis), which attempts to remove these contradictions. This also breaks down for the same reason, and a synthesis is developed which includes the valid elements of the antithesis, and thus, of course, of the thesis also. The synthesis negates the antithesis (the first negation), and is thus the 'negation of the negation'.

The above can best be illustrated by the triad in which Marx was primarily interested – that of feudalism, capitalism, and socialism. The internal contradictions of feudalism lead to its negation by capitalism, which represents an advance upon the earlier stage. But the contradictions of capitalism then lead (or must eventually lead) to socialism, which will be 'the negation of the negation'. Yet, just as capitalism has taken up all that was worth preserving in feudalism, so will socialism take up all that is good in capitalism – its technology, etc. The dialectic is therefore an optimistic doctrine. All development takes place in a kind of spiral, since the reconciliation of every conflict always issues in a higher reformulation. Indeed, it might well be used to prove the existence of a future life. Death is surely the antithesis of life, and as the synthesis of the two must result in a higher reformulation, it is difficult to see what this can be save immortality.

Now it must surely be obvious that it is impossible to found upon the above any sociological or other system which claims to be scientific unless there is a clear definition of what a contradiction or an opposition means, so that we can immediately recognize one when we see it. Yet, as we shall see, it is never made clear upon what principle one thing may legitimately be represented as the negation of another – for example, capitalism as the antithesis or negation of feudalism. For what marxists do is arbitrarily to select any two dissimilar phenomena which it may suit them to represent as contradictions or oppositions, term them respectively the thesis and the antithesis, resolve them into a third phenomenon described as the synthesis, and label the whole process as dialectical. Thus the 'War Communism' of 1919–22 reduced Russia to utter prostration, and forced Lenin to return to private trading under the 'New Economic Policy' – a measure condemned by many of his followers as wholly retrograde, and justified by himself only on the ground of absolute necessity. But present-day marxists hold that such objections as were made at the time revealed an inability to understand the dialectic, and that the N.E.P. was the dialectical antithesis of 'War Communism' of which Stalin's policy from 1924 onwards represents the synthesis. Thus are the defeats of communism converted into its victories.

4. DIALECTIC AND FORMAL LOGIC

Hegel took over from Plato the conception that ideas alone possess reality, but added the notion that ideas themselves are not fixed and are in a continual state of change; and he attacked the philosophers of the eighteenth century on the ground that they had failed to discern the true nature of change because they had applied only the static methods of formal logic. This is that logic which was first systematized by Aristotle, and it is so called because it seeks to define things according to their essential properties, so that a table is defined as such because it contains those features to which a table must *conform* if it is to be a table.

Formal logic rests upon such apparently obvious propositions as that A = A (i.e. that a thing is identical with itself), that A is not non-A (i.e. that a thing is not different from itself) and that a thing is either A or non-A (i.e. that it cannot be both at once). Its mode of argument is the syllogism; e.g. 'All men are mortal; Socrates is a man; therefore Socrates is mortal.' There are, indeed, those who deny the validity of this type of logic, but we cannot enter into their objections which in no way imply any preference for the dialectic which Hegel sought to substitute for it. But we are using formal logic when we say that a cow is a cow and not a horse, or if we go on to state that cows and horses are both animals as distinct from vegetables. For there is a sense in which it must be true that, as Bishop Butler puts it, 'everything is what it is and not some other thing'. The object of formal logic is thus to enable us to make clear-cut distinctions based upon definitions of our subject-matter; and if we are not entitled to do this, it is hard to see how we can think at all. At the same time, we recognize that formal logic is unsuitable for certain types of thinking, as there is also a sense in which the subject-matter of thought, and indeed of being also, must be conceived not as fixed but as changing, so that, as Heraclitus said, 'We never jump into the same river twice'. We become immediately aware of this when we have to deal with abstractions. If, for example, we are thinking about democracy, we quickly become conscious that it is a term used with many different meanings, both in the past and in the present, and that we cannot arrive at its true nature by simply opposing it to monarchy or aristocracy, though such opposition would be permissible if we were merely attempting a rough classification of the various forms of government.

As a revolutionary, Marx was naturally attracted to the dialectic because it represented everything as being in the state of becoming something else, and to this day communists are taught that it constitutes a mode of reasoning which is somehow superior to that of formal logic, which is represented as conceiving of everything in fixed and unchangeable terms and as thus providing a convenient intellectual instrument for reactionaries. Thus, Engels says that the dialectic transcends the narrow horizon of formal logic and contains the germ of a more comprehensive view of the world: and that while formal logic is all very well 'for every-day purposes', it is inadequate to give 'an exact representation of the universe'; though the claim of the dialectic to perform this rests on no more secure foundation that in marxist hands it can be twisted to explain anything.

Again, in an article in the *New International* of March 1940, Trotsky asserts that the relation of the dialectic to formal logic is similar to that between higher and lower mathematics or between a motion picture and a photograph. 'Aristotle lived', he says, 'in a period when the idea of evolution did not exist.' He points out that formal logic starts from the law of identity, that is that $A = A$. But no two things are ever the same, so that a pound of sugar is never equal to another pound of sugar, as a more delicate scale will always disclose a difference. And thus he concludes that the statement that $A = A$ signifies that a thing is equal to itself if it does not change, which means if it does not exist, since everything that does exist is in a state of change.[1]

Now, as Max Eastman rightly observes, all this is most dubious. The idea of evolution was perfectly familiar to the Greeks, and a century before Heraclitus made his famous discovery that all things change, Solon, when asked what was the

1. See also Trotsky's *The Petty-Bourgeois Opposition in the Social Worker's Party* (15 December 1939), and *Defence of Marxism* (1942), p. 49.

best form of government, had replied 'for whom and at what time?' – an answer which many persons who dogmatize on such matters today might consider with advantage. But, as Eastman further points out, when Aristotle says that A=A and that everything is either A or non-A, he is not talking about existent things but about consistent thinking. The principle that A=A means that if we are going to be rational, or in other words talk sense, the meaning of our terms must not shift while we are talking. We cannot even state that pounds of sugar are unequal unless the term 'pound of sugar' is identical with the term itself. That is what Aristotle perceived, and that is what formal logic is about.[1]

Hegel's belief that change is always effected by the fruitful conflict of what he called, indifferently, contradictions or oppositions led him to challenge what he regarded as the barren conflict of affirmation and denial made by formal logic.[2] Unfortunately, he did not at all clearly define what he meant by contradictions, and those to which he refers are of many different kinds. In a given situation, there may be forces that make for peace and others that make for war, and it is doubtless permissible to represent these as contradictions which 'exist in unity'.[3] But there are other types of contradiction which are by their very nature irreconcilable. If, for example, the statement that 'All men are mortal' does not exclude the contrary statement that 'Some men are immortal', it is meaningless. But few writers on dialectical materialism distinguish between the various types of contradiction – between what Jules Monnerot, in his able treatment of this problem, calls *contradictions motrices* and *contradictions paralysantes*.[4] Marxists habitually

1. Max Eastman, *Marxism, Is it a Science?* (1941), pp. 258 ff.; but cp. G. D. H. Cole, *The Meaning of Marxism* (1948), pp. 269 ff.

2. On Hegel's treatment of the Law of Contradiction *see* Hans Kelsen, *The Political Theory of Bolshevism* (California University Press, 1949), pp. 14–17.

3. Sabine, pp. 532–5.

4. Jules Monnerot, *Sociologie du communisme* (Paris, 1949), pp. 214 ff.; *see* also the German Social Democrat, Edouard Conze, *An Introduction to Dialectical Materialism* (n.d.), p. 57, and for a criticism of Conze, David Guest's *A Textbook of Dialectical Materialism* (1939), pp. 78 ff.

describe as contradictory any sequence of events that are in some vague sense contrary to one another; and at the same time imply that the contradictions between them are reconcilable, and that it is only outmoded formal logic which asserts the contrary. Yet while it is legitimate to regard dialectical logic as a development of formal logic, it contains no new function, and the opposition which marxists set up between it and formal logic is quite unjustifiable. We may accept it if we like; but its rejection in no way commits us, as marxists would have it, to regarding everything as fixed and static, and of thus being forever incapable of taking into account the fluidity of the subject matter of thought and of making new judgements as changes in it require them. In fact, marxists do not hesitate to use such expressions as 'feudalism' and 'capitalism' as fixed terms, as indeed they have to do. They talk continually of the 'logic of contradiction', but none of their writings from Marx to Stalin contains any example of reasoning which does not assume that given one thing, another follows from it, which is how we all normally argue.[1]

*

It may assist a better understanding of the dialectic if we give the conclusions which marxists draw from it and the type of illustration which they use to support these conclusions. Within limits the former are reasonable enough, and the claim of marxists that they alone accept them is absurd. The latter are commonly tendentious and misleading, especially when drawn from the current political situation.

First, phenomena do not exist in isolation, but are dependent upon other phenomena. It is therefore in the light of this relationship that they must be studied if their true nature is to be understood. Marxists alone (they claim) recognize that this is necessary.

Secondly, phenomena must be studied in their movement and development. The craving for something stable and eternal is deeply rooted in the human mind, and is exploited by the conservative ruling class, which represents whatever may be the

1. Julien Benda, *Trois idoles romantiques* (Paris, 1948), p. 162.

existing regime as part of the order of nature. In fact, however, society is not static, but is in a continual state of change. Marx was thus able to show by scientific methods that capitalism is simply a transient phase in the flux of historical development, and that it is destined to pass into socialism.

Thirdly, wherever we find opposites we must look for their positive inter-connexion, since opposites are always united, as are, for example, attraction and repulsion in nature. It is only by recognizing this that the problem of a socialist society can be solved. Such a society requires centralized planning. At the same time the control of industry by the workers is of the essence of socialism, and this calls for decentralization. The marxist argues that these opposites are dialectically united in the Soviet Union, through the relation between the Party and the Soviets.

Fourthly, we must look for contradiction both in the processes of nature and of society, since contradiction is the motive force behind all development. It was the inability of the materialist philosophers of the eighteenth century to recognize this that prevented them from understanding the true nature of social change, which can only arise as the result of the conflict and reconciliation of two elements or forces that give rise to a contradiction. Thus capitalism has engendered the contradiction that whereas man should be the master of the products of his labour, he has become their servant. For production, which Marx regards as the central human activity, seeing that almost everyone is in some way engaged in and dependent upon it, has led to what, borrowing a concept used by both Hegel and Feuerbach, he calls 'alienation'. When men no longer produce for their own use but for the profit of others, the works of their hands become 'fetishes' which enslave them. Thus they become 'alienated' or estranged both from themselves and from their fellow men – a state of affairs for which communism alone can provide the remedy, as it has done, according to marxists, in the Soviet Union.

But the two opposed elements or forces in any such given contradiction are not equal, as one will be dying but will be seeking to resist the other which is coming to birth. Hence it is upon this second element that attention must always be focused, since it is this which must finally prevail. The illustration given by all present-day marxists is the Soviet Union itself, which is held to reflect the progressive and democratic forces of society, and is thus involved in a life-and-death struggle with the obsolete and decaying forces of reaction as represented by capitalism and its social democratic 'lackeys'.

All marxist theoreticians are thus committed to applying the dialectic to any problem with which they may be dealing, though the result is often totally to obscure it; and the commonest criticism of any scheme that has miscarried is that its authors failed to carry out beforehand a correct dialectical analysis of the situation. For it is on the dialectic that the *Conclusion* of the official *Short History of the Communist Party of the Soviet Union* bases the claim which it makes for the marxist doctrine, 'the power of which', as it declares, lies in the fact that 'it enables the Party to find the right orientation to any situation, to understand the inner connexion of current events, to foresee their course, and to perceive not only how and in what direction they are developing in the present, but how and in what direction they are bound to develop in the future. Without some knowledge of this mode of reasoning it is thus scarcely possible to understand marxist literature at all. But by reason of its official adoption, it has degenerated into a barren scholasticism such as is taught in all communist centres of learning under the guise of instruction in the art of thinking, of which the best that can be said is that it may perhaps encourage beginners to think historically. Yet we may accept the dialectic as a description of the part played in human affairs by conflicting tendencies and purposes, without necessarily accepting it as a universal law. In the first sense it can be applied with genuine force to the analysis of society, as no one who has read Marx will dispute, and critics like Max Eastman go too far when they condemn it as completely valueless and as a redundant element of marxist theory.[1]

But although the dialectic may give us valuable insights into the history of human development, the marxist claim that it

1. Cp. Karl Mannheim, *Ideology and Utopia* (1936), pp. 115–16.

constitutes the only scientific approach to reality cannot be allowed. It is not, in fact, scientific at all, and it is only in Russia that scientists are required to set out their ideas in pseudo-dialectical jargon, for which Engels's *Anti-Dühring* provides the model.[1] Marxists argue, indeed, that the processes of nature are governed by the dialectic, though if this be so, it is strange that all the great scientific discoveries should have been made without apparent reference to it. Thus, to take the illustration borrowed from Hegel and used by Engels in Ch. xiii of his *Anti-Dühring*, a grain of barley germinates and dies, and from it there arises a plant which is 'the negation of the grain'. This plant grows, and finally produces a stalk at the end of which are further grains of barley. 'As soon as these are ripened the stalk dies and is in turn negated'; and as a result of this 'negation of the negation', the original grain of barley is multiplied tenfold. But such changes cannot just be represented as contradictions, nor does the emergence of ten grains of barley from a single grain constitute a 'qualitative' change (since the grains remain barley), or issue in a 'higher reformulation', such as the dialectic is understood to effect. In fact, the seed-flower-fruit cycle simply brings us back to where we started.[2]

Again, the world of the scientist is not one in which everything is in a state of becoming, for if it were, most scientific investigation would have to be abandoned. As it is, the scientist is aware that the phenomena with which he is dealing change so imperceptibly as to justify him in regarding them as static, and his work becomes possible only because he can, for all practical purposes, isolate them into closed systems. He will, of course, consider his particular group of phenomena in their relation to others; but the idea that they can be comprehended only as a part of the whole is one which belongs to metaphysics rather than to science. And, finally, there is, as Röpke points out, a profound gulf between the attempt to comprehend the

1. *See* Monnerot, p. 215: but cp. J. B. S. Haldane, *Dialectic Materialism and Modern Science* (n.d.), and J. D. Bernal, *The Foundations of Necessity* (1949), pp. 370 ff., 410 ff., 423 ff.
2. Sidney Hook, *The 'Laws' of the Dialectic* (*Polemic*, November–December 1946), pp. 9 ff.

world through the critical intelligence, as the scientist seeks to do within his own field, and the attempt to identify that intelligence with the world. For the process of becoming and our idea of the process are different things, and science lends no warrant to the notion that it is possible to establish a mystical union between the two.[1]

5. MARX'S MATERIALISM AND HIS THEORY OF KNOWLEDGE

Marx rejected, or at least believed he had rejected, the whole of Hegel's idealist philosophy, while retaining his dialectic method. He had many faults to find with Hegel's system, but his fundamental criticism of it is contained in a famous passage in the Introduction to the first volume of *Capital*:

> My own dialectic method is not only different from the Hegelian, but is its direct opposite. For Hegel ... the thinking process is the demiurge (creator) of the real world, and the real world is only the outward manifestation of 'the Idea'. With me, on the other hand, the ideal is nothing else than the material world reflected by the human mind and translated into terms of thought.

Or, as he puts it in a letter to Dr Ludwig Kugelmann, of 1868: 'Hegel's dialectic is the basic form of dialectics, but only after it has been stripped of its mystical form, and it is precisely this which distinguishes my method.'[2]

Marx claimed therefore to have found Hegel on his head and to have 'set him the right way up', and this may be allowed in so far as the material world is for him the ultimate reality, whereas for Hegel it was something immaterial. But it is not true, as Benedetto Croce points out, that marxism is an inversion of Hegelianism, because Hegel had not opposed mind and matter in the way in which the subjective idealism of Berkeley and Kant had done, and, indeed, his system was directed to removing the dualism such an opposition created by representing the mind and the known object as simply different aspects of the whole. His Absolute is not mind, but a self-existent

1. Wilhelm Röpke, *La Crise de Notre temps* (Neuchâtel, 1947), p. 68; Benda, pp. 166 ff.   2. *Correspondence*, p. 234.

realm of being. Thus it is a perversion of his position to suggest, as marxists do, that he regarded mind as real and matter as a reflection of mind, and that Marx performed the service of setting him the right way up by reversing this order and so bringing mind and matter into their proper relation to one another.[1]

For, it must be repeated, in Hegel's philosophy everything that is or ever has been is conceived as a part of the Absolute, which is complete and pure self-consciousness and comprehends all thought and experience according to an ideal logical system. Any event, as for example, the French Revolution, is thus an exteriorization of the Absolute of which our minds that perceive it are only another aspect. The dialectic is thus, as it were, something which is both in us and in things; and this is Hegel's justification for transferring it from the timeless order of thought (for time does not enter into logic) into the temporal order of events. But what Marx does is to take over the essential property of that Absolute upon which, in Hegel's system, both mind and nature depend, and apply it to a material world of which he had declared mind to be simply a by-product.

The marxist version of the dialectic is indeed open to serious objection. The dialectic can properly be applied to the development of ideas through the conflict of contradictions, and Hegel provides a rational explanation of that development. Yet, although dialectical materialism can point to something analogous to contradictions in the material world, not only are these analogies altogether arbitrary, but even if they were not, it would still remain a complete mystery why the material world should exhibit them. Dialectical materialism in fact asserts that matter is matter, but that it develops as ideas do. Only, while we can see why ideas develop as they do, as for example in discussion, there is no conceivable reason why material things should develop in the same way. Eastman maintains, however, that Marx was by no means as successful in getting rid of Hegel as he had supposed, and that having declared the world to be made up of unconscious matter, he then

1. *Materialismo storico et economia marxistica* (ed. Bari, 1944), p. 5; see also Collingwood, op. cit.

found himself obliged to read into matter the very essence of Hegel's Absolute, so that his system is in fact a return to the animism of primitive man which attributes human values to trees and other material objects.[1]

This criticism is perhaps less applicable to Marx than it is to Engels, who both in his *Anti-Dühring* and in his *Dialectics of Nature* maintained that natural processes are dialectical, as modern dialectical materialists continue to do. There are indeed passages in *Capital* which suggest that Marx held the same view, and indeed if the dialectic is a universal principle, it is hard to see upon what grounds the order of nature is to be excluded from its operation. Marx's real interest, however, was in the process of social development, and this he certainly believed to be dialectical. Unfortunately, for a writer who claimed that his work was scientific, he took altogether insufficient pains to make himself understood, and was often obscure and careless in expression. Thus it is not always clear whether his dialectic is one of material economic forces or of the class struggle to which their development gives rise; and his anxiety to stress the importance of the former led him frequently to use language which suggests that they somehow possess the property of developing dialectically, so that by throwing the emphasis upon them rather than upon the human framework within which they can alone operate, he exposed himself to the charge of endowing his material universe with qualities which transcend its physical nature and belong to the order of metaphysics.

Marx radically altered the theory of materialism. The empirical philosophy of the seventeenth century had led in the eighteenth century to a materialist view of the world, which was conceived as a mechanism like a clock operating through all eternity in accordance with fixed laws, the nature of which Newton had been the first to make clear. Descartes had taught that it was by these laws that God willed his universe to be governed; but although this explanation satisfied the orthodoxy of his generation, it relegated the Supreme Being to the position of the *primum mobile*, for God, having once set the world in

1. Max Eastman, *Marxism. Is it a Science?*, p. 23.

motion, could no longer interfere with its processes, and his subsequent role was rather that of the chairman of a committee, the business of which could very well be conducted in his absence. It was therefore not surprising that there should have arisen by the middle of the eighteenth century a school of outright materialists, of which Diderot and Holbach were prominent representatives, which rejected God as an unnecessary hypothesis and conceived of the world in purely materialist terms. Marxists commend this early materialism because it challenged idealism, but they point out that, being mechanistic, it could give no explanation of development, and that scientific materialism only begins with Marx and Engels.[1]

The eighteenth-century materialists believed that they had destroyed idealism. But they were mistaken, and by the end of the century an idealistic reaction had set in, of which Kant and Hegel were the leaders. The basic weakness of the older school is held by marxists to have been its failure to understand the nature of development because it conceived both of the world and of man in terms of mechanics – the dominant science of the times. If, however, the world is a machine, it can only do what it has been made to do and cannot develop any new quality; while if man is so conceived there is no accounting for the origin and growth of his consciousness, since this is something which is part of his nature, and all we can do is to define the mechanism by which it works. What then was needed was a logic or principle of development, and it was to supply this that Hegel propounded his dialectical method which Marx in turn adopted.

Now Marx was a revolutionary, and thus required a philosophy into which his revolutionary theories could be fitted. This philosophy had to satisfy three conditions. First, it had to be scientific, or at least appear to be so, and it had therefore to be materialistic, since science deals with matter and knows no other language. Secondly, it had to show that social development was inevitably moving in the direction of the desired revolution. Thirdly, it could not be a purely mechanistic

1. G. V. Plekhanov, *In Defence of Materialism* (ed. 1947), p. 178; Hook, from *Hegel to Marx*, pp. 28 ff.; Cole, pp. 19 ff.

explanation of the universe, such as, in his *Holy Family* (1845), he accused the French materialists of providing, but had to furnish a guide to revolutionary action or it would remain sterile. He saw therefore that he must deal at the outset with what Engels calls the 'great basic question of all philosophy . . . that concerning the relation of thinking and being';[1] because on this depended the question as to whether any real knowledge of the material world was possible, since if it was not possible, he would have to abandon his attempt to found a purely scientific theory of society upon it.

Marx's treatment of this problem has coloured all subsequent communist thinking. He takes it, of course, as axiomatic that the material world *is* the fundamental reality, and that although it is accessible to thought, it is not constituted by it. But whether the human mind can arrive at objective truth is, he says, not a question of theory at all, but a practical question. The older materialists had taught that our knowledge of the external world – and at the same time our ideas about it – was obtained by the impact of sensations upon the mind, but had regarded these sensations as passive, that is, as not necessarily involving any change in what was perceived. Marx teaches that these sensations, which were held to give us faithful images of the external world, did not provide *immediate* knowledge but only stimuli to knowledge which completed itself in action; for if sensations were purely passive, it was impossible to explain why they should result in conscious activity; and if men were unable to react on their environment and change it, revolutions could no longer be regarded as a form of human activity and were simply incidents in a mechanical process. Hence, he insisted that we only perceive a thing as a part of the process of acting upon it, just as a cat when it sees a mouse immediately pounces on it. This activist theory of knowledge – known today as instrumentalism – which insists that knowledge is indissolubly bound up with action (*Praxis*), is the most distinctive feature of Marx's philosophy as opposed to his theories of history and economics. It was essential to his revolutionary creed, since, as he declared in his *Theses on Feuerbach*: 'All philosophies have

1. Marx–Engels *Selected Works* (2-vol. ed. 1950) II, p. 234.

sought to explain the world; the point, however, is to change it.'
Thus, marxists have always insisted that theory and action are
one. A theory of which the truth is not confirmed by action is
sterile, while action which is divorced from theory is purpose-
less. The two stand in much the same relation to one another as
do faith and works in Christian theology.[1]

On the other hand, Engels, in his anxiety to guard the
materialistic base of dialectical materialism, went back to the
older theory which held the source of knowledge to be sensations. Logically it would seem that this must lead to solipsism
– the position that we only know our subjective states, but can
have no assurance that these correspond to any reality outside
ourselves. Engels, however, rejects this conclusion, and states
dogmatically that our sensations give us accurate 'copies' of
external reality. But this is to assert what it is his business to
prove. For if all we possess in consciousness are copies, and
there is no means of comparing the copy with the original, we
can no more say that the one exactly reflects the other than that
a portrait of a person we have never seen is an accurate likeness
of him. Here, as we shall see, Lenin followed Engels, rejecting
Plekhanov's contention that sensations are simply symbols or
heiroglyphs, and insisting that they give us 'copies, photo-
graphs, and mirror-reflections of things'.

Marxists thus hold that there is an indissoluble connexion
between theory and practice, and this union of the two is one
of the most important elements in their thought. On the one
hand, it is practice which alone determines the truth of theory,
so that, as John Macmurray points out, marxists are highly
suspicious people, and refuse to take the ideas of any political
party at their face value, holding that in order to know what a
party really believes it is necessary to study how it behaves
when it is in power.[2] But on the other hand, theory equally
determines practice, since, if the theory is wrong, its error will
inevitably reveal itself in the sphere of action. This explains the
jealous regard paid to ideological purity, and the immense

1. Max Eastman, *The Last Stand of Dialectical Materialism* (New
York, 1934), pp. 11 ff.
2. *Philosophy of Communism* (1933), p. 36.

importance attached to theoretical indoctrination. Further, it accounts in part for the adulation of Stalin. As the leader of the Party, he was responsible for what it did, and he was therefore also responsible for the theory which lay behind its practice, so that he became 'the greatest living philosopher', though his contribution to philosophy was scarcely an impressive one.

When, therefore, a Party member is given instruction in marxist ideology, the first thing that is impressed upon him is that there exist, and can exist, only two possible philosophical positions, idealism and materialism, the attitude adopted by Engels in his *Ludwig Feuerbach* and later taken over by Lenin, who held that they reflect the class division of society. He is told that there are many forms of idealism, but that all assert that mind is primary, and that matter, if it has any reality at all, is secondary. Idealism contends that we can have no *final* knowledge of the world of phenomena, because such knowledge is conditioned by our senses. A knowledge of 'things in themselves' is thus impossible. To men born in green or red spectacles the snow will appear green or red, and they have no means of discovering that it is, in fact, neither. On the other hand, materialism insists that reality is not mind but matter; that the existence of matter precedes that of mind; that the material world, so far from existing only in our minds, possesses an objective existence apart from our perception of it; and that we can therefore obtain a knowledge of the world which, though incomplete, like a jigsaw puzzle from which certain parts are missing, contains an indestructible core of absolute truth which is continually growing as our knowledge increases. Dialectical materialism is thus represented as the only scientific explanation of reality; while idealism is a non-scientific explanation, and is invariably coupled with religion, both having their roots in ignorance, and being by their very nature hostile to science, just as a witch doctor will always resist a scientific explanation to disease. As the dialectic does not allow for three-cornered fights, there can be no intermediate position, and agnostics who hold the problem of the ultimate nature of reality to be insoluble are simply idealists who lack the courage of their convictions.

6. HISTORICAL MATERIALISM

Historical materialism, or the materialistic interpretation of history, is simply dialectical materialism applied to the particular field of human relations within society.[1] The dialectic supplies the clue to the whole process. In the preface to his *Critique of Political Economy* Marx starts by asking what is the principle that governs all human relations, and his answer is that it is the common end which all men pursue, that is, the production of the means to support life, and next to production, the exchange of things produced. Man has to live before he can start to think. Hence the ultimate determinant of social change is not to be found in his ideas of eternal truth and social justice, but in changes in the mode of production and exchange.

Now two factors enter into production. In addition to the resources provided by Nature, men possess certain instruments of production – their labour and practical skill and (in a primitive society) the implements that they make – and these Marx calls the 'productive forces'. But production also involves a relation between men and men, and this Marx calls the 'productive relations'. In other words, the relation between men and things (productive forces) leads to a second relation between men and men (productive relations), and when the first changes, the second changes also. In a primitive society the relations of production are those of cooperation, or so at least Marx supposed. But at an early stage in the history of man certain members of society acquired a control over the productive forces. This action, which was eventually to lead to the capitalist system, enabled the minority to live by the labour of the majority; and in the marxist scheme it takes the place of the Fall of Man, since the inclination of men to take advantage of one another was a corruption introduced into history by the private ownership of the means of production. As a result, the productive relations henceforth became those of two antagonistic classes; so that, as Marx declares in the *Communist Manifesto*, 'the history of all hitherto existing societies is the history of the class struggle'.

1. Plekhanov, pp. 179 ff.; Venable, *Human Nature: The Marxian View* (1946), pp. 74 ff.

By his own day this was entering upon what he held to be its final phase, the struggle between the bourgeoisie and the proletariat.

Marx goes on to argue that 'the productive conditions taken as a whole constitute the economic structure of society – the material basis on which a superstructure of laws and political institutions is based and to which certain forms of political consciousness correspond'. The economic system of society, which he calls the substructure (*Unterbau*), always provides the real basis; and the religion, ethics, laws, and institutions of society are a superstructure (*Oberbau*) built upon and determined by it. The constituents of the superstructure will invariably be found on analysis to reflect the interests of the dominant class, so that, for example, the system of morals prevailing at any given time will simply be that body of principles by which that class regards it as desirable that society should be directed.

Hence transitions from one phase of social development to another are not effected because of the emergence of new rational principles or of new conceptions of truth and justice, since these belong to the superstructure, and what renders them acceptable is that changes in the productive forces have created the environment which makes them seem the natural expression of what men have come to desire. What, in fact, happens is that a point is reached when, as a result of some new invention or discovery, the productive forces come into conflict with the existing relations of production – and in particular with the prevailing property system – which now so far from furthering their development become fetters upon it. A social revolution will then take place; and owing to the upheaval of the substructure, the superstructure will be gradually or violently subverted.

Take, for example, an agricultural country. Here the productive forces will be primarily land and those implements and aptitudes required for its development. These will bring into existence a type of productive relations appropriate to them, such as that which exists in a community of landowners and peasants; and these productive relations will, in turn, be reflected in the laws and institutions of the community. If it is then found that the country possesses quantities of coal and iron, and if it is decided to develop these resources, a new set of productive forces will come into operation with a corresponding change in the productive relations. The landowner will give place to the manufacturer, and the peasant to the industrial worker; while the laws and institutions of society will be so modified as to make them subserve the new order. The transition will not, however, take place without a struggle, since the new and more productive economy will be resisted by all those who have an interest in maintaining the older and less productive. Indeed, the representatives of the latter may succeed in retaining a considerable degree of political power long after they have lost their economic supremacy, though in so far as they do so they will act as a brake upon their successors.

Marx distinguishes five economic forms, or modes, of production – primitive, communal, slave, feudal, capitalist, and socialist. Under the first, the means of production are socially owned. Under the second, the slave-owner owns them. Under the third, the feudal lord partially owns them, as his men have some property. Under the fourth, the capitalist owns the means of production, but not his men, who he can no longer dispose of as he pleases, though they are compelled to work for him. Under the fifth, which has not yet come into existence, the workers themselves will own the means of production and, with the abolition of the contradictions inherent in capitalism, production will reach its fullest development. Both from the point of view of production and of freedom, each of these stages represents an advance upon its predecessor, this being in accordance with the dialectic principle that every new stage takes up whatever was of value in that which it has 'negated' – the principle that had led Hegel to declare in the Introduction to his *Philosophy of History* that 'the Oriental World knows only *one* that is free, the Greeks and Romans recognize that *some* are free, the German nations have attained to the knowledge that *all* are free'. Thus, Marx commends the early capitalists because they had broken down the barriers imposed by feudalism, but argues that the system has outlived its usefulness and has become an obstacle to the further development of the productive forces.

To understand social revolutions we have therefore to distinguish between changes in the productive forces and the various ideological forms in which men become conscious of the conflict and fight it out. The real cause is always the former; but men are seldom aware of this, and will believe that they are fighting for religion, political liberty or any other ideological motive. Marxists contend that it is, indeed, on the basis of this illusion that most history has been written, the true cause of revolutions having been thus concealed until Marx revealed it. They have to adopt this position because it is an article of their faith that every great movement in history – the rise of Islam, the Renaissance or any other – was ultimately due to an economic cause.

This, then, was the theory which Engels claimed, at Marx's graveside, to have made as great a contribution to the science of social relations as had Darwin's theory to natural science.

Just as Darwin discovered the law of evolution in organic nature, so Marx discovered the law of evolution in human history; he discovered the simple fact, hitherto concealed by an overgrowth of ideology, that mankind must first of all eat and drink, have shelter and clothing, before it can pursue politics, religion, science, art, etc.; and that therefore the production of the immediate material means of subsistence, and consequently the degree of economic development attained by a given people or during a given epoch, form the foundation upon which State institutions, the legal conceptions, the art, and even the religious ideas of the people concerned, have been evolved, and in the light of which these things must be explained, instead of vice versa as had hitherto been the case.[1]

7. THE CLASS STRUGGLE

We have seen that the productive forces at any given period always develop appropriate forms of productive relations, and that, except among the most primitive communities, these are

1. *S.W.*, II, p. 153; *see* also Engel's preface to the 1885 German edition of Marx's *Eighteenth Brumaire*, in which he makes a somewhat similar claim, ibid. pp. 223–4.

always relations of exploitation which divide society into classes. It is, however, characteristic of Marx that having devoted the greater part of his life to writing about the class struggle he should never have defined what he meant by a class, a question that he raised in the last chapter of the third volume of *Capital*, but without answering it. He recognizes, however, that classes are not homogeneous, and that there will be as many of them as there are well-marked degrees of social status. But he is not much concerned with their functional differences, because, for the purpose of the class struggle, he holds that all classes are ultimately divisible by two, one of which controls the means of production, while the other does not, and that the antagonism to which this gives rise creates a profound contradiction. Yet it is through this very contradiction that progress is effected, since, as we have seen, it is through the conflict of thesis and antithesis that we reach the synthesis which brings us one step nearer to our goal.[1]

The force which lies behind the dialectic of history and moves the world is not therefore the clash of nations, as Hegel and the majority of historians had supposed, but the clash of classes or the class struggle. Class interest thus takes the place of national interest, which is always found upon examination to be no more than the interest of the ruling class. Marx did not pretend to have discovered the class struggle; but he claimed to have proved that the existence of classes is bound up with a 'particular historic phase in the history of production', that it must inevitably lead to the dictatorship of the proletariat, and that the dictatorship will be a transitional stage which will end with the abolition of all classes and the establishment of a classless society.[2]

The class struggle is thus held to offer an explanation of phenomena for which traditional history cannot account, and in particular of the trend towards increasing productivity. Men

1. On the class struggle see K. R. Popper, *The Open Society and its Enemies* (1945) II, pp. 103 ff.; Venable, pp. 98 ff.; J. L. Gray, *Karl Marx and Social Philosophy in Social and Political Ideas of the Victorian Age* (ed. F. J. C. Hearnshaw, 1933), pp. 141 ff.

2. Letter to Weydemeyer of 5 March 1852, *Correspondence*, p. 57.

work blindly within a social system which forces them to act in accordance with what they believe to be their class interest, and it is vain to blame them for so doing. As all are caught in the network, they can do nothing to change its nature. This is one of the reasons why Marx does not believe in social technology, and incidentally why marxism is no guide to the practice of government, as Lenin was later to discover. Yet all the time the class struggle is inevitably leading to the transformation of society. As the productive forces change, the class which has hitherto controlled them is confronted by a new class, which claims to be able to administer them more efficiently; and just as the merchants and craftsmen were able to challenge the feudal lord of the later Middle Ages, so will the wage-earner challenge the capitalist and wrest economic power from him. Thus there will be brought about the final emancipation of mankind, seeing that there is no class below the proletariat, which is at the bottom of the social scale. But to accelerate this process, the class-consciousness of the worker must first be developed, that is, he must be made to realize his class interest and become conscious of that same power with which Hegel had endowed the nation. The class-conscious proletarian is thus the worker who is not only aware of his class situation, but is also proud of his class and assured of its historic mission.

Yet Marx nowhere seeks to prove that the worker *is*, in fact, fitted for the role assigned to him; nor does it occur to him that the negation of capitalism may lead to the emergence of a wholly new class which is strictly speaking neither capitalist nor proletarian. The belief in human perfectibility that he had inherited from the eighteenth century led him to believe that a classless society, inherently desirable on ethical grounds, must be the next stage in social evolution; while as a revolutionary and agitator he saw in the working-class movement the only available instrument for the achievement of this aim in the immediate future, and was thus induced to regard it as the final 'negation of the negation'.

The belief in the class struggle as the 'inner essence' of history vitiates the thinking of marxists by leading them to attribute to the proletariat attitudes and judgements which are in fact, confined to little groups of revolutionaries.[1] The classical economists were in the habit of generalizing widely about a class of factors of production which they called 'labour', and to which they opposed an equally chimerical general monopoly of employers. But this classification breaks down upon analysis. So also does the marxist version of the class struggle. It is, in fact, a myth, and the very exhortation of the workers to unite is an admission that there is no natural proletarian solidarity, as is attested by the relations in any particular country between male and female labour, skilled and unskilled, white and coloured. Still less is there an identity of interests between workers in different countries. Measures which perpetuate the poverty of the workers in one country are beneficial to those in another; while in no advanced country will the workers accept cheap foreign labour. And, again, all experience has hitherto proved that whenever the existence of any country appears to be threatened from without, its preservation is regarded as the dominant interest by all classes.[2]

Finally, Marx's thesis that all conflict among men arises from the class struggle, albeit of undoubted tactical value as calculated to convince the masses that their misfortunes are attributable to the capitalist system and will disappear with the victory of the proletariat, is none the less fallacious. For the supreme source of conflict in life is the inevitable opposition between the claims of the individual and those of society – a conflict which is not reducible to the class struggle and cannot be dialectically resolved (even were it desirable that it should be) because it is a part of the unchanging human situation.

8. CRITICISM OF HISTORICAL MATERIALISM

Marx's philosophy of history is regarded, even by his critics, with a greater respect than any other part of his doctrine,

1. Max Eastman, *Stalin's Russia and the Crisis of Socialism* (1940), p. 217.
2. L. H. Robbins, *The Economic Basis of the Class Struggle* (1939), pp. 17 ff.; Franz Borkenau, *Socialism, National or International* (1942), pp. 14 ff.

though it did not exert much influence until after his death. It rests on two theses. The first is that economic causes are fundamental, and the second that they operate in accordance with the dialectic principle. The latter is nowadays accepted only by marxists, but the former commands a much wider allegiance.

The claim that the dialectic furnishes the clue to history cannot, indeed, be seriously defended, even if we are prepared to accept it as an explanation of the processes of thought. Any proposition, such as that 'All property is theft', can be developed dialectically because it supplies a starting point. But as Karl Federn points out in his most valuable study, history proceeds as an unending stream of which no one knows the beginning or the end. It provides no *terminus a quo*, and thus makes it impossible to determine which of its stages are thesis, antithesis or synthesis.[1] Any historical event can be shown with equal plausibility to be a synthesis of two contradictory elements in the past, or as a thesis for which some other event will then be chosen to provide the antithesis. Thus, the Norman Conquest can be represented as a synthesis of Roman and Anglo-Saxon cultures, or as a thesis of which the age of the Plantagenets and that of the Tudors are respectively the antithesis and the synthesis. Such irresponsible treatment simply reduces history to a game for which the only qualifications are a lively imagination and much ignorance.

Further, we have seen that the dialectic, as used by Hegel, is essentially an optimistic doctrine, since every synthesis is an advance towards the Absolute; while Marx similarly contends that every successive stage of society which arises on account of the internal contradictions of the preceding stage constitutes a 'higher' form. If history were a continuous record of progress, this would be well enough. But it is as much a tale of dis-

1. Karl Federn, *The Materialistic Conception of History* (1939), pp. 209 ff.; for a recent statement of the marxist thesis *see* Jean Bruhat, *Destin de l'histoire* (Paris, 1948); *see* also M. M. Bober, *Karl Marx's Interpretation of History* (Harvard University Press, 1927), pp. 297–315; for a well reasoned statement of the marxist case *see* R. Mondolfo, *Il materialismo storico in Federico Engels* (1912 ed. Florence, 1925); H. B. Acton, *The Illusion of the Epoch* (1955), pp. 107 ff.

solution and decay; and to this part of it the dialectic cannot be applied.[1]

Again, the dialectical approach to history becomes extremely dangerous when it is accepted *de fide*, as it offers no objective standard as to the sense and rationality of action; and the fanatical devotion to it of the Russian leaders is certainly a hindrance to them rather than a help. The inter-war years abound in examples of policies, allegedly based on dialectical analyses, which served neither Russian nor communist interests. A notable instance was the discovery that the pre-condition of a communist victory in Germany was that Hitler should enjoy what it was assumed would be only a brief spell of authority. The communists were therefore instructed to attack the social democrats instead of combining with them against the common enemy, with the result that he came into power and crushed them both.[2] Similarly, the line which Stalin imposed upon the Chinese communists, in support of which a whole literature of theoretical justification was forthcoming, proved singularly unfortunate. They were ordered to adopt a policy which lay beyond their power to carry out, or at least to do so as Stalin desired, and thus played into the hands of the Kuomintang, which wellnigh exterminated them. The party was driven into the remoter districts, to emerge many years later under conditions which had never been foreseen, and are unlikely to have been viewed by Moscow with entire satisfaction.[3]

But Marx's first thesis, that the economic factor is fundamental for all social institutions and particularly for their historical development, is of much greater importance. It has exercised a profound influence, and all modern writers are indebted to him even if they do not know it. Any return to pre-marxist social theory is inconceivable. Indeed, as K. R. Popper

1. John Plamenatz, *What is Communism?* (1946), pp. 39–40.

2. A. L. Rowse, *The Use of History* (1946), pp. 136–7.

3. Stalin defended his policy in his speech to the Central Committee of 1 August 1927, printed in *Marxism and the National and Colonial Question*, pp. 232 ff. For a criticism of it see Harold R. Isaacs, *The Tragedy of the Chinese Revolution* (1938, revised edition, Stanford, 1951) and Robert C. North, *Moscow and the Chinese Communists* (Stanford, 1935), pp. 66–121.

points out, his thesis is sound enough so long as we use the term 'fundamental' loosely and do not lay too much stress upon it; and practically all social studies will profit if they are conducted against the background of the 'economic conditions' of society. In this qualified sense his 'economism' represents a valuable advance in the methods of social science, and has suggested many lines of inquiry that have greatly extended our knowledge.[1]

None the less, it is open to serious criticism in the extreme form in which Marx presented it. He asserts in the *Critique of Political Economy* that there are two factors in production, the productive forces and the productive relations which derive from them. Conceived in purely economic terms, they constitute the substructure, which is primary; while all the manifestations of the mind of man as reflected in his religion, laws, institutions and the like, constitute the superstructure, which is secondary. In other words, the mind and all that it creates is a part of the superstructure which is determined by the economic substructure. We are therefore left to suppose, as was pointed out above, that the productive forces somehow develop automatically, though in fact they *are developed, e.g.* by new discoveries, the responsible agency being the intelligence of man and the use which he makes of it.[2] As Koestler put it, 'marxist society has a basement-production and an attic-intellectual production; only the stairs and lifts are missing'.[3]

That Marx was aware of this difficulty is shown by the many passages in which he treats the political and social institutions of the superstructure as part of the substructure, as indeed he is obliged to do if he is to make sense of his theory, since it is obvious that it is only in proportion as men reach a certain level of political and social development that they are likely to make discoveries or possess the resources to exploit them. His disciples do likewise, and, as John Plamenatz says, no good marxist will ever hesitate to include elements of the superstructure in the substructure whenever he finds it convenient to do so.[4] The truth is that while Marx was ultimately led to admit an inter-

1. Popper II, p. 99.   2. Federn, pp. 15 ff.; but cp. Bober, pp. 11–27.
3. *The Yogi and the Commissar* (1945), p. 70.   4. Plamenatz, p. 35.

connexion between the two, he never clearly worked out what it was, and that if he had attempted to do so he would have had to abandon his theory.

Now it is quite certain that the forms of production have far-reaching consequences and are of the greatest importance in history. But, as Federn observes, the question is whether it is true that the intellectual, cultural, and political forms of any community not only depend for their existence upon economic production, but are in all their modifications also determined by it. When Marx said that 'men must be able to live in order to be able to make history', he did not simply mean that society depends on production for its existence, as this would have been a view that no one would have contested. Air is an essential condition of life. But if a scientist should succeed in proving that institutions and opinions depend upon the particular composition of the atmosphere, he would have made a very important discovery indeed. What Marx meant was that the way in which men produce determines the entire complex of ideas and institutions which make up the social order.[1]

The proofs which marxists adduce to substantiate this are taken either from pre-history or from history; the method is to show that an economic change occurred at a certain time, that some decades or centuries later a change took place in the ideas or institutions of the same people, and then to attribute the second change to the first. Thus, Kary Kautsky accounts for puritanism in England by saying that 'the transition from a natural to a monetary system of economy caused the lower classes to fall a prey to a sombre puritanism'. Why this should be so is not explained; in fact, the transition to a monetary economy had been completed by the fourteenth century, whereas puritanism did not appear until towards the end of the sixteenth century. Again, Antonio Labriola explains why the aborigines of North America did not attain a high degree of civilization on the ground that it was the Europeans who introduced wheat and domestic animals which had previously been lacking. But not only were there other forms of food, but vast herds of bison roamed the North American plains which the

1. Federn, pp. 30 ff.

Red Indians might have tamed, just as the negroes did the buffalo and the mongols the yak. That they did not do so was simply because it was not among their gifts.[1]

Marxist writers thus forever repeat the truism that men must eat and clothe themselves before they can undertake political activity and the like. But this is to confuse the condition of such activity with its cause. It is significant that it is to primitive society that they turn whenever possible for their illustrations, since the more primitive a community, the greater will be the part which physical necessity plays in its life – as is equally true of the individual. As civilization advances, men become possessed of more complex desires, which cannot be so easily related to elemental needs, such as the love of power which has led to so many conflicts. But having decided that every movement must have an economic cause, marxists do not study the movement in order to find out what really lies behind it, but look round for any economic cause that may possibly explain it.[2]

In finding such a cause they are assisted by the equivocal use that they make of the concept of 'historical necessity' which Marx and Engels borrowed from Hegel. 'Necessity' means something – whether good or bad is immaterial – which is bound to occur because it is the inevitable result of a cause. Yet marxists commonly apply it in the quite different sense of 'desirable'. Thus, we are told that England had a liberal constitution because she needed strong personalities to develop her commercial empire; whereas it would be far nearer the truth to say that because she had a free constitution, and other countries had not, the strong personalities had full scope and were in a position to found it. Again, the emergence of a great man at a critical period in a nation's history is attributed to 'necessity', so that Engels points out that Napoleon 'did not come by chance, and that if he had not come another man would have taken his place'. Yet no great man emerged to save the civilizations of Greece and Rome.[3] But then marxists invariably belittle the role of 'so-called great men', arguing that they do no

1. Federn, pp. 36–8, 40–1.   2. ibid. p. 73.
3. op. cit. pp. 220–2.

more than identify themselves with conditions which are independent of them. As Croce puts it, 'Homer had sung, Plato had philosophized, Jesus and Paul had transformed moral consciousness, quite unaware that they were simply the instruments of an economic process to which all their work was ultimately reducible'.[1] For to concede that such men shape history would be inconsistent with the principle that it is determined by economic forces, and these last have, therefore, to be made responsible for their emergence. Thus, Hessen maintains that Newton was not inspired to discover the law of gravitation by being hit on the head by an apple, as the discovery was demanded by the economic needs of his time.[2]

Nor do marxists make any allowance for the contingent element that enters into history. Bertrand Russell gives some brilliant examples of seemingly fortuitous events which have had a decisive influence. It was, as he points out, touch and go whether the German Government would allow Lenin to return to Russia in 1917, and if the particular minister had said 'No' when in fact he said 'Yes', it is difficult to believe that the Russian revolution would have taken the course it did. Again, if Genoa had not ceded Corsica to France in 1768, Napoleon, born there in the year following, would have been an Italian and would have had no career in France. Yet it can scarcely be seriously maintained that without him the history of France would have been the same.[3]

The social relations which form the subject-matter of history are, in fact, far too complex to be determined by any single cause. Historical materialism does not explain why peoples living under similar conditions of production have developed widely divergent civilizations.[4] It does not explain why the Christian religion was independently accepted by races as dif-

1. *Sul problema morale dei nostri tempi* in *Pensiero politico e politica attuale* (Bari, 1946, pp. 7–8).

2. B. Hessen, *The Economic Roots of Newton's Principia* (1931). On the general marxist thesis, all manifestations of intellectual and artistic activity are determined by the state of the productive forces in any given age; see Plekhanov, op. cit. pp. 200 ff.

3. *Freedom and Organization* (1935), pp. 228–9.

4. Bober, pp. 278 ff.

ferent as the civilized Romans and the semi-barbarous Slavs and Irish. Nor, incidentally, does it explain why totally different ideologies should be held by men who share the same cultural background, so that the founders of socialism, including Marx and Engels themselves and most of the leaders of the nineteenth-century labour movement, should have belonged to the bourgeoisie. As Federn puts it, the relation between the economic substructure and the superstructure resembles that between the soil of a field and the plants growing in it. We know that the plants sprang from the soil, and that if there were no soil there would be no plants; but we do not know who sowed the seeds, or where they come from, or why those plants grow there and not others.[1]

Finally, Marx had no right to appeal to economics in support of his theory. As L. H. Robbins points out, economics is not, as was once held, the study of the causes of material welfare, but of those aspects of behaviour which arise from the scarcity of means to achieve given ends. As to whether the ends in themselves are good or bad, it is strictly neutral; but if the attainment of one set of ends involves the sacrifice of others, it has an economic aspect.[2] The notion, entertained by men like Carlyle and Ruskin, that economics is concerned with purely material ends is false, though they may perhaps be excused for having held it, as it was generally accepted by the economists of their day. Nor can it be urged, save on the basis of the crudest Benthamite psychology, that the economic motive always prevails.

Again, economics is not to be confused with technology. It is not interested in technique as such, but only in so far as it is one of the influences that determine scarcity. The manner in which men will apply the various skills of which they become masters will largely depend upon considerations which are psychological and having nothing to do with economics. But Marx's economic interpretation of history explains all major events by changes in the *technique of production*, thus implying that

1. Federn, p. 100.
2. *The Nature and Significance of Economic Science* (1932), pp. 7 ff., 24–5.

ultimate valuations are merely its by-products, and without taking into account the very different ways in which men may use it. His doctrine, as Robbins puts it, 'is a general statement about the causation of human motive which, from the point of view of economic science, is sheer metaphysics. The label "materialist" fits the doctrine. The label "economic" is misplaced. Economics may well provide an important instrument for the elucidation of history. But there is nothing in economic analysis which entitles us to assert that all history is to be explained in "economic" terms if "economic" is to be used as equivalent to the technically material. The materialist interpretation of history came to be called the economic interpretation of history, because it was thought that the subject-matter of economics was the cause of material welfare. Once it is realized that this is not the case, the materialist conception must stand or fall on its own merits. Economic science lends no support to its doctrines.'[1]

*

The claim that historical materialism rests upon scientific laws contained the implication that history was an exact science, and that it was thus possible to foretell its future development. Yet neither Marx nor Engels was a historian, and the value of their work lies solely in their penetrating observation of a certain number of contemporary facts. In his *Capital* Marx does indeed make considerable use of history to support conclusions at which he had arrived independently, but the book in no way proves historical materialism to be true, and in fact, assumes that as it is self-evident no proof is required. His anxiety to represent history as an exact science, and his 'historicism' which made him believe that the main function of science was to predict the future, led him, however, constantly to maintain that society was governed by 'inexorable laws' operating independently of the will of man, and thus beyond his power to change. 'When a society', he says in the Introduction to *Capital*, 'has discovered the natural law that determines its own movement . . . it can neither overleap the natural phases of its evolution nor shuffle out of them by a stroke of the pen.' All it

1. ibid. pp. 43–4.

can do 'is to shorten and lessen the birth pangs'. But this committed him to a view of history not altogether consistent with that implied by his theory of knowledge as *Praxis*, of which the function is to 'change the world', so that, as he and Engels both declare, 'history does nothing' seeing that 'man makes his own history, even though he does not do so on conditions chosen by himself'.[1] Doubtless what they both wished to convey was that man was able to become the master of his destiny; but in their desire to stress the scientific character of their doctrine they succeeded in making a great many people think that they meant the exact opposite, and that the course of history was wholly predetermined.[2]

By the nineties Engels had become aware of this, and in a letter to Joseph Bloch he admits that many contemporary marxists were turning out 'a rare kind of balderdash':

According to the materialist conception of history, [he says,] the determining element ... is *ultimately* the production and reproduction in real life. More than this neither Marx nor I have ever asserted. If, therefore, somebody twists this into the statement that the economic element is the *only* determining one, he transforms it into a meaningless, abstract and absurd phrase. The economic situation is the basis, but the various elements of the superstructure ... also exercise their influence upon the historical struggle, and in many cases preponderate in determining their form. There is an interaction of all those elements in which, amid all the endless *hosts* of accidents ... the economic movement finally asserts itself as necessary ... Marx and I are ourselves partly to blame for the fact that younger writers sometimes lay more stress on the economic factor than is due to it. We had to emphasize this main principle in opposition to our adversaries, who denied it, and we had not always the time, the place or the opportunity to allow the other elements involved in the interaction to come into their rights.[3]

Marxist writers hold that the above puts the whole matter in a just perspective. Yet, in fact, Engels has to admit an interaction between the superstructure and the substructure, which

1. Hook, *From Hegel to Marx*, pp. 38 ff.   2. Wilson, pp. 180 ff.
3. 21 September 1890, *Correspondence*, pp. 475–6.

is, indeed, assumed by the appeal 'Workers of the World, Unite!'; for if there were none, it was useless to preach revolution, and there would be nothing for the proletariat to do save passively to await the working out of the dialectical process, of which it was the ultimate beneficiary. But he does not seek to explain its nature, and repeats that the 'economic situation' is the basis which always 'ultimately' asserts itself. His concession, as T. D. Weldon puts it, is 'an elaborate attempt to have it both ways, to accept the incompleteness of the marxist hypothesis and to pass this off as a matter of no great moment.'[1] In practice, marxists habitually write as if economic factors were the sole determinants, and rarely if ever make allowances for any others.

As, however, Marx and Engels are concerned with the origin of the superstructure rather than with its influence upon the development of society, they tend to assign to it a purely passive role. In his *Dialectical and Historical Materialism* (1938) Stalin goes further, and insists that once a superstructure has arisen, it becomes 'a most potent force which facilitates . . . the progress of society'. Indeed 'new social ideas and theories arise precisely because they are necessary to society, because it is impossible to carry out the urgent tasks of the development of the material life of society without their organizing, mobilizing and transforming action'.[2] He returned to this theme in his *Concerning Marxism in Linguistics* (1950): 'The superstructure is a product of the basis, but this does not mean that it merely reflects it, that it is passive, neutral, indifferent to the fate of its basis, to the fate of classes, to the character of the system. On the contrary, having come into being, it becomes an exceedingly active force, actively assisting its basis to take shape and consolidate itself, and doing everything it can to help the new system finish off and eliminate the old basis and the old classes.'[3]

This would seem to be a more positive view than that of Marx and Engels. Yet two points should be noted. First, Stalin is only

1. *States and Morals* (1946), p. 158.
2. *History of the Communist Party of the Soviet Union* (Moscow, 1943), pp. 116–17.
3. p. 4.

able to represent the superstructure as a 'potent force' because, as all marxists do, he attributes to the substructure or base the property of being able to produce 'new ideas and theories' whenever the material needs of society require them, though no explanation is given as to why this should be so. Secondly, as he was himself largely responsible for the form the superstructure had assumed in Russia, he could very well represent it as playing an 'active' role, and indeed could scarcely do otherwise.[1]

While, therefore, Marx and Engels have much to say about the power of men to transform nature and, in so doing, to transform themselves and the society in which they live, and while both maintain that it is in the knowledge of external reality and the power to use that knowledge for definite ends that human freedom consists, they never resolve the central problem. If man is to be in any real sense the master of his destiny, it can only be through his ideas and opinions. But these belong to the superstructure, and the form they take is determined by the substructure. All they will admit is that an interaction takes place between the two, though upon what principle they do not tell us. But once an interaction has been conceded, the whole thesis is undermined, since we are no longer dealing with a purely economic factor, but with one which has been itself in part determined by non-economic factors. To say after this that the economic factor must always be decisive is meaningless.

The common-sense view is surely this. Man is a being endowed with intelligence, and this develops as he rises in the scale of civilization. Through it he provides himself with the means of subsistence, and at the same time with the laws, art forms, and the like that he regards as necessary for his security and well-being. The two are part of the same process, and there is no occasion to bring them into opposition and to make the one dependent upon the other. If it be true that the way in which men think and the various institutional and other forms to which their ideas give rise are influenced by the manner in

1. For a full discussion of Stalin's views see Henri Chambre, *Marxisme en Union Soviétique* (Paris, 1955), pp. 457–83.

which they make their living, the converse is equally true. Marx is a good servant but a bad master. He was quite right in drawing attention to the importance of the economic factor, which had been seriously neglected, but he gave it an undue prominence and thus over-simplified the complexity of the social situation, as his followers have continued to do to this day.

According to Engels, the vagaries of his French disciples 'of the late seventies' led Marx to declare on more than one occasion that 'all I can say is that I am not a marxist'.[1] This disclaimer is often quoted as evidence that with the passing of the years his views became more moderate, though it is only valid within its specific context, and we are not told of what he was complaining. Doubtless he was not uninfluenced by the growth of humanitarian sentiment and the development of representative institutions in the second half of the nineteenth century, and in the preface to the 1872 edition of the *Communist Manifesto* he and Engels declare that the passage at the end of Section II dealing with revolutionary measures 'would in many respects be written differently today', as it had 'in some details become antiquated'. Yet apart from this admission, he never openly disavowed any part of his revolutionary creed. Nor did increasing age lead him to regard with greater forbearance views different from his own. 'I remember', H. M. Hyndman records, 'saying to him once that as I grew older I became more tolerant. "Do you?" he said, *"do you?"* It was quite certain that he did not.'[2] Perhaps if he had written a book on dialectical materialism, as he once said that he intended to do when he had finished with *Capital*, we should have known better where he stood. But though he came to detest economics – 'economic shit' as he calls it in his correspondence with Engels – once he had started upon *Capital* he could never escape from it. Yet his real interest in the dialectic was that it provided a support for his economic and revolutionary theories, and he left its exposition as a logical system to Engels, who had been more influenced than himself by the climate of scientific materialism,

1. Engels to Conrad Schmidt, 5 August 1890 (*Correspondence*, p. 472).
2. *Lenin on Britain*, p. 86.

and was thus more concerned, though at the same time less qualified, to provide for it a philosophical basis.[1]

Hence there has been some controversy as to how Marx's position should be defined. Popper argues that he was at heart a dualist for whom the world was a conflict between the flesh and the spirit (but one in which the flesh is always primary), and his real concern was with 'the kingdom of freedom', and that what he sought to show was that men can enter into it only in proportion as they bring the material circumstances of life under their control, as they can never do in a class-divided society.[2] On the other hand, G. D. H. Cole maintains that he would today have called himself a realist, that is, that he was only concerned to assert that being is independent of consciousness, while leaving it an open question as to whether the nature of being is spiritual or material, the position that Lenin later adopted, though he failed to maintain it consistently.[3] Yet while it was undoubtedly Marx's primary concern to insist upon this independence, it is hard to believe that he did not at the same time share the prevailing scientific view of the nature of reality, which was certainly materialist. At the time when he attained maturity, the prestige of the natural sciences was immense and they emphasized the view that man is a part of nature, with the result that man's opinions soon came to be regarded as equally a part of the natural order. In the field that he made his own, Marx gave this view a greater precision by arguing that such opinions could, and indeed must, be related to economic forces, and that they changed when these forces changed – a creed which its adherents call materialism and which can hardly be described in any other terms.

1. I. M. Bochenski, *Der Sowjetrussische dialektische Materialismus* (Bern, 1950), p. 28; Sabine, p. 576.

2. op. cit. II, pp. 95–6.

3. op. cit. pp. 20 ff.

5. Marxist Economics

MARX'S economic system derives from that of the classical school of British economists, which started with the publication in 1776 of Adam Smith's *Wealth of Nations*. The main object of this school, which came into existence at a time when society was rapidly passing from the feudal (or pre-capitalist) into the capitalist stage, was to remove the innumerable restrictions imposed both upon domestic and foreign trade by the mercantilist system. Under this system a nation was regarded wealthy in proportion to the amount of gold that it was able to acquire by cutting down imports and increasing exports, although the Dutch, who lived solely by trade and whose country did not possess an ounce of gold, had defeated and bankrupted Philip of Spain, who owned or controlled all the gold mines in the world. Mercantilism thus not only imposed restrictions upon free enterprise at home, but also upon free trade abroad; and as the classical economists held with good reason that the development of the nation's wealth was thereby hampered, they were quite justified in taking their stand upon the principle of *laisser-faire, laisser-aller*.

The British school had adopted the theory of value first outlined by Locke, who had defended private property on the ground that a man was entitled to that to which he had given value by his labour, and they had thus made labour the criterion of value. They assumed, however, that buyers and sellers of labour operated on equal terms in a free market, and that each received what he had earned. Thus, Ricardo put forward, with certain reservations, a theory of value according to which 'the value of a commodity' depended 'on the relative quantity of labour necessary to its production'; and he held what Lassalle was later to call the 'Iron Law of Wages', that is, that the value of labour itself, or the rate of wages, similarly depended upon the cost of the labourer's subsistence. Marx, and other champions of labour, seized upon this theory of value, and turned it to ends which its sponsors had not foreseen. For if the whole value of a commodity was due to the labour which had gone into it, why, they asked, should it not be paid to the men who had produced the commodity?[1]

For the purposes of political economy, value may be defined as the amount of other commodities for which a given commodity will exchange; but as in civilized countries the exchange is effected in terms of money, it has come, in fact, to mean the price paid under certain circumstances. But in Marx's day, and long after, there was a widespread conviction that in economic theory a separate theory of value should precede a theory of prices, on the ground that behind money there were certain factors which led men to attach more value to one object than another, and that money simply introduced an additional complication.[2] The need for some such theory of 'real value' (that is, of value as divorced from prices) continued to be felt when subjective theories of value, such as that of marginal utility, began to be put forward in the seventies by Jevons and the Austrian economists, since such theories largely conceived of value in terms of the psychological process which induces people to pay more for one thing than for another. But whereas the classical economists had treated value primarily as a function of supply, and had then gone on to relate it to what they called the natural or normal price – that is, the price to which commodities tended if supply and demand were in equilibrium – the new school emphasized rather the complementary function of demand. Thus, the way was prepared for a concept of value that could be related to current prices, so that today most economists hold that for all practical purposes value means price, and attach no significance to any theory of economic value which cannot be related to prices.

In Volume I of *Capital* Marx certainly gives the impression that he, too, is seeking to relate value to price, as he gives many illustrations of how a given quantity of one commodity exchanges against a given quantity of another, or even against

1. Bertrand Russell, *Freedom and Organization*, p. 129.
2. Gustav Cassel, *Fundamental Thoughts on Economics* (1925), pp. 38 ff.

a given quantity of gold, the measure by which prices are reckoned. Cole contends, however, that he never sought to establish any such connexion, as he did not believe that value could be related even to the normal price of the classical economists, much less to market prices. All he meant to convey was that two commodities embodying the same amount of labour would possess the same exchange value, as he believed that labour itself did tend to sell at its real value. He was chiefly concerned at this stage of his book with the conditions governing the sale of labour, and did not wish to complicate his argument by introducing considerations which could be treated more appropriately later.[1]

Indeed, whatever may have been Marx's intention, and it is to be regretted that he did not make his position clearer, it is certain that when he talks of value he does not mean price. What he is concerned with is to discover the property that all commodities possess in virtue of which a given quantity of one is exchangeable against a given quantity of another. Now if a commodity is to possess value, it must have two characteristics – it must be useful, that is somebody must want it, and it must have cost some labour to produce. No commodity lacks value which possesses both these characteristics, and no commodity has value which lacks utility. Air, for example, has utility, but it lacks value because no labour has gone to produce it. On the other hand, an object may embody years of labour, but if there is no demand for it, it has no value.[2] But while Marx is obliged to recognize that any exchangeable commodity must be useful, he refuses to admit utility into his definition of value. The only property he is prepared to accept as common to all commodities, or at least to all with which he proposes to deal, is that they are the result of labour.

At this point, however, Marx introduces a modification into the labour theory of his contemporaries. They had taught that, at any rate on a first approximation, all actual prices were determined by the value of the commodity measured in terms of the number of labour hours required to produce it. Yet it was

1. Cole, pp. 226–7.
2. John Rae, *Contemporary Socialism* (1891), p. 165.

evident that the employer, by virtue of his superior economic power, was able to make agreements with his workers which were not determined by the number of hours they worked; and that therefore wages, or the price of labour, did not correspond to values. But if the theory that labour was the sole value-producing agency did not apply to wages, might it not be that it did not apply to other prices also? Marx came to the rescue with an ingenious notion which temporarily saved the theory. What the employer buys and pays for is, he pointed out, not *labour hours* but *labour power*, and the value of this last is the average number of labour hours required by a worker to enable him to support life and reproduce his kind.[1]

Further, to make the labour theory work, Marx was obliged to qualify his definition of labour, because the statement that the value of a commodity depends upon the quantity of labour put into it would be ridiculous if taken literally, as it would mean that the same article produced by two workers, one of whom worked hard and the other did not, would have differing values. His labour is thus not *actual* labour, but what he calls *simple average labour*, to which category all types of labour, skilled and unskilled, are held to be reducible. What the co-efficient of reduction is is not stated; but Marx says that it is arrived at 'by experience', and that there is a 'social process', the nature of which he does not define, which determines that a skilled worker should get so much more than a day labourer. Yet this is to argue in a circle. The value of a commodity is first stated to depend on the amount of simple average labour embodied in it; but what this amount is cannot be determined until we know the value at which the commodity exchanges.[2]

On the basis of the view that labour is the only value-producing agency, Marx put forward the theory of surplus value which is often taken to be his distinctive contribution to economic theory, though he never claimed to have invented it, as Engels points out in the Introduction of the second volume of *Capital*. It was, indeed, almost as much of a truism in his generation as the labour theory of value, for Adam Smith had declared that 'the value which the workers add to their materials resolves itself into two parts of which one pays their wages and the other is the profit of their employer'. What Marx did was to call the second of these parts 'surplus value' and to represent it as fraudulent.

We have already seen that it is the Marxist contention that at some remote and unspecified period of history society became divided into two classes, one of which obtained control over the means of production, while the other possessed nothing but its labour power. This labour power, which Marx calls 'variable capital', the capitalist (the contemporary representative of the possessing class) buys and sets to work on the various means of production – raw materials, machinery and the like – that constitute what he calls 'constant capital'. Now, labour possesses the unique property of being able to produce more than is required for its subsistence and replacement. The worker receives as wages only what is sufficient to maintain him; and if it took a whole day's work to produce this, the question of surplus value would not arise, nor incidentally would it be to anyone's advantage to employ him. What, in fact, happens is that a man works for ten hours, and in the first, say, five of these (which constitute what Marx calls 'socially necessary labour') he produces all the value he is to receive as wages. Of the value produced during the second five hours he gets nothing, and it is stolen from him by his employer. The difference between the value created during the period of socially necessary labour and that created during the period in excess of it is what Marx calls 'surplus value', and is the measure of the worker's 'exploitation'. Thus the value produced by the worker far exceeds the value of his means of subsistence, that is, the value of his labour power which he receives from the capitalist as wages. But by remunerating labour in the form of wages, the division between paid and unpaid labour time is concealed.

Variable capital, i.e. labour, alone produces value, and constant capital produces none. Machinery is simply 'stored up labour', that is, something upon which labour has already been expended. Sources of wealth, such as unworked mineral deposits, have, indeed, an exchange value, because people are prepared to give money for them, but this is only on account of their potential value, that is, the value they will have when labour is applied to them. Orthodox economic theory teaches that the production of anything that has value calls for the co-operation of four agents – land (raw materials), labour, capital, and organization (management) – and that each agent receives its share of the product: land as rent, labour as wages, capital as interest, and management (or more strictly the element of uncertainty which enters into production) as profits. Marx rejects this view, and isolates labour from the other agents of production. It alone is the source of value, and is alone entitled to the value it is alleged to create.

In the first volume of *Capital* Marx argues that as profit is created solely by surplus value, and as labour is the sole value-producing agency, the rate of profit will depend upon what he calls the 'organic composition of capitals', that is, the proportion of labour (variable capital) to machinery (constant capital) employed in a given undertaking; and that it will thus tend to fall in proportion as technological improvements lead to the employment of less labour. Yet although this conclusion logically followed from his premises, it was demonstrably false in practice. Marx was aware of the difficulty, to which he refers in a letter to Engels of August 1862.[1] But he did not face it at the time, and set it aside for further treatment. There the matter rested until 1883, when he died.

Engels had seriously miscalculated the time that would be needed to put in order the unpublished portion of *Capital*, and the second and third volumes did not appear until 1885 and 1894 respectively. Meanwhile, as E. H. Carr has pointed out, certain followers of the German economist Rodbertus had accused Marx of plagiarizing from the works of their master, and Engels had retorted by challenging them to produce the solution to the above problem, thus drawing increased attention to it.[2] It was, indeed, eagerly awaited, but when it appeared in the third volume it caused widespread disillusionment. For it was now contended that although the rate of profit did depend on the relation of variable to constant capital if the whole capital of the world was taken into account (and of this no proof

1. *Briefwechsel* III, p. 77.   2. Carr, *Karl Marx*, pp. 270–1.

was given), this did not apply to the profits of particular businesses, which tended to equalize themselves according to the state of trade. As Joan Robinson points out, Marx's demonstration simply amounts to the tautology that if wages are constant (and elsewhere he denies that they are) the rate of profit will fall as capital per man increases.[1]

What, after all this, is left of the labour theory of value? We are asked to believe that there is an abstract property called 'value' which belongs to any labour-produced commodity, and which, while purporting to be its exchange value, does not, in fact, correspond to its price or even to its average price. And we are further asked to believe that there is a second abstraction, called 'surplus value', which determines profits in general but not profits in particular, and bears no relation to the standard of wages of the workers whose exploitation it is supposed to measure. Marx first says that the value of a commodity corresponds to the amount of labour put into it, and if he had stuck to this, he would, as Plamenatz points out, at least have made clear in what sense he was using the term. But he then goes on to call this value 'exchange value', and to spend many pages describing just how the value of one commodity is expressed in terms of another, thus inevitably suggesting that they do actually tend to exchange in accordance with the relative amounts of labour required to produce them. He then has to confess that they do not, in fact, exchange in this manner, and would only do so if the same proportions of capital and labour were employed in their production; and thus, he ends by confusing both himself and his readers.[2] Actually, he is ultimately driven to admit that exchange value is governed by the market, that is, by the law of supply and demand, which makes nonsense of his theory that it is derived from labour only.

From the theory of surplus value Marx deduces three laws:

1. *The Law of Capitalist Accumulation.* Competition forces the capitalist to accumulate capital, that is, to install more and more labour-saving machinery in his factory in order to pro-

---

1. *An Essay on Marxian Economics* (1949), p. 36.
2. Plamenatz, pp. 33–4.

duce more goods. Yet in so doing he acts to his own hindrance, because any increase in the proportion of constant to variable capital is liable to result in a fall in his profits.

2. *The Law of the Concentration of Capital.* Under competition the number of capitalists will contract, as the weaker will be driven from the field and will swell the ranks of the wage-earners. As Marx puts it, 'One capitalist kills many'. Thus capitalism inevitably leads to monopoly in the form of trusts, cartels, and the like, since these alone are strong enough to withstand the recurrent economic crises.

3. *The Law of Increasing Misery.* As a result, the misery of the workers will continually increase. The individual capitalist is not to be blamed, for he is subject to a pressure that he has to pass on, and is forced to compensate for the decline in his profits resulting from the replacement of labour by machinery by intensifying his exploitation of the worker from whom he extorts more and more hours of unpaid labour. Meanwhile, the unemployed worker is driven into what Marx calls the 'industrial reserve army', and this enables the employer still further to force down wages. Hence, the more capital there is in circulation, the greater will be the production, but the less will be the labour employed and the wages it receives. Yet Marx nowhere explains how this degradation of the proletariat is to be reconciled with its development as a class, which, according to the dialectic of history, will eventually render it more competent than the bourgeoisie to direct the productive forces, and provides the justification for its doing so.

Marx had no sympathy with anything inefficient, and he was quite prepared to concede that by increasing production capitalism had rendered a service to mankind. Yet he contended that on account of its internal contradictions the system was bound to break down, and that the superstructure of laws and institutions which had arisen to safeguard it had long since become fetters upon the productive forces. Capitalism could not be reformed and must be destroyed. But this was impossible without a revolution, if only because the dying order would strive to the utmost to prevent the emergence of the new order that was being born. When, however, the revolution had been accomplished, the productive forces would be liberated, and would henceforth be directed to their proper end – to give to every man the work of his own hands. It is on this note of prophecy that Marx ends his chapter on 'The historical tendencies of capitalist accumulation in the first volume of *Capital*:

Along with the constantly diminishing number of the magnates of capital, who usurp and monopolize all advantages of this process of transformation, grows the mass of misery, oppression, slavery, degradation, exploitation; but with this too grows the revolt of the working class, a class always increasing in numbers, and disciplined, united, organized by the very mechanism of the process of capitalist production itself. The monopoly of capital becomes a fetter upon the mode of production, which has sprung up and flourished along with, and under it. Centralization of the means of production and socialization of labour at last reach a point where they become incompatible with their capitalist integument. This integument is burst asunder. The knell of capitalist private property sounds. The expropriators are expropriated.

Marx's economic doctrine may therefore be summarized as follows. Labour alone creates value. All profits are derived from unpaid labour time. Capitalists are driven by competition to accumulate capital, which becomes concentrated in fewer and fewer hands, with the result that the smaller businesses disappear and their owners are driven back into the working-class. The accumulation of capital in the form of labour-saving devices reduces the use of human labour and at the same time the profits of the capitalists, who are therefore compelled to offset their losses by intensifying the exploitation of their workers, over whom the increase of unemployment has given them an even stronger hold and who are now prepared to work on any terms. Hence the misery of the workers, eventually almost the entire population, will progressively become more and more unendurable. This will lead them to combine for their own protection, and so create a force which will eventually destroy the whole system.

It has been necessary to dwell upon Marx's theory of value at some length because he regarded it, as do all marxists, as the cornerstone of his system, though it only introduces an element of confusion, and he has nothing of importance to say which could not have been expressed equally well without it. We have seen that it is not a theory of value at all, and that his value and surplus value are pure abstractions. It is in fact a theory of exploitation, designed to show that the propertied class has always lived on the labour of the non-propertied class. It is therefore on the assumption that labour – by which is meant wage-labour – is the only value-producing agency, that the theory stands or falls. But it is a false assumption because, as is characteristic of marxist dogmas, it concentrates upon one single factor in a highly complex situation to the exclusion of all others. Thus capital is itself a product of labour. Someone has laboured to produce it, and has then decided to forego the immediate consumption of the value created in order to create further value, as it is clearly in the interests of society that he should do. As, however, not everyone is willing to do this, the owner of capital finds himself in possession of something that has a scarcity value and thus commands its market price. The marxist argument that capital produces value only when labour is applied to it is simply that of the medieval schoolmen. Labour without capital is equally unproductive. The capitalist system is open to abuses like any other. Yet those who desire to abolish it would do well to reflect that the only alternative to the profit-and-loss motive that has so far shown any indication of being equally effective is the fear of punishment imposed by a totalitarian State.

Moreover, as Popper points out, the whole of Marx's theory of value is redundant. For if we assume, as is fundamental to his case, a free market in which there is always a greater supply of labour than there is a demand for it, the law of supply and demand becomes sufficient to explain all the phenomena of 'increasing misery' without bringing value into it.[1] Marx was on strong grounds so long as he restricted himself to the conditions prevailing under *laissez-faire* capitalism at the time when he was writing, and his analysis of these conditions was an important contribution to the study of social relations. He was quite right in pointing out that labour was not receiving its

1. op. cit. II, p. 165.

fair share; but he failed to see that there might be other ways of dealing with the problem than by revolution, and that he himself had provided one of the most effective of these by calling upon the workers to unite. The organizations of labour, collective bargaining and State intervention in its various forms were to revolutionize the situation and to make nonsense of the law of increasing misery, save in so far as it applies to Russia, where the promise of the millennium remains unfulfilled and all verbs, it has been said, are conjugated in the future tense.

Nor did Marx discern that the middle-class, so far from being crushed out of existence, would greatly increase in strength. The capitalist to whom Engels had first called his attention was commonly the owner of his business. But the great extension of jointstock companies in the second half of the century – following in this country upon the Companies Act of 1862, which extended the principle of limited liability – had the effect of creating a new type of capitalist in the person of the shareholder, who had no part in the management of the concern, which he delegated to paid officials. The result was at least temporarily to broaden the basis of the capitalist system by creating a new middle-class which had an interest in retaining it either as investors concerned with their dividends, or as members of the managerial salariat, whose lower ranks felt themselves superior to the proletariat from which they had been largely recruited.

Keynes has described *Capital* as 'an obsolete economic text book ... not only scientifically erroneous, but without interest or application for the modern world'.[1] Yet the modern world continues to take an interest in it, for, like every great revolutionary treatise, its power lies rather in its central idea than in the arguments used to support it, which may often enough be found untenable. To the Victorians the capitalist system appeared the embodiment of permanence and stability, and, in general, this belief persisted up to 1914. From that conflict many held that it had emerged even stronger than ever. Yet, as Carr has shown, its character had changed. The old-fashioned Capitalism – what Marx called 'bourgeois capitalism' – had

1. *Essays in Persuasion* (New York, 1932), p. 300.

broken down, partly because it had evolved away from a free competitive system of individuals and small units into a highly organized system of large-scale enterprises; and partly because of the increasing strength and organization of the workers, who were bound to resent the old privileged order, and to insist that the new order should contain increasing elements of Socialist-planned economy which made for a more equal distribution of goods. This transformation had taken place over most of western Europe by the First World War; after that war capitalism in the older sense never came back, and there was an uneasy interregnum during which the two rival systems jostled one another without finding any working compromise.[1] These years were marked by violent economic crises, accompanied by greater mass unemployment than had been known since the Industrial Revolution started. The concentration of capital proceeded; while labour continued to organize itself, though it is claimed that the workers did not thereby become revolutionary-minded. Then came the Second World War, and few will contend that the capitalist system is the stronger for it. Many of Marx's prophecies have, indeed, been falsified. Yet, looked at objectively, it is too early to say that his central thesis has been disproved; and we should do well to recall Jung's observation upon Columbus, who 'by using subjective assumptions, a false hypothesis, and a route abandoned by modern navigation, nevertheless discovered America'.

For, when every criticism has been made, *Capital* remains a very great book, and if the greatness of a book is to be measured by its influence, one of the most important ever written. Marx presents a view of the world which cannot be disregarded – a world in which, as Edmund Wilson puts it, 'commodities bear rule and make men their playthings'. His highly abstract reasoning provides the clue to this economic labyrinth. 'It is', Wilson says, 'his great trick to hypnotize us by the shuttling of the syllogisms which he produces with so scientific an air, and then suddenly to remind us that these principles derive solely from the laws of human selfishness which are as unfailing as the

1. *Problems of Writing Modern Russian History* (*The Listener*, 7 October 1948, pp. 548 f.)

force of gravitation.' The exposition of his theory is always followed by a documented picture of the capitalist laws at work, until 'we feel that we have been taken for the first time through the real structure of our civilization, and that it is the ugliest that ever existed – a state of things where there is very little to choose between the physical degradation of the workers and the moral degradation of the masters'.[1]

But this account of the matter is not altogether satisfactory. Marx does indeed hold that the capitalist system is morally objectionable, though he fails to show how its evils will be removed by getting rid of the capitalists, as they certainly have not been in the Soviet Union. Yet he is careful not to ascribe these evils to the capitalists themselves, nor to impute to such persons a larger share of original sin than other members of the community possess. For they are, like the workers they exploit, the prisoners of a system. They have to operate in accordance with its laws, and these are not 'laws of human selfishness', but the laws which govern the development of the productive forces, and which demand that it must inevitably take the particular historical form it has done, though they will equally inevitably end by destroying it. It is true that communist propaganda is designed to convince the workers that capitalism is simply the expression of the selfish interests of a minority which deliberately exploits the majority for its own advantage. But this was not Marx's teaching – at least when he was writing seriously.

1. op. cit. pp. 271–2.

6. The Marxist Theory of the State and of Revolution

THE history of political theory reveals wide differences of opinion as to the origin and nature of the State, the limits of its authority and the degree of obedience to which it is entitled. But behind these divergencies there has been a general recognition that it exists, or should exist, to promote the welfare of its citizens, and that with the development of civilization it has become more conscious of its mission and nearer to fulfilling it. Marxist theory, however, denies this. The *Communist Manifesto* declares that the State is 'the executive committee of the bourgeoisie'. In his *Anti-Dühring* Engels maintains that it is not a natural institution, that it only arises 'when society is cleft into irreconcilable antagonisms which it is powerless to repel'; and that as it is simply the product of the class struggle, it will disappear – or to use his famous phrase will 'wither away' – when a classless society has been established. At the end of his Introduction to the 1891 edition of Marx's *Civil War in France*, he resumes his attack. 'The state is nothing more than a machine for the oppression of one class by another.' He adds that this is as true of a democratic State as of a monarchy, and that when the proletariat comes to power it will be thrown upon the scrap-heap as 'useless lumber'.

At first sight this hostility to the State appears singular in men who were not only Germans but disciples of Hegel. But it was, in fact, a matter upon which they felt deeply, as is shown in their correspondence with one another when they are expressing their views without an eye upon the public. If all they had wished to convey was that the class that owns the means of production will tend to control the State, and will use its apparatus to safeguard their ownership and repress any ideas which challenge it, their position would have been reasonable enough. But their theory of the State went much further than this, and was to prove so embarrassing that Soviet ideologists have long since abandoned it.[1] For Marx and Engels concentrate almost exclusively upon those coercive functions which can be represented with a certain plausibility as the conscious or unconscious expression of class interests at the expense of those other functions into which such interests do not enter. In any civilized community murderers are arrested without inquiry into their class status, nor is there any class discrimination in the postal service. They are indeed obliged to recognize the necessity, even in a classless society, for an organization which will discharge such functions, but they maintain that it will no longer be a State, because the State is, by definition, an instrument of class oppression. Thus in an article which Engels wrote against the anarchists in 1873 he explains that what 'all socialists' understood by the disappearance of the State was that 'public functions would lose their political character and be transformed into the simple administrative functions of watching over real social interests'; or as he put it in his *Anti-Dühring*, 'the government of persons is replaced by the administration of things', though how the one is possible without the other he does not tell us.[2]

What then is fundamental to the marxist doctrine is that States are essentially evil because they are class products, and that they will therefore disappear with the classless society. Marx and Engels were strengthened in this conviction by their study of the work of an American anthropologist, Lewis H. Morgan, published in 1877 with the title *Ancient Society. Researches into the Lines of Human Progress from Savagery through Barbarism to Civilization*, which professed to show that primitive man had lived under an order which was both communal and Stateless. Marx had made extensive notes of this book, and at the time of his death was intending to publish an account of it in which the author's views would be combined

1. For an interesting treatment of this matter *see* Vernon V. Aspaturian, 'The Contemporary Doctrine of the Soviet State and its Philosophical Foundations' (*American Political Science Review*, December 1954, pp. 1031 ff.)

2. Carr has pointed out, however, that the distinction was one commonly recognized by socialist writers: *The Bolshevik Revolution*, I. p. 326n.

with his own; and this task Engels discharged in his *Origin of the Family, Private Property, and the State* (1884), a work of the first importance for an understanding of the doctrine of historical materialism, and the most complete exposition of the marxist theory of the State. Lenin devoted to its interpretation the first chapter of his *State and Revolution*.

If, however, the State is simply an organ of class oppression, the assertion that it will 'wither away' when there are no more classes is a tautology; whereas if it is something more than this, the establishment of a classless society will not guarantee its disappearance.[1] In any case, there can be no assurance that the victory of the proletariat will bring such a society into existence, or that the individuals who form the proletariat will retain their class unity once the struggle against the common enemy has been won. On *a priori* grounds it would seem probable that the leaders will soon come to constitute a new class – reinforced by the technicians and specialists whose services they will require if they are to maintain themselves in power – though they will attempt to conceal this by retaining as much as possible of the revolutionary ideology, and by appealing to the danger of counter-revolution.

But for Marx and Engels the State belongs pre-eminently to that superstructure which is created by the productive forces of society, and reflects the relations of production as defined by the class struggle; and thus it stands guardian over the economic order, which it protects with its army, legal system, police, and other organs of physical or moral compulsion. In any society which is divided, as capitalism is represented as being, into two antagonistic and irreconcilable groups, the State cannot be democratic – indeed a democratic state is a contradiction in terms, seeing that a true democracy would be classless and would need no State. The exploited masses do indeed succeed in wringing certain concessions from their oppressors, but these are so contrived that the real power always remains in the hands of the dominant class, so that as Marx puts it, the franchise only gives the people the right to decide, 'once in every three or six years which member of the ruling class is to misrepresent

1. Hans Kelsen, *Sozialismus und Staat* (Leipzig, 1923), p. 18.

them in Parliament'.[1] Hence communists lose no opportunity of disparaging parliamentary democracy, to which they oppose their own version of 'proletarian democracy'.

The above thesis calls for some comment, as we have had abundant opportunity in recent years of observing the consequences of its application. In the west there has been a tendency to stress the *political* aspect of democracy rather than its *economic* aspect, and although at times this may have been carried too far, the fault is on the right side, seeing that a people which surrenders its political rights in return for promises of economic security will soon discover that it has made a bad bargain, as it is helpless if the promises are not kept. Communists, on the other hand, invariably stress the *economic* aspect, in accordance with the marxist principle that the economic basis of society is primary; and thus they argue that no country can claim to be 'democratic' unless the land and the means of production 'belong to the people', which in communist-controlled countries means the workers and the peasants (who are represented as separate but no longer antagonistic classes) and a stratum of intelligentsia recruited from both. Hence they contend that until the foundations of such a society have been laid, it is idle to speak of 'democratic' institutions, and that those which profess to be so are fraudulent. Unfortunately, under communism, the land and the means of production only 'belong to the people' in a purely formal sense, while the political institutions set up are not 'democratic', at least as the term has been traditionally interpreted, that is, as conferring upon the 'people', in the wider sense of the various sections which make up the community, the right to determine how they are to be governed.

It follows from the above that the first task of the revolution which Marx held to be the inevitable outcome of the class struggle for a new economic order is the capture of the State by the proletariat, and its utter destruction, since every part of its apparatus is contaminated with bourgeois ideology, as are all those associated with its administration. Indeed, so fundamental did Marx hold this to be that he introduced in 1872 what Lenin

1. *The Civil War in France, S.W.* I, p. 472.

contended to be the only amendment he ever made to the *Communist Manifesto*, in which he declared that the proletariat must smash the 'existing state machine', which the Commune had failed to do effectively, and could not simply take it over and use it for its own purposes. Above all, the proletariat must avoid any such compromises as the bourgeoisie would certainly seek, whereby some part of the existing order would be retained.

Marx's theory of the dialectic of revolution rests upon two main principles.[1] The first was based on an appreciation of the class struggle as it presented itself in his time. In scarcely any country had it yet become a straight issue between the proletariat and the bourgeoisie, because the bourgeoisie – the rising class – was itself engaged in a struggle with feudalism as represented by absolute monarchy and its various survivals. He foresaw therefore that the revolution would develop in two phases. In the first, the bourgeoisie would be seeking to assert its claims, and as these were in the line of progress, it would be the duty of the nascent proletariat to support them and then await the second phase, when it would make its own bid for power. He held that it was unlikely that the two phases would be accomplished in a single revolution, and his statement that this might be possible in the case of Germany was probably made with an eye to the Communist League, most of whose members were German revolutionary workers. For the claims of the bourgeoisie would always be more readily conceded than those of the proletariat because they were less far-reaching; and thus as soon as it was in power, it would throw over its allies, with whose more radical claims it had no sympathy. The alliance of the proletariat with the bourgeoisie was thus tactical only, and in no way concealed the fundamental antagonism between the two classes.

1. The most complete exposition of Marx's theory of revolution is his *Eighteenth Brumaire* (1852). *See* also *The Communist Manifesto*, *The Address to the Communist League* (1850), *The Class Struggles in France* (1850) and *The Civil War in France* (1871) and Engels's Introduction of 1891 to the last-named. Laski gives an interesting summary of the theory in the introduction to his edition of *The Communist Manifesto* (1948), pp. 41 ff. *See* also *The Communist Manifesto* in E. H. Carr, *Studies in Revolution*, pp. 15 ff.

Marx held that the classic example of the betrayal of the proletariat by the bourgeoisie was the 1848 revolution in France. In February of that year both classes had fought shoulder to shoulder; but in June, Cavaignac had secured the bourgeois revolution and staved off the proletarian revolution by massacring the class-conscious workers. England escaped the revolution because the middle-class had consolidated its position and was firmly established. The Chartist movement was simply the attempt of the workers to continue the struggle after the middle-class had abandoned them in 1832.

In the second phase, the bourgeoisie, having destroyed feudalism, would itself be destroyed by the proletariat in alliance with left-wing bourgeois elements which would later be discarded. Marx recognized that the struggle would not be wholly clear-cut, as there were certain elements – small traders, peasants, slum dwellers and the like – which did not strictly belong to either group. Yet this complication did not much affect the pattern of revolution. Living as he did in England, he identified the proletariat with the *industrial* workers. The petty bourgeoisie did not form part of it, since its interest was to maintain its semi-bourgeois status. Nor did the peasantry, a class which both Marx and Engels always regarded with suspicion. Nor, finally, did that submerged working-class element which they called the *lumpen proletariat* and held to be altogether unreliable. It was left to Lenin in the next century to work out a more exact analysis of the class forces, and in particular to effect that alliance between the workers and the peasants on which the October Revolution was founded.

The role of bourgeois democracy was thus to act as the foster-mother of the proletariat during the stage of pre-emancipation. The reforms that it effected, such as extensions of the franchise or of the workers' right to combine, not only softened the reactionary crust of society, but also provided the conditions under which the proletariat gained the experience required to enable it to fulfil its historic mission. Such reforms were, of course, only palliatives, and in fact their failure to free the workers would make the latter see that their only hope lay in revolution. Indeed, the more democratic in appearance the bourgeois State became, the more violently should its short-comings be exposed, since on the one hand its democratic tendencies revealed a weakness of which the revolutionary element should take advantage, while on the other there was always the danger that the proletariat would mistake this spurious democracy for the real article and lose its revolutionary zeal.

Marx would certainly have agreed with Lenin that there must be no playing with revolution, which must not be undertaken until the time for it was ripe. After the collapse of the Paris Commune of 1871 it had no chance whatever of success, and to continue to advocate 'putschism', as the Communard exiles were doing, could only weaken the proletarian cause. In April 1870 Marx had declared that England was 'the most important country for revolution', that to bring it about was therefore 'the most important task of the International', and that this should be done by playing up trouble in Ireland, an anticipation of the tactics later developed by Lenin.[1] Yet in September 1872 he told the Amsterdam section of the International that he did not deny that there were countries such as England and the United States 'where the workers will be able to achieve their aim by peaceful means', though he added that 'this was not true of all countries'.[2] Again, in a letter to Hyndman of 1881 he said that his party did not hold a revolution to be 'necessary', but only, on historic precedents, 'possible'.[3] In his introduction to the English translation of *Capital* in 1886 Engels repeated the first of these statements, though he somewhat weakened its force by pointing out that while Marx's 'lifelong studies' had led him to this conclusion, 'he never forgot to add that he hardly expected the English ruling class to retreat without a "pro-slavery rebellion" against this peaceful and legal revolution'.

How far such statements were made for tactical purposes or

1. Marx to S. Meyer and A. Vogt, 9 April 1870, *Marx and Engels on Britain*, p. 507.

2. G. M. Stekloff, *History of the First International*, Eng. trans. 1928, pp. 240–1.

3. Boris Nicolaievsky and O. Maenchen-Helfen, *Karl Marx* (1936), p. 380.

represented a genuine change of front it is hard to say. Certainly Marx and Engels had lived long enough to have seen reforms brought about which should have been impossible according to the Law of Increasing Misery, and were in fact a challenge to their theories. Thus Engels attributes the failure of a workers' movement to develop in England to the fact that 'the ruling classes have set themselves the task of carrying out, parallel with other concessions, one point of the Chartists' programme after another';[1] and he declared that 'since 1848 the English Parliament had been the most revolutionary body in the world'.[2] Such judgements are scarcely consistent with their elsewhere wholesale condemnation of governments in general and of bourgeois governments in particular. It may be argued, of course, that the transition from capitalism to socialism constitutes a revolution however it is effected, and that neither Marx nor Engels absolutely commit themselves to the view that it must involve a popular uprising. Yet it is towards violence that the balance is inclined, especially in their early writings. Indeed Engels never abandoned his belief in its inevitability. In 1895 he contributed an introduction to a new German edition of Marx's *Class Struggles in France*, which appeared with certain excisions in the *Neue Zeit*, and has been called his 'testament', as he died in the same year. In it he dwells with enthusiasm upon the use which the German workers had made of universal suffrage. Only, as Cole has noted,[3] he makes clear that this alone would not enable them to seize power, and he explains, in a passage prudently suppressed by the editors, that street fighting would still be necessary, and that in view of the increased strength of the armed forces, it would have to be 'carried out with even greater force'.[4] Yet violence is after all a relative term, and in one passage Marx declares that the revolution may involve less bloodshed than the suppression of a slave revolt in Roman times. It was, he held, effective only

1. Article entitled 'The English Elections', dated 22 February 1874, in *Marx and Engels on Britain*, p. 466.

2. Engels to J. P. Becker, 15 June 1885, *Correspondence*, p. 439.

3. *History of Socialist Thought. Marxism and Anarchism* (1954), pp. 434–5.

4. *S.W.* I, p. 122.

within certain limits. It is, he says, 'the midwife of progress; it delivers the child, but can do no more for it'. For Stalin it was rather the mother of progress.

However this may be, Marx's followers soon became divided into two schools, each of which appealed to his authority – the moderates who believed in the peaceful transformation of society, which came in fact to signify the reforming of the existing order by constitutional means, and the extremists who held that the existing order must be swept away, and that this could not be done without violence, though it was the resistance of the capitalists that would be responsible for this. The communists belong to the second of these schools. They deny that Marx ever modified the position he adopted in the *Communist Manifesto* and continued to maintain in the *Civil War in France* and elsewhere, and they assert that the fact that a contrary opinion came to be entertained towards the end of the last century was due to the 'opportunism' of the social democrats, seeing that, as Marx puts it, the 'peculiar character of social democracy' is that 'it demands democratic-republican institutions not as a means of doing away with two extremes – capital and wage-labour – but of weakening their antagonism and transforming them into harmony'.[1]

Marx's second principle is a corollary of the first. Just as the establishment of bourgeois democracy is a pre-requisite of the proletarian revolution, so also must be the full development of capitalism, which is the essential expression of bourgeois society, since, as he says in the *Critique of Political Economy*: 'A social system never perishes before all the productive forces have developed for which it is wide enough; and new, higher productive relationships never come into being before the material conditions for their existence have been brought to maturity within the womb of the old society itself.' For, according to the dialectic, every new phase in human development is a higher one which includes within it all that is of permanent value in that which it has superseded, and thus the proletariat could not take over such elements in the capitalist system if that system existed only in a rudimentary form. It appeared there-

1. *Eighteenth Brumaire, S.W.* II, p. 249.

fore to follow paradoxically that in backward countries the interest of the proletariat was to hasten the development of capitalism even if, according to the law of increasing misery, this could only render its situation worse than before. Towards the end of his life Marx somewhat modified this principle, at least in so far as it applied to Russia; but his more orthodox followers viewed any such concession with disfavour, for if it were possible to advance from the thesis of feudalism to the synthesis of socialism without the intervening antithesis of capitalism, what would become of the dialectic?

Both the above principles were taken over by the Russian marxists as essential elements of the dialectic of revolution. The relation between the bourgeois-democratic and the proletarian revolutions was long to be a controversial issue; yet both bolsheviks and mensheviks believed, possibly up to 1917, that the revolution which they regarded as inevitable would not be a *socialist* one, as the country had not yet passed through its industrial stage. These convictions illustrate not only the authority that Marx's teaching had acquired, but also the influence that the dialectic exerts upon minds disposed to accept it; and to this day one of the most serious charges that can be brought against any policy is that it 'jumps a stage' in whatever orthodox marxist theory (or Moscow's interpretation of it) holds to be the true dialectical development of a given situation.

As to what organization would replace the bourgeois State, both Marx and Engels were somewhat reticent. But in the *Critique of the Gotha Programme* (1875), in which Marx comes nearest to defining the difference between the existing order and that which is to be, he lays down that between the abolition of the bourgeois State and the establishment of a communist society there lies a transition stage which he calls the 'dictatorship of the proletariat' – an expression, possibly borrowed from the French revolutionary Blanqui, which he had used in almost exactly the same sense in his *Class Struggles in France* (1850). During this phase, the State will continue as an organ of coercion, but with the difference that the coercion will be exercised by the proletarian majority against the bourgeois minority. Hence, it will not constitute a free society, and certain features of the old order, including inequalities of pay, will continue. We shall see later how Lenin eagerly fastened upon this when he was trying to find some authority in Marx's teaching for the regime set up after the October Revolution.

In his Introduction to the 1891 edition of Marx's *Civil War in France* Engels identified the dictatorship with the regime set up by the Commune, though in fact this had owed more to the ideas of Proudhon than to their own; and in criticizing the Erfurt Programme of 1891 he said: 'If anything is certain, it is that our own party can only come to power under the form of a democratic republic. Precisely this is the scientific form of the dictatorship of the proletariat, as the great French Revolution [the reference is again to the Commune] has already shown'.[1] This last statement is frequently quoted as evidence that Engels held that the dictatorship would be a democratic republic. But this was certainly not his meaning, as he follows Marx in holding that the 'democratic republic' is simply, as he told Bernstein, 'the last form of State or bourgeois domination, that in which it is broken to pieces'.[2] His reference to it in connexion with the Erfurt Programme was thus made in no complimentary sense, and all he meant was that, as he had explained in his *Origin of the Family*, it was 'the highest form of State which, under our modern conditions of Society, is becoming more and more inevitable, the form of State in which the last decisive struggle between the bourgeoisie and the proletariat will be fought out'.

What is clear therefore is that Marx held that the bourgeois State would be replaced by a form of government to which he gave the name of the dictatorship of the proletariat. He admitted that it would be obliged temporarily to retain the coercive machinery of its predecessor, as it would not be possible immediately to eradicate all traces of the old order. Yet both he and Engels were chary of calling it a State. This was in part

1. *Correspondence*, p. 486.
2. Letter of 27 August 1883, *Briefe von F. Engels an E. Bernstein*, pp. 129–30: cp. *Eighteenth Brumaire*, *S.W.* I, p. 232; *Critique of the Gotha Programme*, ibid. II, p. 31.

due to their identification of the State with the economic oppression of one class by another, as this was something that would no longer exist after the revolution, seeing that the proletariat would not 'exploit' the bourgeoisie but would eliminate it. But, as Engels admitted in a letter to August Bebel of 18–28 March 1875, it was also due to the fact that they were being accused by the anarchists of wishing to retain the State.[1] In fact, both parties were agreed in theory that the revolution would destroy it, only whereas the anarchists made this its sole object, Marx held that its primary object was the destruction of the capitalist system, the transference of the means of production to the proletariat, and the setting up of a centralized planning economy. He seems genuinely to have believed that as a result of this the State would disappear. Yet the anarchists had good grounds for suspecting that the type of economy he envisaged would render its retention a necessity; and indeed his assurance to the contrary rests on no more secure foundation than his conviction that the revolution would so transform human nature as to render it superfluous, save for the discharge of certain innocuous functions.[2]

When, however, Marx goes on to describe the communist State of the future, his language becomes as utopian as that of the French socialists, from whose influence he had never wholly freed himself.[3] It has been suggested that he rightly limited himself to the analysis of contemporary society, and that he did not feel called upon to concern himself with problems that would doubtless be settled when they arose; while it has also been maintained that the establishment of a new social order of justice calls for an act of faith, and that it is thus unreasonable to demand any precise description of how it will operate. Yet neither of these arguments is altogether convincing, since it is surely incumbent upon those who seek to destroy the existing order to have some clear ideas as to how society will be affected

1. *Correspondence*, p. 336.

2. *See* Kelsen, op. cit. pp. 81 ff.

3. For the Utopian strain in Marx *see* Croce, *Come il Marx fece passare il communismo dall'utopia alla scienza* (Bari, 1948), pp. 24 ff.; *see* also Abram L. Harris, *Utopian Elements in Marxist Thought* in *Ethics* (University of Chicago, 1950), pp. 195–224.

by their action. All we are told, however, is that during the transition period the State will dialectically encompass its destruction and give place to a true communist society based upon voluntary association. Yet how this society will be held together is not revealed. Nor does Marx tell us whether the dialectic ceases at this stage, though on his premises it must do so, seeing that the division of society into classes, which has been the cause of conflict throughout history, has been removed. The apotheosis of the historical process is, however, best described in his own words:

In the higher phase of communist society after the enslaving subordination of individuals under division of labour, and therewith the antithesis between mental and physical labour, has vanished; after labour has become not merely a means to live, but has become itself the primary necessity of life; after the productive forces have also increased with the all-round development of the individual, and all the springs of cooperative wealth flow more abundantly – only then can the narrow horizon of bourgeois right be fully left behind, and society inscribe on its banners 'From each according to his ability, to each according to his needs'.[1]

*

There is a double strain in Marx. He has been called 'the father of modern sociology', and he well deserves the title as the author of the most penetrating analysis of social relations which appeared in his generation. But he has also been called 'the last of the prophets', and this is true also, for his predictions regarding the 'higher stage of socialism' are, indeed apocalyptic rather than analytic. A generation later Georges Sorel was to argue that every movement which aims at capturing the masses must possess its 'myth', that is, something which has the power to seize their imagination and inspire them to action. It is the belief in an impending event which will transform the world. What that event is and how it will come to pass is never clearly defined, for if it could be it would lose its potency; but there is always something praiseworthy or glorious in contributing to its consummation. It is Marx's in-

1. *Critique of the Gotha Programme, S.W.* II, p. 23.

cursions into prophecy which have furnished communism with its *mystique*.

Marxism, as Isaac Deutscher puts it, was the illegitimate and rebellious offspring of nineteenth-century liberalism.[1] Yet although it hated its parent, it professed to share with it a common belief in democracy. Marx has been reproached for failing to discern that the application of his revolutionary doctrine would lead to a greater tyranny than that which it sought to overthrow. Certainly he erred in supposing that the revolution would take place in a highly industrialized country, in which the way for it would have been prepared by the liberal bourgeoisie, whereas it actually did so in an industrially backward country with no democratic tradition, in which it could only be maintained by intensifying that autocratic rule from which its people had always suffered. Yet it may well be argued that wherever a revolution of the marxist type occurs it will lead to much the same form of government, seeing that it is impossible to introduce communism without resorting to extreme sanctions, as was discovered by the early Christians and attested by the fate of Ananias and Sapphira. For the essence of the dictatorship of the proletariat is that it is the rule of a single section of society whose mission is to eliminate all other sections as 'counter-revolutionary'. Yet this is the negation of democracy, which is 'the rule of the people', the term 'people' in this context transcending that of 'class', so that the merchant, farmer, and small shopkeeper belong to it with as good a right as do the industrial worker or agricultural labourer. Democracy, if it has any liberal content, accepts that in any society there will be conflicts of interest, and thus provides the necessary machinery for reconciling them. Marx's position is altogether different. It is that the class that controls production – by his day the bourgeoisie – has, by virtue of this, *all* political power in its hands, and uses it to dominate and oppress. Thus the immediate purpose of the revolution is to deprive the bourgeoisie of its economic control, in which event it will lose its political power also; and it is unthinkable that he would ever have permitted its members to organize themselves politically

1. *Stalin* (1950), p. 343.

in order to defeat the objects for which the revolution had been carried out. Lenin, as we shall see, held the same view, and his conception of the role of the dictatorship of the proletariat – a matter which will be considered in its place – was thus a legitimate interpretation of Marx's views.

7. The Marxist Ethic

IT would be hard to find among the writings of the mid-nineteenth century a more generous tribute to the capitalist system than is paid to it in the *Communist Manifesto*. In a short space of years it had wrought unparalleled wonders. It had established 'the universal inter-dependence of nations'. It had 'drawn all, even the most barbarian, nations into civilization'. By creating great cities it 'had rescued a considerable part of the population from the idiocy of rural life'. It had, in a word, 'subjected Nature's forces to Man'. 'What earlier century', Marx asked, 'had even a presentiment that such productive forces slumbered in the lap of social labour?' He did not, indeed, pause to enquire whether this was altogether an advantage. Yet he can scarcely be blamed, as few Victorians would have denied that production was the chief duty of man; and we may surely admit Marx to their company after the many years he lived among them.

Yet the *Communist Manifesto* is none the less a declaration of war against capitalist society, which the workers are to overthrow by violence; and marxists hold that any means are permissible which contribute to this end. That Moscow should proclaim this doctrine might be argued to reflect the amoralism which early manifested itself in the Russian revolutionary movement. For every communist is taught that his first duty is to his party; and all communist parties have shown themselves willing to adopt the Leninist principle that the criterion of right action is the degree to which it assists the cause of revolution. Here, indeed, the single exception proves the rule. In his *Left-wing Communism: an Infantile Disorder* (1920) Lenin condemned terrorism (e.g. political assassination) because the bolsheviks held at the time that it weakened the proletarian movement by encouraging the masses to believe that the revolution could be won for them by a few 'heroic individuals', whereas it was their duty to carry it out for themselves. But he was careful to point out that his objection was 'of course only based on considerations of expediency'; and marxists have long since been permitted to use such methods if they are likely to be successful. Nor, indeed, had Lenin himself hesitated to make use of them in his earlier years.

This attitude has disturbed many persons otherwise sympathetic to much that marxism stands for. In an article published in the *New Statesman* of June 1946 Kingsley Martin strongly condemned it as contrary to the Greco-Roman-Christian tradition, which insists on the primacy of the individual conscience; while H. J. Laski referred to the 'grave issues created by the ethical behaviour of communist parties outside Russia since 1917', which he held to have been marked by deception, ruthlessness, contempt of fair play, willingness to use lying and treachery to gain some desired end, and complete dishonesty in the presentation of facts – accusations that marxists scarcely trouble to refute, merely contending that their opponents are as bad or worse. Such charges raise, however, the question as to whether marxism possesses any ethical basis, and if so what it is; to which marxists reply that they certainly do not repudiate ethics, but have their own system which differs from others only in being grounded on sound principles instead of false. The great increase in Soviet, and generally in marxist, influence today makes this a burning issue, and attention should therefore be paid to it.

The marxist ethic derives logically from the general philosophic position which Marx adopted. Here three points should be noted.

First, the hegelian dialectic denied the existence of any eternal and immutable principles upon which a system of ethics or of anything else could be founded, since ideas themselves were in a continual state of change.

Secondly, Kant had taught that while we could have no real knowledge of the external world, we do reach solid rock in the moral consciousness; and he had formulated certain principles of conduct – his famous 'categorical imperatives' – by which morality, in the sense of private morality, should be regulated and for which he claimed a universal validity. But Hegel could not accept such an ethic as final, since he was concerned with a grand historical process, directed by reason and operating through the dialectic, under which civilizations rose and fell; and to justify this process he *had* to show that there was a higher and dynamic ethic upon which the judgements of 'world history' rested, since it was obvious that no nation reaches a dominant position through obedience to the precepts of private morality or by turning the other cheek. The Norman Conquest, for example, cannot be justified by ordinary moral standards. But historians do not therefore condemn it, but agree that it was of the utmost benefit to this country. It could, of course, be argued that this only proves that in certain cases good may come out of evil. But that would not have satisfied Hegel, as it would have introduced a fortuitous element into a process which he wished to exhibit as wholly rational. He therefore held that Kant's imperatives were vapid when they were not actually dangerous; and that many of the moral injunctions of Jesus were inapplicable to a 'bourgeois society', and would speedily bring about the ruin of any State that attempted to apply them.

Thirdly, Marx agreed with Hegel in rejecting what is called abstract ethical idealism, that is, the view that there exist certain principles of right and wrong which are universal. He held that there was no such thing as 'human nature' in the abstract, and that men's ideas of what is good and bad were determined by the economic structure of the social organism of which they formed a part. He, too, was not concerned with the morality of individuals but with that of groups, though for him the group was a class and not the nation. The force behind the dialectic of history was the class struggle, and this generated its own ethic. Here, however, Marx went farther than his master. Hegel had pointed out that actions which could not be justified by the moral standards of the police-court might ultimately be approved by 'world history', which adopted a different standard. But he never said that nations or their leaders were free to act as they pleased on the chance that their actions might be thus approved.

Marx teaches that the ethical system of any community, like

its religion and laws, is simply a part of the superstructure created by the conditions of production, and always reflects the interests of the dominant class. Its values are thus no more than expressions of 'class morality', and as long as the class system persists, no useful purpose is to be served by discussing them. When that system has been destroyed and not before, it will be possible to put ethics on a sound basis. The *Communist Manifesto* is the most powerful indictment of the capitalist order ever written, but it contains no word of 'right' or 'justice', and no appeal to any 'moral law'. Nor does Marx's use of 'exploitation' in *Capital* directly imply an ethical condemnation; it is not, as least ostensibly, the expression of a moral judgement, but rather a description of social relations. His main charge against the French utopian socialists, and particularly Proudhon, had been precisely their obsession with 'justice', whereas his object was to convince every thinking person that the capitalist system was doomed to disappear for reasons which lay within its very nature and which had nothing to do with metaphysical abstractions.[1]

Yet again there enters that ambivalence which we have already noted between Marx the scientist and Marx the revolutionary agitator. His *Capital* purports to be a strictly scientific demonstration of the fate which must ultimately overtake the capitalist system. Yet every page reveals Marx's abhorrence of that system. Capitalists may be obliged to act as they do; but this is only because they are operating within a system which is inherently corrupt. Indeed, if Marx had held it to be otherwise, his demonstration could have aroused only an academic interest, and would have not stirred men's passions as it was intended to do. Yet his moral indignation raises an awkward question. For if the capitalist system is evil, it can only be because it is in conflict with some objective moral principle. But the existence of any such principle has been denied.

The two classical formulations of the marxist ethic, to which all apologists invariably refer, are those of Engels and Lenin. The first is in the *Anti-Dühring*.

1. Venable, p. 205.

We therefore reject every attempt to impose on us any moral dogma whatsoever as an eternal, ultimate, and for ever immutable moral law on the pretext that the moral world too has its permanent principles which transcend history and the differences between nations. We maintain on the contrary that all former moral theories are the product, in the last analysis, of the economic stage which society had reached at that particular epoch. And as society has hitherto moved in class antagonisms, morality was always a class morality; it has either justified the domination and the interests of the ruling class, or, as soon as the oppressed class has become powerful enough, it has represented the revolt against this domination and the future interests of the oppressed. That in this process there has on the whole been progress in morality, as in all other branches of human knowledge, cannot be doubted. But we have not yet passed beyond class morality. A really human morality which transcends class antagonisms and their legacies in thought becomes possible only at a stage of society which has not only overcome class contradictions but has even forgotten them in practical life.[1]

Lenin's contribution is contained in his *Address to the 3rd Congress of the Russian Young Communist League* of 2 October 1920 – not the most inspired of his writings :

Is there such a thing as communist ethics? Is there such a thing as communist morality? Of course there is. It is often made to appear that we have no ethics of our own; and very often the bourgeoisie accuse us communists of repudiating all ethics. This is a method of throwing dust in the eyes of the workers and peasants.

In what sense do we repudiate ethics and morality?

In the sense that it is preached by the bourgeoisie, who derived ethics from God's commandments ... Or instead of deriving ethics from the commandments of God, they derived them from idealist or semi-idealist phrases, which always amounted to something very similar to God's commandments. We repudiate all morality derived from non-human and non-class concepts. We say that it is a deception, a fraud in the interests of the landlords and capitalists. We say that our morality is entirely subordinated to the interests of the class struggle of the proletariat. Our morality is derived from the

1. *Anti-Dühring* (ed. C. P. Dutt), pp. 109–10.

interests of the class struggle of the proletariat. . . . The class struggle is still continuing . . . We subordinate our communist morality to this task. We say: morality is what serves to destroy the old exploiting society and to unite all the toilers around the proletariat, which is creating a new communist society. . . . We do not believe in an eternal morality.[1]

It will be seen that Lenin accepts the sharp division drawn by Marx between the bourgeoisie and the proletariat, which are represented as two entirely different human types whose relations resemble those of a white minority exploiting a coloured majority. But while this distinction is adopted by all marxist writers and has an obvious propaganda value, it is an altogether arbitrary one and is rooted in a static conception of society as seen at a particular period of time. Marx was a great admirer of Balzac, upon whom he had intended to write a book, and it is a pity that he had not read the *Comédie humaine* with a greater discernment, as it admirably illustrates that movement, continually operative in society, as a result of which members of the proletariat rise in the social scale, for reasons often not unconnected with their superior intelligence and capacity for hard work, while members of the bourgeoisie similarly descend, possibly again for lack of such qualities. But this arbitrary class division is maintained by all marxist writers, and is rendered even more artificial by their practice of transferring to the bourgeoisie or petty-bourgeoisie any section of the workers with whom they may be in conflict.

Stalin, perhaps to his credit, did not venture into ethical theory; nor have modern Soviet apologists made any contribution to it, so that a talk on 'communist morality' given by Professor Kalbanovski over the Moscow Radio in October 1946, and subsequently reprinted in the European communist press, was no more than a repetition of what Engels and Lenin had said, padded out with abuse of 'bourgeois' and 'fascist' morality and eulogies of the ethical standards which had been achieved in the Soviet Union. Yet if the above passages from Engels and Lenin are read in conjunction with such glosses as western marxists have made during recent years, the main lines

1. *Selected Works* (2-vol. ed. 1947) II, p. 667.

of the marxist ethic become clear enough.[1] It is strictly materialist and naturalistic. Man is the product of nature and is bound by nature's laws; and it is in accordance with these laws, and not with his dreams and ideals, that society develops. A scientific study of society at once reveals that the class struggle is fundamental, and from this is born the doctrine of the social revolution, which transforms marxism from a theory into a militant activism. And, as Trotsky puts it, 'the highest form of the class struggle is civil war, which explodes in mid-air all moral ties between the hostile classes'.[2]

The basis of the marxist ethic is thus what present-day marxists often call 'the concrete human situation' in which the conditions of production are the determining factor. It is an ethic which is rooted in demands, not in intuitions, and which rejects every 'transcendent' element.[3] A recent American writer on the *Communist Manifesto* observes that the workers do not seek to derive the principles which lead them to demand the abolition of the capitalist system from anything except their own interests, which, it is explained, are ultimately those of mankind in general, since those who make them represent the enslaved of all ages. Hence he declares that the marxist ethic is simply the expression of the desires of the workers, but that these are justified because they accord with the inevitable course of social evolution. That proletarian morality is still class morality is recognized. But it is an advance on bourgeois morality, because it is that of the class dialectically predestined to triumph and ultimately to create a society the ethics of which will possess an absolute value because class distinctions will have disappeared.[4] Indeed, as J. D. Bernal pointed out in an article in the *Modern Quarterly* of December 1945, the new planned society into

1. *See*, for example, Roger Garaudy's *Le Communisme et la morale* (Paris, 1946). This makes the usual question-begging claim that only when the capitalist system has been abolished will men be free to develop their personalities to the full, and that marxism is thus the true humanism.

2. *Their Morals and Ours* (New York, 1940).

3. Hook, *From Hegel to Marx*, pp. 47 ff.

4. Howard Selsam, *The Ethics of the Communist Manifesto in Science and Society*, Vol. XII, No. 1, 1948, pp. 22–32; see also his *Socialism and Ethics* (New York, 1943; London, 1947), p. 12.

which we are now entering already calls for a radical change in ethical values. Some of the old virtues will remain; but virtues such as thrift, which have their roots in an outmoded individualism, will be replaced by others based on a livelier sense of social relations.

It should be noted, finally, that marxists use the term 'proletarian morality' with a certain ambiguity. At times it is held to mean the morality of the proletariat during the transition period which lies between the revolution which abolishes the bourgeois State and the creation of a classless society, that is, the phase of the dictatorship of the proletariat which Lenin characterized as one of 'violence unrestricted by law'; while at others it is used to denote the morality of the classless society of that 'higher stage of socialism' which lies in the future, but to which the dictatorship of the proletariat will eventually give rise.

*

It is only possible to make a few brief comments on the foregoing.

1. We do not need Marx or Engels to tell us that standards of behaviour vary from age to age and that every generation has to work out its own moral problems. If this was all they wished to say, they could only be charged with uttering a commonplace. In fact, however, as appears clearly in the *Communist Manifesto*, their intention was to invalidate all ethical criticism of their teaching by denying that it could rest upon any universal principles and by representing it as no more than the expression of class interest. But this is to reject the existence of any objective standard. Every great work of literature reflects the social condition of its age; but it also contains aesthetic values which are universal. Equally, there are absolute and immutable ethical principles which have commanded assent all down the centuries. For underlying the flux of history there is, as A. L. Rowse has pointed out, a certain continuum to which all ethical judgements can be related, and which lead men to agree that Socrates was a good man and Nero a bad man, and that truth and charity are better than falsehood and malice. At all times

men have agreed that it is better to assist their fellow creatures than to injure them, though the extent to which they have been prepared to render such assistance and the particular form which they have felt that it should take have depended on the moral insights of their generation.[1]

Present-day marxists may point out that Marx and Engels would never have contested the above, and would thus have agreed that bourgeois morality contained certain permanent elements which a classless morality would take over. But although this is doubtless what they meant, it is not what they said; and their condemnation of all ethical systems other than their own is so sweeping as to make it difficult to see what elements in them they regarded as worthy of survival, or by what criterion they would be selected. Indeed, it is not uncommon for marxists to argue that such virtues as kindliness are not virtues in their own right, but only become such if and in so far as they are harnessed to the proletarian cause.

2. Marxism greatly exaggerates the power of communities in general, and in this case of classes, to evolve genuine ethical systems. The morality of all collectivities is invariably low, if only because the sense of personal responsibility is diluted; and it is a commonplace that boards and committees will often act as none of their individual members would dream of doing. It is, of course, perfectly true that private morality is the outcome and product of social morality. Yet it is equally true that every advance in the moral standards of a community is the work of individuals. Later we shall find Lenin right in contending that the proletariat, if left to itself, never develops a revolutionary ideology. But neither will it develop an ethical system worthy of the name as long as the criterion is solely its own class interests, while it is less likely than other classes to produce the type of leader who will transform whatever system it does evolve into a better. The ideology of marxism itself derives from men who, like Marx and Engels, were bourgeois and not proletarians.

3. Even if we accept the marxist thesis that all ethical systems simply reflect the interests of the dominant class, it would

1. op. cit. pp. 151–2.

only follow that proletarian morality will do the same, and not that it is superior to other forms of morality. In the absence of any objective standard, bourgeois and proletarian morality are only different sets of feelings about right and wrong, and there can be no proof that one set is better than another. To prefer proletarian morality because the victory of the proletariat is guaranteed by the dialectic is incompatible with any view of ethics, since a thing is not necessarily desirable because it is unavoidable.[1]

4. It is certainly a logical inference that if all morality is class morality, the only way to get a classless morality is to do away with classes. But it does not follow that the destruction of the bourgeoisie, or of whatever class may be regarded as in the ascendant, will create such a society; and, indeed, the more highly developed is the social order in which a marxist revolution has occurred, the more inevitably will there arise a new class stratification, the upper levels of which will tend, precisely as in the past, to impose their ideas upon the lower. The new class of managers, technicians, and the like which has arisen in Russia has quickly enough revealed the same prejudices as the older class which it has replaced.

5. It is quite true that in some sense moral obligation does derive from human demands. Yet is this the end of the matter? All civilized people condemn murder. But does this condemnation spring only from the very 'concrete demand' that they should not have their throats cut? Or does it not imply some perception of the sanctity of human life, a consideration which a marxist might well dismiss as 'transcendent', and which it is certainly not easy to represent as the rationalization of an economic interest? This at least appears to be the lesson of Dostoyevsky's *Crime and Punishment*. The gifted student Raskolnikov is conscious that he possesses all the qualities which will enable him to make a name for himself, and at the same time be of service to the community. One thing only is lacking – money. Yet this he can have if he murders an old usuress who is detestable and a burden upon society. He murders her, but only to find himself caught up in something he had not foreseen

1. *See* J. M. Cameron, *Scrutiny of Marxism* (1948), pp. 46 ff.

– a struggle between the human will and an eternal moral imperative. What Dostoievsky is trying to say is that the moral order ultimately rests not upon man-made prohibitions and injunctions, but upon a mystical element – a still, small voice which puts to silence all the babel of human argument and counter-argument.[1] This element has nothing to do with self-interest. Still less is it derived from the class division of society, or from any economic or other factor which underlies this division.

6. The marxist contention that any action is justified if it assists the cause of revolution raises the difficult question of ends and means.[2] John Lewis, the editor of *Modern Quarterly*, has quoted with approval a statement to the effect that 'an end will always justify the means if the end is good and the means adapted to promote it' which is simply the old maxim (erroneously fathered upon the Jesuits) that 'the end justifies the means', since it is naturally assumed that the end is good and no one has ever suggested that any end justifies any means.[3] There are those who hold that, as we cannot define absolute standards, we are obliged to use the above principle and habitually do so. It is difficult to see the force of this contention. People of normal moral instincts do not pursue ends by means which they know to be bad, or, if they do so, they do not pretend that they are acting rightly, save in so far as they unconsciously deceive themselves. It is no uncommon experience for a man to abandon an end, the realization of which might in his view advance some cause or interest which he has at heart, because he comes to see that it can only be attained by methods which he holds to be disreputable. Machiavelli puts the case well. If, he says, a man wishes to obtain domination over the State, but then decides that he can do so only by assassinating a dangerous rival, he must renounce his design if he objects to employing such methods, though if he persists in it, he must use

1. Stanislaw Mackiewicz, *Dostoyevsky* (1947), pp. 117–18.

2. For an interesting discussion of this much debated theme *see* H. Gompertz, *When does the End justify the Means?* in *Ethics* (University of Chicago, April 1943), pp. 173 ff.

3. For a more recent statement of his views see *The Modern Quarterly* (Summer, 1950), pp. 195–224.

all those means which are necessary to its attainment. What he must not do is to seek the end while trying to evade the means for this is altogether contemptible. But Machiavelli does not attempt to show that this pursuit of ends by appropriate means has anything to do with moral goodness. It calls rather for that quality which he calls *virtù*, which is ethically neutral and does not concern itself with whether the end is good or bad.

It is true that Machiavelli goes further than this in maintaining, albeit with bitterness and pessimism, that political life has its own laws, and that the ruler may thus be forced, in the interests of the state, to act in a manner impermissible in a private individual. Croce has recently lent the weight of his authority to this familiar doctrine. Political sense, he maintains, is the power to act according to expediency, and however lofty a statesman's moral feelings, if he acts contrary to expediency he does not possess it. This is the true foundation of political philosophy. To deny it only leads to a false dualism between political and moral action, and to illogical talk about the necessity of doing evil to attain good. Such men as Frederick the Great and Cavour might, he holds, have spared themselves their misgivings, seeing that, as may be assumed, they were not acting from ambition 'but for the sacred protection, the development or the rebirth of the State'. For 'the struggle for liberty . . . does not object to rebellions and wars when they are necessary, and does not shrink from the blood that man has always shed in order to make the history of mankind bear fruit'.[1] Yet this is to concede everything to the marxists, who may interpret 'liberty' with as good a right as Croce himself. And it is at least arguable that policies adopted from motives of expediency and without regard to principle have ultimately recoiled upon the nations that have pursued them. Richelieu sought by every means to destroy Austria, with the result that, when Germany became strong, Austria was unable to exert upon her any restraining influence. Napoleon plunged Europe into war for a generation, and left France smaller than he found her. And how far did Bismarck's policy advantage those whom it sought to benefit?

1. Croce, *Politics and Morals* (1946), p. 92.

That 'the end justifies the means' is thus rightly to be regarded as a dangerous doctrine. Doubtless it may possess a certain application to practical questions of administration, as for example to schemes of planning, almost every one of which causes injury to someone. If the widening of a road necessitates the pulling down of certain houses which the occupiers are most unwilling to vacate, and if the scheme is generally held to be in the public interest and reasonable compensation is paid, the conscience of the community is undisturbed. But here we are dealing with a strictly determinate end, and one which can be shown to be readily attainable. To apply the doctrine when the end is as indeterminate as the creation of a new society is a very different matter, as all sorts of moral issues enter upon which it is impossible that there should be agreement. Unless we are prepared to claim omniscience, we cannot be certain that the establishment of a communist society will of necessity be a good thing. Even if it were, we are not in a position infallibly to determine the means best adapted to promote it, and still less are we justified in using any means which we hold to be so adapted. For if it is decided to commit a wrong action, the action will be committed; but there can be no guarantee that it will bring about the end we desire. In fact, there is good reason to suppose that it will not, seeing that men and not measures are the *ultima ratio*, and measures become what men make them. And, again, once we have decided to use means which are only justifiable in view of the end to which they are applied, we have set out on a course which may lead us farther than we had intended, just as Raskolnikov, contrary to his intentions, had not only to kill the old usuress but also her good and innocent sister, though he so bungled the matter that he even failed to secure the money for the sake of which the crime had been committed.[1] The central error of present-day marxists, apart from their fundamental lack of charity towards their fellow-creatures, is their attempt to set up by any and every means a planned Absolute of social justice. We do well to strive after justice. Yet in an imperfect world we can never hope to reach more than an approximation to it; and if our presumption

1. Rex Warner, *The Cult of Power* (1946), p. 52.

carries us farther, all we are likely to achieve is a greater injustice. *Summum jus, summa injuria.*

That our marxist ideologist thinks otherwise is partly because the doctrine of the class struggle has taught him to regard life as an unending battle in which no quarter must be given; and partly, and perhaps even more, because he has been trained to believe that he is helping to plan society in strict accordance with scientific laws. Dialectical materialism repudiates mechanistic interpretations. Yet in practice marxists accept them. Society, they hold, is like a machine which will only work properly if it is put together in the right (or marxist) way. Hence our ideologist feels as little compunction in ridding himself of an opponent as does a mechanic who throws some faulty bolt upon the scrap heap when he is assembling an engine. He will point out that the dialectic shows that at the present stage of history nothing matters except the victory of the proletariat which will usher in the classless society, and that he prefers to cooperate with this inevitable process rather than oppose it. And that he reasons thus should be a sufficient answer to those who underrate the role that the dialectic plays in the marxist system.

PART TWO

THE DEVELOPMENT OF THE EUROPEAN SOCIALIST MOVEMENT UP TO 1914

*

8. The Precursors of Marx

EUROPEAN Socialism derives from two sources:

a. The Industrial Revolution, which riveted capitalism upon a society hitherto largely feudal and thus radically changed the connexion between what Marx called the productive forces and the productive relations. This is a matter of economic history, and it is not necessary to pursue it farther here.

b. The ideas of the French Revolution as expressed in the formula 'Liberty, Equality, and Fraternity'. Yet while the French Revolution had led to a great deal of declamation, it was not a popular movement save for a brief period under Robespierre in 1794 and for the Babeuf conspiracy of 1796. It was essentially a rising of the *tiers état*, of which the bourgeoisie was the most important element, against the monarchy and the privileged orders, and the lists of grievances submitted to the States General in 1789 show a most respectful regard for the rights of property.[1]

Although the French Revolution was a bourgeois-democratic revolution, it can scarcely be fitted into the marxist dialectical pattern. In so far as it was directed against feudal survivals, it provides an illustration of the class struggle. Yet, as Plamenatz points out, to make it a marxist revolution of the approved type, it would be necessary to show that the productive relations of the time were impeding the development of the productive forces, that is, that the middle-class could not fail to make full use of the new methods of production because of the survival of feudal institutions jealously defended by those who had an

1. H. J. Laski, *The Socialist Traditions in the French Revolution* (1930), pp. 7 ff.; *The Rise of European Liberalism* (1936), pp. 224 ff.

interest in retaining them. In fact, however, the Crown had not only done much to stimulate trade and industry, but had also rigidly excluded the nobility from the administration of the State, in favour of members of the middle-class. The inefficiency of the administration was, indeed, a great hindrance to commerce; but it was not a feudal administration, and there was no reason why the country should not have been as well governed as Prussia, where there were many more feudal survivals. In France the nobility were rather a class of hereditary pensioners than of rulers. That they paid no taxes was an economic grievance; but the fact that the middle-class had to pay for expenditure of which it disapproved did not mean that its economic activity was being seriously hampered.[1]

But while the French Revolution ended by establishing the domination of the bourgeoisie, it taught the lesson that it would never again be safe for any government wholly to disregard the workers; and it further caused a number of intellectuals to feel dissatisfaction with the capitalist system and to look round for ways of ending it, or at least of mitigating its evils. Thus there arose a school of socialist thinkers, of whom the most important were Saint-Simon (1760–1825), Fourier (1772–1837), Louis Blanc (1811–82), and Proudhon (1809–65).[2] They exercised considerable influence over Marx, who borrowed a number of their ideas while dissociating himself from the specific remedies which they recommended.

Saint-Simon, the founder of French socialism, is the apostle of the 'business government', though in a form which would make little appeal to those who ordinarily demand one. He believed that economic problems were more important than political problems, and that the French Revolution had failed because, while putting an end to various forms of privilege, it had neglected the most important of them all – the privilege of wealth. He had been deeply impressed by the industrial and

1. Plamenatz, pp. 41 ff.; Federn, pp. 134 ff.

2. For a general discussion of the views of these writers *see* Karl Diehl, *Über Sozialismus, Kommunismus und Anarchismus* (Jena, 1920), pp. 181 ff.; Charles Gide and Charles Rist, *History of Economic Doctrines* (ed. 1947, Eng. trans. 1948), pp. 211–42, 255–73; A. Gray, *The Socialist Tradition* (1946), pp. 135–256.

financial developments of his time and was enthusiastically in favour of them. He called therefore for a government of industrialists, bankers, and technicians, though these high priests of the new order were to be appointed by the State and be responsible to it. All the means of production should belong to a 'social fund', as he held the view, later developed by Marx, that society was moving inevitably towards socialism, and that it was the duty of the State to establish it. But he was not a communist, because he did not believe in a classless society, and he had no objection to anyone making a large income provided he earned it, though if the income was derived from inherited property it was exploitation.

Fourier was a 'perfectionist' who believed that all evils were due to restraints imposed by society, and that once these were removed men would work together in a spirit of cooperation. This constituted his principle of the 'harmony of passions', the enunciation of which set him, as he believed, upon the level of Newton. Society should be organized in *phalanges* of 1,600 persons, each group occupying a *phalanstère*; and in 1832 an unsuccessful attempt was made to start one of these near the Forest of Rambouillet. He applied to Rothschild for support, just as Robert Owen sought to interest the Tsar and Metternich in his socialist experiments; and he was as far removed from the realities of life as though he had been the inhabitant of another planet. He is of interest, partly as an extreme representative of the sort of utopianism which Marx had to combat, and partly as one of the principal channels by which French socialist ideas reached America. Further, he had a considerable influence upon the precursors of Russian Narodnik socialism, and particularly upon Chernyshevsky.[1]

Louis Blanc, the historian of the French Revolution, was a more practical thinker, and his ideas are set out in his *Organisation du travail* of 1839, which, despite its superficiality, had a vogue in its day. He held the evils of society to be due to competition, and the remedy for them to be the control of industry by the State – regarded as a beneficent institution – which set up *ateliers nationaux* in which the workers would be

1. Franco Venturi, *Il populismo russo* (Turin, 1952), pp. 141, 233–4.

guaranteed employment at a fair wage – an experiment later
attempted under his direction with disastrous results. But no
one before him had so clearly taught that the State must be
used to set up a new social order. He was the first to see the
close inter-connexion between political and social reform. It
was not enough to lay down general principles; the real problem was to give effect to them, and this was a question of power,
that is, of the State. Unfortunately he accepted office in the
provisional government of 1848, and is therefore regarded by
marxists as a renegade.

Proudhon was a prolific writer with a natural gift of style,
who assembled an immense number of contradictory propositions leaving his readers to reconcile them as best they could.
He came to the front with his *Qu'est-ce que la Propriété* (1840)
with its celebrated answer *'La Propriété, c'est le vol'*. But while
it might be supposed from this that he was opposed to
property, he was, in fact, wholeheartedly in favour of it. For
the basis of his system, if it can be so described, was a thorough-
going individualism which led him to reject the State and *a
fortiori* all forms of collectivism; and he thus held that property
(provided it did not give rise to unearned income) was a bulwark against the power of the State. His particular brand of
socialism was 'mutuellisme', and its most distinctive feature
was an exchange bank at which the worker would deposit the
fruits of his labour, and receive coupons which would serve as
money. What was to happen if no one wanted the particular
type of product deposited was a difficulty which he did not face,
and which led to the speedy collapse of such banks of the kind
as were set up by way of experiment.

None the less, Proudhon is extremely important because of
one idea which was to have repercussions, the force of which is
still not wholly spent. Both he and Marx agreed in demanding
an economic reorganization of society. But at this point their
ways diverged. Proudhon held that what was wrong with the
French Revolution was not that it had been inaugurated by
the bourgeoisie, who had then betrayed the workers – though
doubtless this had occurred – but that it had been a *political*
revolution, since all that political revolutions could ever do was

to shift the balance of power *within* the State, and it was to this power, of which the State was the embodiment, that he was unalterably opposed. Hence he argued that the existing economic order would only be changed when all power was abolished and the adjustment of economic interests was left to the exertions of the private individual. But for this purpose no revolution was necessary, save a revolution in the minds of men, since he had persuaded himself that they would be willing to do what the very existence of the state of affairs he condemned proved that they were not. By thus sharply differentiating between economic and political action, and by repudiating the latter, Proudhon became the founder of French anarchism, and was later regarded as the father of anarcho-syndicalism, though this is only true in the sense that the arguments he advanced against collective ownership of any kind were used by the anarcho-syndicalists to attack that form of it of which they disapproved. His theories exercised over many years an immense influence upon Russian revolutionary thinkers, and in particular Bakunin; while they so exasperated Marx as to lead him to set out his own with a greater precision in the *Poverty of Philosophy* (1847).[1] He is of interest as responsible for the much overworked phrase 'the exploitation of man by man'.

At the same time, there existed in France a small revolutionary group under the leadership of Louis Blanqui (1805–81). It drew its inspiration from the jacobinism of the French Revolution, and particularly from 'Gracchus' Babeuf (1760–97), the founder of the only socialist movement of that period. Babeuf was not a communist save in so far as he proclaimed that 'nature has granted to every man the equal right to enjoy all her goods', which was common form in contemporary declamation. A notary's clerk, who had made a living by looking after the property of the landed gentry of his native Picardy, he rejected Rousseauist attempts to bring men back to the state of nature, and advocated a society in which there would be neither rich nor poor, and every man would work and own a certain amount of property. He set forth his opinions in the

1. For Marx's relations with him *see* Pierre Haubtmann, *Marx et Proudhon* (Paris, 1947).

Tribun du Peuple, of which he was editor; and in 1796 he founded a secret society, the Societé des Égaux, which was to overthrow the Directorate. But, although a pioneer in conspiratorial technique, his group was early penetrated by the police, and he was arrested and executed.[1]

Among Babeuf's lieutenants was a certain Filippo Buonarroti, a descendant of Michelangelo, who published, in 1828, *Le Conspiration pour l'égalité dite de Babeuf*, which became the breviary of the younger revolutionaries of 1830. Blanqui became associated with Buonarroti as fellow-members of a secret society, the Carbonari, and through him was indoctrinated with babouvist ideas. A precursor of Lenin in his belief that revolution could only be accomplished by a body of professionals, he organized a succession of secret societies. But these were ineffectual as lacking all contact with the masses; and when one of them, the Société des Saisons, staged a conspiracy in Paris in March 1839, it was completely unsuccessful, as the workers had no idea what it was about.

Thereafter Blanqui spent most of his time in prison, though he emerged for a few weeks during the 1848 revolution and again during the Commune. In 1879 he was amnestied as a result of an agitation for his release, and was at once elected deputy for Bordeaux. But this was not what the Government had intended, and his election was declared invalid, though he was defended in the Chamber by Clemenceau. He now became a public figure, touring the country and being everywhere received with ovations. But he was an old man, and in 1881 he died, appropriately enough from an apoplectic fit while addressing a meeting. A revolutionary pure and simple, he had no scientific basis for his theories, nor any power to deal with situations as they arose. He despised trade unions, and held every form of working-class activity other than revolution to be suspect. Essentially an individualist, he came near to anarchism, and if he did not accept anarchist theory it was only because he ignored all theoretical questions. As he told the Paris correspondent of *The Times* in 1879: 'I have no theories. I am not a professor of politics or socialism. What exists is bad, something

1. *See* David Thomson, *The Conspiracy of Babeuf* (1947).

else must take its place, and gradually things will come to what they ought to be.' Above all he held the destruction of religion to be essential.[1]

Yet fantastic as Blanqui was, he kept alive the jacobin tradition, though the technique of conspiracy was to be revolutionized by the Russians, and in particular by Lenin, who solved the problem of how a secret organization could also maintain contact with the masses. Further, however unrealistic their treatment of the future, the 'utopian socialists' – by whom Marx and Engels meant Saint-Simon, Fourier and Robert Owen, but not Proudhon, with whom they differed fundamentally – had made none the less an important and positive contribution to socialism. They were the first to make it a genuine public issue; while their criticism of the existing order, their analysis of history and their insights into social psychology provided Marx with much valuable material. He might attack them, but he would not permit others to do so, and reminded his readers that, for all their shortcomings, they were among the greatest men that history had produced, since, as Engels explained, they were utopians only 'because they could be nothing else at a time when capitalist production was so little developed'.[2]

1. Niel Stewart, *Blanqui* (1939), pp. 329–30.
2. *Anti-Dühring* (ed. C. P. Dutt), p. 298.

9. The Communist League

NOT long before Marx paid his first visit to Paris, there had come into existence there a small society of German exiles, the 'League of the Just', of which the most prominent member was Wilhelm Weitling, an eager disciple of Blanqui. It was a very small affair, and its meetings consisted of from ten to twenty artisans who met in a back room in the suburb of Vincennes. But its members took part in Blanqui's coup, and after its failure some of them came to London and founded the 'German Workers' Educational Society', which was non-revolutionary and resembled one of those mutual improvement societies which were a feature of early Victorian England. When Marx came to England in 1845, Engels introduced him to this group. Marx was favourably impressed, and on his return to Brussels he founded a 'German Workers' Association' on similar lines, in connexion with which Engels organized a Paris committee. In the summer of 1847 a congress of the Brussels, London, and Paris committees was held in London, and it was decided to form an international 'Communist League', and to approve its constitution and programme at a second congress to be held in November. Marx had not attended the first congress, but he now felt that it was time to take a hand. He did not regard the constitution as of much importance, but it was most desirable that the programme should follow the right lines. He therefore joined the sub-committee set up to prepare it; and as he was far abler than any of its members, he was soon asked to draft it himself, which he and Engels did. The result was the *Communist Manifesto*, which was printed in German in February 1848. It is one of the outstanding political documents of all time, and has exerted an influence comparable to that of the American Declaration of Independence of 1776 and the French Declaration of Rights of 1789. It is still accepted as the classic formulation of the marxist creed, and on the occasion of the centenary of its publication in 1948 the British Socialist Party acknowledged its indebtedness to it by issuing an officially sponsored edition.

The events of 1848 made the Communist League a proscribed society in France and Germany, and London became its centre. But its executive was divided, its president Karl Schapper calling for immediate revolutionary action in accordance with the tactics which had been laid down for the especial benefit of the German workers in the *Address to the Communist League* of March 1850, whereas Marx, though bitterly resentful of the defection of the bourgeoisie, had now come to see that there was no immediate prospect of a successful revolution, and that a long period of preparation would be necessary before the masses would be fit to seize power. The issue came to a head at a meeting on the following September 15th, when Marx accused the extremists of being idealists rather than materialists in representing 'will by itself as the motive force of revolution', and declared: 'We tell the workers: you have to go through fifteen, twenty, fifty years of civil wars and international struggles not only to change the international situation, but *to change yourselves*, and make yourselves fit for political power.'[1] Marx won a nominal victory. But as he recognized that the rank and file were against him, he carried a resolution transferring the executive to Cologne, where he possessed a group of secret adherents, and this marked the effective end of the League. The German Workers' Educational Society persisted, and Marx gave its members popular lectures on political economy. This was to be for many years his only contact with any proletarian movement.

1. Michel Collinet, *La Tragédie du marxisme* (Paris, 1948), pp. 135–6; Mehring, p. 233.

10. Marx and Lassalle

AFTER the failure of 1848, France settled down under the Second Republic, and no socialist leader of eminence emerged to continue the struggle. In England the Chartist movement was undermined by the anti-Corn-Law agitation. A large part of the working-class accepted the middle-class leadership of Cobden and Bright, and abandoned its dream of winning political power in favour of the ideology of free trade. But in Germany there began to grow up a type of socialism which Marx was able to influence, though by no means to the extent he would have wished, or indeed to which he might have aspired had he not so long delayed to publish a full exposition of his doctrine. The leader of this movement was Ferdinand Lassalle (1825–64), the founder of the first working-class political party, whose relations with Marx form one of the most curious episodes in their lives.[1]

Lassale was a Jew from Eastern Germany – he was born in Breslau (Wroclaw) – and had attached himself to Marx's group in 1848 when the latter was editing the *Neue Rheinische Zeitung* in Cologne. At the end of the year he had been imprisoned for revolutionary activity, and by the time he was released Marx had settled in London. Thus the two did not meet again for more than ten years, though Lassalle performed a number of services for Marx, and in particular obtained a publisher for his *Critique of Political Economy*. But although Marx could never withhold an involuntary admiration for Lassalle's energy, he entertained an intense dislike for him, as is shown by the epithets – 'Jewish Nigger' and the like – under which he referred to him in his correspondence with Engels. The cause of this was partly jealousy that Lassalle, whose abilities he accounted far inferior to his own, should cut a figure in Berlin, while he himself lived in exile, poor and neglected; and that he

1. Diehl, pp. 292 ff.; Arthur Rosenberg, *Democracy and Socialism* (1939), pp. 156 ff.

should be under financial obligations to him was an additional aggravation. The result was that, as Mehring points out, he was unjust to Lassalle, persistently underrating his very real ability, and contemptuously throwing aside his writings which 'had given new life and new hope to hundreds of thousands of German workers'.

In 1863 Lassalle founded the Allgemeine deutsche Arbeiterverein, but in the following year he was killed in a duel, and after an interval the leadership passed into the capable if authoritarian hands of Johann von Schweitzer. In 1863 there was also founded, at Leipzig, the Arbeiterbund, of which Marx's pupils August Bebel and Wilhelm Leibknecht (the father of Karl Leibknecht) were the principal leaders, and this affiliated to the International of 1868. In 1869 it changed its name to the Sozialdemokratische Arbeiterpartei at a congress held at Eisenach, and its members thus became known as the 'Eisenachers' as opposed to the 'Lassalleans'. The two movements amalgamated as the Sozialistische Arbeiterpartei Deutschlands at the Gotha Congress of 1875, on a programme to which Marx vainly objected. At the Erfurt Congress of 1891 it took the name of Sozialdemokratische Partei Deuetschlands, and adopted what was, despite certain criticisms by Engels, an essentially marxist programme.

Although under von Schweitzer the lassalleans had adopted a friendly attitude towards the International, Marx would have nothing to do with them. On the theoretical side, his principal objection was that Lassalle had taken his stand upon the 'Iron Law of Wages', the name the latter had given to Ricardo's thesis that under capitalism wages inevitably tend to fall to the subsistence level. Marx had committed himself to much the same view in the *Communist Manifesto,* but this was before he had developed his theory of surplus value, which asserted that the essential evil of capitalism was that the workers were defrauded *whatever wages they received.* This was a much more formidable controversial weapon than the 'Iron Law', which was liable at any time to be falsified if wages were to rise, as Marx admitted they might do under certain circumstances. It was this wage theory that led Lassalle to disparage the role of trade unions, and as Marx attached great importance to them, this was an additional grievance.

Yet while Lassalle may have been inferior to Marx as an economist, he was his equal as a revolutionary, and had also a better understanding of the situation in Germany. Marx held dogmatically to the tactics he had advocated in 1848, namely that the workers should enter into an alliance with the progressive bourgeoisie against feudal elements, and he held that Lassalle should adopt this course and so bring about a bougeois-democratic revolution. But Lassalle had the deepest distrust of the bourgeoisie, which albeit opposed to autocracy strongly supported *laissez-faire* and was hostile to any form of working-class combination. He believed that the unification of Germany was likely to be achieved in the near future under the hegemony of Prussia, and he therefore entered into negotiations with Bismarck, the representative of the Prussian Junkers, who was then looking round for popular support, with a view to obtaining universal suffrage, and other benefits, for which he would then claim the credit. He had no more love than Marx for the Prussian State, but as a hegelian he did not share Marx's antipathy to States in general or regard them as instruments of class oppression, and held that there could be no sort of objection to them provided they were controlled by the people. He argued that were there a German parliament to be set up, it would at first be weak, but would none the less provide a basis upon which the socialist movement could develop; and here the event was to prove him right, for although when Bismarck did eventually introduce universal suffrage the workers were not immediately the gainers, they profited by it in the end. It is true that the outcome of this policy was the emergence of a brand of socialism that was non-revolutionary, at least in the marxist sense, and it sought to work through the State and not by destroying it; but Lassalle can hardly be blamed for this seeing that the destruction of the bourgeois State was never practical politics.[1]

1. *See* Diehl, pp. 296 ff., 307–9; Mehring, pp. 308 ff.; Cole, *History of Socialist Thought*, Vol. II, pp. 71–87.

11. The First International

In the summer of 1862 a party of French workers visited London to see the International Exhibition, and were entertained by a party of British workers to what *The Times* described as 'a very excellent and substantial tea' at the Freemasons' Hall in Great Queen Street. This tea-party was to have important consequences. In July 1863 a group of British trade unionists organized a meeting in support of the Polish revolutionaries, and the French sent over a delegation; and on 26 September 1864 a second meeting, at which French, German, Italian, Swiss, and Polish workers were represented, was held at St Martin's Hall to consider a British proposal for cooperation against the practice of importing cheap foreign labour. It was now decided to found an 'International Federation of Working Men', pledged to destroy the prevailing economic system', and an executive committee was formed, of which Marx was a member. The drafting of a constitution was at first entrusted to a lieutenant of Mazzini's; but the statutes he drew up were felt to be more adapted to a secret society than to an international workers' movement; and as Marx's learning, experience, and self-assurance had quickly brought him to the fore, it ended with his drafting them himself for submission to the 2nd Congress, held at Geneva in 1865, which approved them. As with the Communist League, the statutes were less important than the profession of faith, which Marx also drafted in the form of an inaugural address, and into which he introduced as much of his doctrine as he could persuade his colleagues to accept. It concluded with the tail-piece of the *Communist Manifesto* – 'Workers of all Lands, Unite'.

From 1866 to 1869 the First International held annual congresses either in Switzerland or Belgium. Marx and Engels did not attend them, for neither thought such gatherings of much importance as long as they themselves controlled the General Council in London. In their view the International fulfilled its

main purpose by existing at all, and they did not regard with
any particular concern its resolutions on political and economic
matters, which were, indeed, colourless enough.[1] For although
the statutes called for an 'eternal union of brotherly cooperation', the elements of which the International was composed
were too heterogeneous to render possible agreement on any
positive policy. The attitude of each country was determined by
its own particular history and problems. The English, on whom
the International was largely dependent for its financial resources, were primarily interested, and particular after the
extension of the franchise in 1867, in strengthening the trade
unions and in securing reforms; the Germans were divided into
marxists and lassalleans; while the French were so bound to
Proudhon's anarchist theories as to refuse to agree to a maximum working day, desired by the English, as being opposed to
the principle of freedom of contract.[2]

None the less, the First International did much to encourage
a sense of proletarian unity such as had not existed, for
example, at the time of the Chartist movement, when the
various working-class sections had refused to cooperate. It grew
yearly in numbers. By the end of the sixties it was believed to
have a regular dues-paying membership of 800,000. Its power
was increased by alliances with other labour groups, and thus
its press boasted a total strength of 7 million, while police
estimates put is as high as 5 million. It organized a collection
for the Paris bronze workers in 1867, and secured a 25 per
cent increase in their wages; and in 1869 is issued an appeal 'to
the workers of Europe and America' in aid of the victims of
the strike in the Belgian iron industry. Such activities corresponded to the English conception of the functions which an
International should perform. Marx approved of them, but
regarded them as important only in so far as they embarrassed
the employers and promoted the international solidarity of the
workers for proletarian revolution.[3] He saw in the International
great possibilities. *'Les choses marchent'*, he wrote to Engels in

1. Letter of 11 September 1867 (*Briefwechsel* III, p. 407).
2. Rosenberg, pp. 166 ff.; cp. Diehl, pp. 331–2.
3. Carr, *Karl Marx*, p. 77.

September 1867. 'By the time of the next revolution, which may perhaps be nearer than it seems, we (that is you and I) will have this powerful engine in our hands. ... We may consider ourselves very well satisfied.'[1]

The revolution came at last with the Paris Commune of 1871, but its result was to destroy the International, though it was left to Bakunin and the anarchist to administer the *coup de grâce*. The Commune, the greatest of the many revolts of the Parisian workers, began on 17 March, and was not finally suppressed until 28 May, by which time at least 20,000 people had been killed, most of them in cold blood. It was now generally admitted that the brutality of the government forces was much greater than that of the insurgents, but this was not the official version which appeared in the European press. Up to this time the public had been scarcely aware of the existence of the International; but as a number of its leaders had played a prominent part in the rising, it was now held up to execration, and the more moderate trade unionists hastened to leave it.

Marx had done nothing to encourage the Commune, and in an Address from the General Council of the International, dated 9 September 1870 and drafted by himself, he had exhorted the French workers to accept with a good grace the republic of which, as he pointed out, the Germans had made them a present, to put out of their minds the ideas of 1792 and not to embark upon a rebellion which was bound to fail. Both he and Engels desired a German victory – in which they were incidentally at one with British public opinion – partly because the keystone of their revolutionary strategy was the unification of Germany and the consequent weakening of Russia – held by all good liberals to be the bulwark of reaction – and partly because, as he told Engels in a letter of 20 July, it would mean the triumph of 'our theory' over that of Proudhon. Yet when the masses, inspired by Bakunin and Blanqui, took to the barricades, it seemed that the long-expected revolution had come at last, and he became an ardent champion of *défensisme*. The event was to prove that his earlier estimate had been the right one. But the condemnation of the Commune by the

1. *Briefwechsel* III, p. 406.

European middle-class and the more respectable elements of
labour was in itself sufficient reason to lead him to defend it;
and this he did very effectively in his *Civil War in France*,
written two days after its collapse, in which he openly identified
it with the International, thus annexing its memory, and making
it a part of the communist legend, so that until the Bolsheviks
seized power it remained the most conspicuous achievement of
the revolutionary working-class.[1]

Yet for Marx its failure meant the end of the revolutionary
plans to which he had devoted his whole life. The initiative of
the French workers was destroyed for at least a generation, as
he and Engels had predicted; and this meant that the proletariat of other countries would be helpless for a long time to
come.[2] But new hope was to dawn in an unexpected quarter.
In 1872 Marx's *Capital* was published in a Russian translation –
the first to appear in any country – the censor having apparently
decided that it was a purely scientific work.[3] Marx hardly
knew what to make of this. 'It is an irony of fate', he told
his friend Kugelmann, 'that the Russians whom I have fought
for twenty-five years, and not only in German but in English
and French, have always been my "patrons"'; and he could
only attribute this to the fact that 'they always run after the
most extreme ideas the West has to offer'.[4] Yet he now so far
responded to their interest as to devote considerable attention
to Russian problems and to attempt to learn the language.

The final dissolution of the First International was due to
Marx's controversy with Michael Bakunin (1818–76), the most
formidable adversary he was ever to encounter.[5] It is impossible
to enter into the details of this, which certainly reflect no credit
upon Marx. As Herzen noted, the tragedy of Bakunin was that
he possessed immense latent powers which he could not use in
his own country, and which drove him, by way of frustration,
into the crack-brained extremism of his later years. He accepted
Marx's social diagnosis, and held that the State must be de-

1. Rosenberg, pp. 202–3.   2. Carr, p. 77.
3. Mehring, p. 385.   4. Wilson, p. 350.
5. *See* E. H. Carr, *Bakunin* (1937); T. G. Masaryk, *The Spirit of Russia*
(1919) I, pp. 430 ff.

stroyed. But this was the limit of their agreement. For while Bakunin held exploitation to be an evil, he regarded it as only part of the greater evil of tyranny. He repudiated all authority, whether of God or man, since in his view atheism and anarchism were almost interchangeable terms; and he was opposed to any plan or organization. Such opinions, and the chaotic form in which he expressed them, or allowed them to be expressed by others, appeared outrageous to Marx, who held, as a German, that there should be order and system in revolution as in everything else; and it was impossible that the two should ever have worked together on any terms.

Marx had first met Bakunin in Paris in 1844, and they were again associated in Brussels on the eve of the 1848 revolution. Then their ways fell apart, and Bakunin embarked on the adventures which were to take him to Siberia and thence round the world. In 1864 he was passing through London on his way to Italy, and the two men had an unexpectedly friendly meeting. In 1867 he left Italy for Switzerland, where he became a member of the Executive Committee of a radical bourgeois organization at Geneva known as the 'League of Peace and Freedom', and by Marx as 'the Geneva Windbag', which combined the advocacy of peace with that of the union of Europe under a republican government. He now tried to amalgamate this body with the International, of which he had become a member, a proposal which Marx peremptorily rejected and which led to Bakunin himself being excluded from the League. He thereupon formed a league of his own, the 'International Social-Democratic Alliance', with branches in Italy and Spain, where the International had never secured a following; and he succeeded in getting hold over certain working-class organizations in Switzerland and the Jura. His personality dominated the Basle Congress of 1869 – which Marx did not attend – and a resolution drafted by Marx was voted down by a large majority. Marx therefore became persuaded that Bakunin was out to capture the International; and thus he and Engels attended the next congress, held at The Hague on 2 September 1872, when they succeeded in getting him excluded. But his influence in the International was still dangerously strong; and rather than allow it to come under his control, Marx carried a resolution transferring its headquarters to the United States – then largely cut off from Europe – where it was finally dissolved at the Congress of Philadelphia of 1876.

Soon after the Hague Congress, Bakunin drafted a lengthy exposition of his case in the form of a letter to be published in the Belgian newspaper *Liberté*, but as so often happened with his writings, it was never completed, and did not therefore appear in his lifetime. On 15 September, however, his anti-authoritarian followers held a congress at St Imier at which they refused to recognize the new General Council and formed themselves into a rival International. Both organizations held congresses at Geneva in September 1873, but when Marx realized that that convened by the General Council, now established in New York, would be a failure, he declined to have anything to do with it. In the same month Bakunin announced his decision to retire from the political stage on the ground of ill health, and to this he adhered, if we except some abortive revolutionary activity which he undertook in mid 1874 in the neighbourhood of Bologna. In a letter of 15 February 1875 he told his fellow-anarchist, the geographer Élisée Réclus, that he had set himself to study 'the evolution and development of the principle of evil', now clearly triumphant in a world that had turned its back upon revolution;[1] but this not inconsiderable task must again be numbered among his unfinished projects, for on 1 July 1876, he died.

1. K. J. Kenafick, *Michael Bakunin* (1948), p. 304.

12. Anarchism

ANARCHISM is one of the two main heresies against which revolutionary Marxism has had to contend, the other – to be discussed in its place – being revisionism or reformism, which did not become important until the close of the century. It is perhaps as much a mental disposition as a doctrine, though it possesses a theoretical basis. It exerted a great influence over Russian revolutionary thought; but in the west it has tended to be confined to the Latin countries, where marxism was slow in taking root.

What, then, is anarchism? It must not be confused with anarchy, though this is a condition to which it may well lead. In its western form it derives from three main sources:

a. William Godwin's *Political Justice* (1795), which Pitt refused to suppress on the ground that a three-guinea book could do no harm. Godwin ascribed all social justice to the coercive nature of the State, and believed that if it were abolished men would live together in accordance with those principles of right reason upon which he claimed to speak with absolute authority.

b. Max Stirner – the pseudonym of Johann Caspar Schmidt – who insisted in his *Der Einzige und sein Eigentum* (1844) on the absolute sovereignty of the individual which was the only reality. A precursor of Nietzsche and the first *immoraliste*, he argued that the real enemy of freedom was the tyranny of abstract ideas, and that if a man could once rid himself of them, he would get down to the bed-rock of his personality and so find freedom.[1] Stirner was an important influence in intellectual circles, and he is of interest as the first adversary against whom Marx measured himself, in his *Der heilige Max*, the second section of the *Deutsche Ideologie*. Marx objected alike to Stirner's egotism and his idealism. Ideas are not private

---

1. Macmurray, pp. 27 ff.; Gide and Rist, pp. 612 ff.; Croce, *Come il Marx fece passare il communismo dall'utopia alla scienza* (1948), p. 37.

property out of which the individual can somehow think himself, but belong to the common stock of society and derive from human relations which are in turn determined by economic reality.

c. The writings of Proudhon, who was the real force behind western anarchism, though his position was later challenged by Bakunin. As already noted, Proudhon was opposed to all compulsion, and held that the State should be replaced by free, decentralized, self-governing communities – a view which greatly influenced the first generation of Russian *émigrés* as being in line with their native anarchist tradition and with the type of revolution, based upon the peasant commune, that seemed most realizable in Russia.

Bakunin's violent brand of anarchism, as opposed to the peaceful doctrine of Proudhon, continued to be preached after the collapse of the First International by the 'Jurassic Federation', which was responsible for convening a number of congresses in the seventies; and in 1881 an anarchist International was founded in London which thereafter held occasional meetings. It was this body that sponsored the anarchist terrorism of the nineties, particularly in France. In 1893 Ravachol dynamited houses in Paris; in 1894 Auguste Vaillant threw a bomb in the Chamber and went to the guillotine; and in the same year the Italian anarchist, Caserio, assassinated President Carnot to avenge Vaillant. Public opinion was profoundly disturbed by these excesses, which in time died down except in Russia, where the Social Revolutionaries for many years kept alive the tradition of political assassination.

In essence, western anarchism is simply liberal individualism, based upon the alleged 'right of man' pushed to its extreme limit. Its goal is the complete freedom and equality of the individual, and thus it repudiates the jacobin tradition, adopted by the socialists, in which the individual is subjected by the State to the social group. This attitude towards the State is primary. It carries with it the rejection of every form of political activity in favour of economic activity only; and it involves the condemnation of parliamentary democracy in accordance with Proudhon's dictum that 'universal suffrage is counter-revolution', since the concession of the vote is simply a device for preventing the individual from governing himself, and its effect is thus to weaken his sense of responsibility. Anarchists contend therefore that even if the workers were to achieve every reform in their programme, but through the agency of a bureaucratic government, they would only have exchanged one form of tyranny for a worse; and thus present-day anarchists regard the Soviet regime as a complete betrayal of the proletarian revolution.[1]

When the trade union or syndicalist movement started in France, and in the Latin countries generally, in the last quarter of the nineteenth century, its leaders were much influenced by Proudhon's ideas, and the movement became known as anarcho-syndicalism. Thus, the constitution of the Confédération Générale du Travail—the *Charte d'Amiens* of 1906—laid it down as a fundamental principle that the organization was to have no affiliation with any political party, whatever its programme, a position to which Léon Jouhaux's Force Ouvrière now represents a partial return. This attitude was to lead to some strange accommodations. When, for example, the C.G.T. excluded the Communists after the German–Soviet Pact of September 1939, a group known as the Syndicats and led by René Belin protested on the ground that such action on a political and not an economic issue was contrary to the *Charte d'Amiens.* It was therefore no accident that it was Belin and his followers who later accepted office under the Vichy Government and tried to enforce the Labour Charter. It was they who had been the exponents of 'planning' within the pre-war C.G.T., and the particular framework into which the plan would be integrated counted for little with men who had always scorned political action.[2]

Yet the marxist contention that the anarcho-syndicalist movement was avowedly anti-marxist in origin, intent, and practice is unfounded. Anarchism, in general, repudiated the class struggle; but anarcho-syndicalism accepted it, and in so

1. *See* Diehl, pp. 77 ff.; Gide and Rist, pp. 610–56; Rudolf Rocker, *Anarcho-Syndicalism* (1938).

2. Henry W. Ehrmann, *French Labour* (1947), p. 245.

doing held itself to be the true heir of the marxist revolutionary tradition, and deplored the manner in which it was everywhere becoming compromised by reformism.[1] It insisted upon the working-class character of the movement, since Marx had taught that the emancipation of the workers could only be achieved by the workers themselves; and it did not therefore welcome bourgeois intellectuals into its ranks, so that Georges Sorel had no personal contact with it, though his *Réflexions sur la violence* made him its most distinguished exponent. But its leaders never faced the problem of how the revolution was to be brought about. Their panacea was the 'general strike', when the workers would leave their factories until, after a brief period of chaos, they would be invited to return to them as owners – a crisis which Sorel thought might well be surmounted in a spirit of mutual forbearance and good humour. They failed to see that the general strike could not in itself produce a revolutionary situation, since it could not take place unless such a situation already existed. And, finally, Sorel himself developed an irrational Bergsonian logic which converted the general strike into a 'myth' of purely emotional significance, thus undermining the whole marxist scientific analysis of revolution. Yet Max Eastman, a severe critic of Sorel, none the less holds that, like anarchism, anarcho-syndicalism did make the working-class movement appear more practical to non-scientific minds, as it represented a tendency away from that 'everlasting theoretical insanity' of which Bakunin accused Marx, though Bakunin himself did not wholly escape from it, and Proudhon only did so through ignorance.[2]

Anarchists agree with marxists that revolution is inevitable, and that the proletariat is destined to play a preponderant role in it. But they reject the political struggle, which is fundamental to marxism; and they equally reject the dictatorship of the pro-

1. Sidney Hook, *Towards an Understanding of Marx*, pp. 48 ff.
2. *Marxism: Is it a Science?*, pp. 206–7. On Sorel, *see* Jacques Rennes, *Georges Sorel et le syndicalisme révolutionnaire* (Paris, 1936); S. Beracha, *Le Marxisme après Marx* (1937), pp. 169 ff.; Gaëtan Pirou, *Histoire des doctrines economiques en France depuis 1870* (Paris) (1925 ed. 1947).

letariat and the guiding role of the party, both before and after the revolution, which is fundamental to leninism and stalinism. Above all, they reject the State, and advocate an equalitarian society based on free, self-governing communes. Anarcho-syndicalists differ in regarding the trade unions as constituting a ready-made apparatus capable of taking over the administration and organization of production. But anarchists object to trade unions, and at the congress of the Italian Anarchist Party, held at Florence in May 1948, it was laid down that no party member should belong to one.

This aversion to central authority has made the anarchists refractory to any but the most rudimentary form of party organization, with the result that the strength of the movement had lain rather in its powers to produce leaders. Yet it is still a force to be reckoned with, at least in western Europe, since it reflects that distrust of authority which is as deeply rooted in the Latin mind as is its exaltation in that of the German. For, as La Fontaine put it long ago, *Notre ennemi, c'est notre maître*. The prime and everlasting duty of the citizen is to resist the central power, for unless he does so, it will always become a tyranny, whether you have a king by divine right or a Prime Minister elected by Parliament. Power is itself evil, and corrupts all men who wield it: that is the ultimate lesson of moral psychology. But the ordinary man can watch this and stop it. Thus, at least, do most Frenchmen reason. It does not make for internal stability. But then the Germans were always prepared to do everything the State told them, which was of little ultimate advantage to them, or to the rest of the world either.[1]

1. Denis Saurat, *Modern French Literature* (1946), p. 82.

13. The Second International

AFTER the dissolution of the First International, Marx made no attempt to found another. In his view its reputation had been made by the Commune, and it had thus fulfilled its end. In a letter to Bebel of January 1873 he explained that it would have been killed had a compromise been reached at the Hague Congress of 1872, while as it was its spirit had survived, and it was now stronger dead than it had been living. When therefore the Brussels Congress of the Belgian Socialists decided in 1880 to call a Congress at Zürich to revive the International, Marx was against it. As he told a Dutch socialist correspondent in February 1881:

Doctrinaire anticipations of the programme of action for revolution in the future only divert us from the struggle of the present. . . . It is my conviction that the critical juncture for a new International Workingmen's Association has not yet arrived, and for this reason I regard all workers' congresses, particularly socialist congresses, in so far as they are not related to the immediate given conditions in this or that particular nation, as not merely useless but harmful. They will always fade away in stale, generalized banalities.[1]

Engels was of the same opinion. In a letter to the German Social Democrat, Sorge, of September 1874 he said that 'any further attempt to galvanize the International into new life would be folly'. 'But', he added, 'I think that the next International – after Marx's writings have had some years of influence – will be directly communist and will openly proclaim our principles.'[2] This prophecy was not, however, to be fulfilled.

From 1871 to the Fall of Bismarck, conservative forces were in power in Europe. Yet socialism gained in strength, particularly in Germany, where, at the Reichstag elections of 1890,

1. Letter to Domela Nieuwenhuis, 22 February 1881, *Correspondence*, p. 387.   2. ibid. p. 330.

the Social Democrats polled nearly a million and a half votes and returned thirty-five deputies, though it would have been unthinkable under the Kaiserreich that any of the latter should have been asked to join the government, or that, even if they had been, they would have consented to do so. It was by far the largest political labour group in Europe, and its leaders were regarded, even by the Russians, with an extreme respect. In England the Democratic Federation' was founded in 1881 by H. M. Hyndman, and became known in 1884 as the 'Social Democratic Federation'. Hyndman, although a well-to-do stockbroker, was in sympathy with Marx's ideas; but unfortunately when he came to introduce them in his newspaper, *England for All*, he did not mention Marx by name, but only referred to 'the work of a great thinker and original writer which ... will be accessible to the majority of my countrymen'; at which Marx took such violent offence that he and Engels broke off all connexion with the s.d.f., though it continued to regard itself as a marxist party.[1] But marxism never took much root in England, where the promotion of socialist ideas was mainly the work of the Fabian Society (founded in 1883), whose members, coldly reasonable people nourished upon blue books and statistics, while sharing Marx's centralizing views, had no interest in his dialectical philosophy, nor any inclination to idealize the proletariat or regard it as possessed with an historic mission. In France the Parti Ouvrier Français had been founded in 1879 by Jules Guesde, and Marx had drawn up its statutes. Guesde was an ardent marxist; but his intransigent temper did not appeal to all working-class sections, and there arose a number of rival groups, which did not unite into a single party until 1907.

In 1889 two congresses were held in Paris, the one attended by marxists, and the other by non-marxists. The two, however, were persuaded to combine; and thus on 14 July, the centenary of the capture of the Bastille, there was founded, at a meeting held under the joint chairmanship of Liebknecht and Édouard Vaillant, the Second International, which held con-

1. G. D. H. Cole and Raymond Postgate, *The Common People* (1946), pp. 415–16.

gresses every two or three years up to the first world war.[1] It
formally adopted Marx's basic principles – the class struggle,
international unity, proletarian action, and the socialization of
the means of production; but these were principles all of which
lent themselves to a wider or narrower interpretation. It is
clear from Engels's letter to Sorge of 17 July 1889 that he was
well aware that the International contained many non-marxist
elements, but that he was prepared to support it as he was confident that the marxists would obtain control. What must be
recognized is that marxism had not become the rigid creed into
which the Third International, under Russian influence, was to
convert it; and that the Second International neither was, nor
could be, a marxist body. As its communist historian, Lenz,
points out:

> To have admitted only these organizations which took their stand
> on the basis of the revolutionary class struggle would have meant
> excluding the mass organizations of the proletariat at a time when
> the real need of the day was not direct revolutionary action, but
> rallying the masses and winning them to socialism.[2]

Hence, the Second International admitted any political party
or labour group which gave a general adhesion to its principles,
though it early excluded the anarchists, with whom there had
been a decisive breach after the Hague Congress of 1872; and
it is Croce's contention that with their departure the possiblity
of ever establishing communism disappeared.[3] For it must be
understood that behind all the confusion of anarchist thought
lay the desire for a decentralized society under which the introduction of a communal way of life became at least a theoretical possibility. But such a society implied a return to a
simpler mode of production, which was not at all what Marx
advocated. He held that the productive forces should be developed to their fullest capacity in accordance with what he
called a 'common plan', and that this development would only

1. For its history and a bibliography *see* Cole, *History of Socialist
Thought*, Vol. III (1954), pp. 1–103 ; James Joll, *The Second International*
(1955).
2. J. Lenz, *The Second International* (New York, 1932), pp. 16–17.
3. *History of Europe in the Nineteenth Century* (1924), p. 301.

be possible when they were liberated from the 'fetters' of capitalism. Yet on the rare occasions when he allowed himself to reflect upon what this 'common plan' would involve, he saw that it would inevitably necessitate the establishment of a centralized authority, and should have seen that under such a regime communism would not be possible, save in so far as it was imposed from above. It may be remarked, in parenthesis, that it was his conviction that the capitalist system could not be reformed and must therefore be completely abolished that led him to condemn all experiments in social planning conducted within its framework as foredoomed to failure, and calculated to weaken the revolutionary fervour of the masses.[1]

While therefore the First International had had a genuine revolutionary trend, though there was a disagreement as to methods, the Second International was a loosely knit assembly of workers' organizations of varying degrees of maturity and representing many shades of opinion. Again, the delegates of the First International had been chosen at its congresses; but those of the Second International were the elected representatives of the affiliated bodies, and were bound by the mandates they had been given. Finally, the Second International possessed very slight disciplinary powers, and it was not until 1900 that its only central organ, the International Socialist Bureau, was set up in Brussels.

But of even greater significance than the above was the change that had come over the European labour movement during the last decades of the century. It may perhaps best be illustrated by conditions in this country. To the early Victorian economists, as Graham Hutton puts it, the industrial revolution was no time for easy living or wide social benefits. It was, on the contrary, a time for austerity, saving, and investment, so that within a generation the machines, railways, ships and the like should get built and start producing consumer goods. Then would come what the Americans call the 'pay-off'. They were right. The period from the 'hungry forties' to the sixties of the cotton famine were the lean years. But between 1865 and 1875 there took place an immensely rapid accumulation

1. Martin Buber, *Paths in Utopia* (1949), pp. 82 ff.; Popper II, p. 79.

of capital, and the people began to reap the benefit of a generation of hard living.[1]

The beginning of the 'great divide' of the Victorian age coincided almost to a year with the appearance of Marx's *Capital*, and it falsified his prediction that the lot of the worker would continually worsen. Between 1873 and 1895 there was a steady fall of prices, estimated at 45 per cent, while average money wages over all trades rose by 5 per cent, thus constituting a rise of real wages of 35 to 40 per cent. From 1896 onwards the price trend was reversed; but up to 1900 wages kept pace with it, and it was calculated in that year that they were 15 to 16 per cent higher than in 1873, and that their purchasing power was 42 to 43 per cent higher. It followed therefore that the employed worker had only to avoid wage reductions to enjoy a steady rise in his standard of living.[2]

Further, capitalism was changing its character, as the principle of limited liability assisted the divorce between the ownership and the business administration of capital. Wealth became less individual and more impersonal, and thus increasingly a matter for State action and intervention. And the demand for such action was supplied by the workers, who had now organized themselves in fields of industry in which organization had been once thought to be impossible.

Hence the Second International inevitably found itself committed to defending and improving the economic interests of the workers by demanding reforms within the framework of the existing order, rather than with attempting to destroy that order in accordance with its principles. And it was the less inclined to revolutionary action as it was in substantial agreement with liberal-bourgeois democracy in demanding peace abroad, legality at home, free trade, universal suffrage, and the extension of parliamentary institutions.[3] It may be taken as a universal principle that no labour organization, whatever its professed creed, will seek to overthrow the capitalist system so long as this is making large profits, since the leaders are well aware that the

1. *The Victorian Conception of Wealth* in *Ideas and Beliefs of the Victorians* (1949), p. 315.

2. Cole and Postgate, pp. 441–2.   3. Rosenberg, p. 313.

rank-and-file are mainly concerned with obtaining that higher standard of living which they know that the system can well afford to give them. A different situation arises when capitalism has been sufficiently weakened, either by war or by other causes, as to be no longer in a position to make concessions, as the worker will now readily support the practical application of those doctrines which he has hitherto contented himself with applauding when uttered upon the platform. Marx was perfectly aware of this, and held that it was the duty of socialist parties, always provided that they were aiming at revolution, to continue to extort concessions until the limit had been reached. Then there would come about that change from quantity into quality which would introduce socialism. But the leaders of the Second International could not conscientiously pretend that their policy was marxist in this sense, as few of them had any desire to see capitalism abolished in their time. As Sidney Hook says, they salved their consciences by accepting socialism as an objective science. Marx had proved that the class struggle was as objective a fact as the law of gravitation, and that socialism was inevitable. If you welcomed it, it might come a little sooner. If you did not, it would come anyway – perhaps a little later. In neither case did your attitude make much difference. Thus was the will to revolutionary action still further paralysed.[1]

In particular did this apply to the German Social Democrats, whose party was by far the largest and the one most unreservedly committed to revolutionary marxism, at least after the adoption of the Erfurt Programme of 1891. Its membership was, indeed, overwhelmingly proletarian. But numerous nonproletarian elements had entered; and these, by virtue of their technical skill or social connexions, made their way to the top as functionaries, theoreticians, or political representatives. Parallel with the party was the trade-union movement, which had greatly extended, and in so doing had created an immense administrative machine of officials whose higher standard of living cut them off from the workers, and who tended, with every additional year of office, to acquire the mentality charac-

1. Hook, *Towards an Understanding of Karl Marx* (1933).

teristic of the German bureaucrat. It was therefore no accident that the most concrete theoretical defence of 'reformism' – as this deviation from revolutionary action is called – should have come from a leading German Social Democrat, Eduard Bernstein, in the form to become known as 'revisionism'.[1]

Bernstein was the editor of the *Sozial-Demokrat*, which had been founded at Zürich during the period when the Social Democratic Party was proscribed by Bismarck, but had been transferred to London, whence copies had been smuggled into Germany. While in London, he had been converted to communism by Engels; but he had also been much impressed by the progressive ideas of the Fabians, and it was this influence that eventually prevailed. He first set out his opinions in a series of articles in the *Neue Zeit* (1896–7), which he expanded and published in book form in his *Voraussetzungen des Sozialismus und die Aufgaben der Sozialdemokratie* (1899), and developed still further in his *Wie ist wissenschaftlicher Sozialismus möglich?* (1901). He declared that social democracy 'should find the courage to emancipate itself from a philosophy which has, in fact, long been outmoded, and be willing to show itself for what it really is – a democratic socialist party of reform'. He entirely approved what social democracy was doing; but his intellectual honesty forbade him to approve that its practice should be in flat opposition to its theory. He pointed out, further, that the economic trends predicted by Marx, *e.g.* the accumulation of capital in fewer and fewer hands and the increasing misery of the worker, were not currently discernible; and that all the contemporary manifestations of capitalism proved Marx to have been a false prophet.

All the inconvenient facts which Bernstein adduced could have been answered within the marxist framework, as Marx had pointed out, for example, that there might be periods of rapid capital accumulation when the price of labour power would

1. The fullest account of Bernstein's position is Peter Gay's *Dilemma of Democratic Socialism* (Columbia University Press, 1952); *see* also Cole, *History of Socialist Thought*, Vol. III, Pt I (1956), pp. 249–96; Hook, pp. 75 ff.; Diehl, pp. 314 ff.; *see* also Karl Kautsky, *Le Marxisme et son critique Bernstein* (Fr. trans. 1900).

show a rising tendency. His 'melorium' was indeed as much a reflection of the boom conditions prevailing at the time in the more advanced capitalist countries as was Marx's 'increasing misery' that of the conditions of the mid-nineteenth century. But, in fact, his criticism went much deeper. The irreconcilable element that he introduced into the controversy was his condemnation of the material philosophy of socialism. He maintained that socialism as a science gave an explanation of the causes and conditions of the socialist movement, but that it could offer no justification of it, as this depended on ethical motives which it excluded. What socialism required was an objective moral code such as materialism could not supply, and which must be found in a return to some form of idealist philosophy. Max Eastman thinks that it was a pity that Bernstein raised this issue, as he holds that marxist materialism was already dying a natural death and that Bernstein's action only rallied the genuine revolutionaries to support it.[1] But whatever the truth of this, it was the spearhead of his attack.

Its effect was to undermine the whole marxist position, which denied the existence of any objective ethical system and held all morality to be class morality. Marx had said that the worker had no country and belonged only to his class. This class had rights, and other classes had no rights. Bernstein pointed out that now that the worker had been enfranchised this was no longer true, and that he also owed a duty to his country. Thus, there began that confusion between the conflicting claims of class and country which was to lead to the victory of the latter in August 1914.

In France a somewhat similar problem arose in 1897 when the socialist Millerand (later the radical-socialist Prime Minister) accepted office in the Waldeck-Rousseau government, thus creating the issue to become known as 'ministérialisme'. His action was particularly galling to the socialist extremists, as Waldeck-Rousseau's War Minister was that General Galliffet who had made himself notorious in 1871 by his treatment of the Communards. The socialist leader, Jean Jaurès, regarded Millerand's acceptance of office as a victory for democracy; but

1. *Marx, Lenin and the Science of Revolution* (1936), p. 190.

Guesde carried a resolution that 'the class struggle forbids the entry of a socialist into a bourgeois government'; and Lenin stigmatized Millerand's acceptance of office as 'an excellent example of practical Bernsteinism'.[1] Millerand resigned from the party; but the controversy dragged on until 1904, when Guesde appealed to the Amsterdam Congress, which condemned ministerialism, and with it the revisionism of Bernstein. Thereafter no socialist was a member of any French government until Guesde himself, and that *enfant terrible* of the party, Marcel Sembart, joined the Government of National Defence at the end of August 1914.

Yet marxist ideology was slow to establish a hold over French socialist opinion, always jealous of its own revolutionary tradition. When Lenin visited Paris in 1895 and told Marx's son-in-law Paul Lafargue that the Russian revolutionaries were studying Marx's writings, the latter replied that even after twenty years no one in France understood them.[2] His materialism failed to appeal to that sense of justice and fraternity which was dear to French socialism, and with the turn of the century ideas similar to those of Bernstein began to circulate. In his *Les origines du socialisme en Allemagne* (1897) Charles Andler stressed the ethical side of the movement as opposed to its scientific aspect, maintaining that socialism could not be scientifically demonstrated and called for *l'adhésion du cœur*. Similarly, in his *Paroles d'Avenir* (1904) Georges Renard, while affirming the naturalistic and non-metaphysical nature of Socialism, relegated its scientific demonstration to the background by declaring that if it was contrary to reason and justice there would be no grounds for supporting it even if it could be shown to be economically inevitable.[3] Again, French socialism contained a large admixture of individualism, and was wholly opposed to that centralization of authority which was implicit in the marxist system. In his *Esquisse d'une organisation socialiste* (1895–6) Jaurès advocated a 'decentralized collectivism' which would be respectful of personal liberty, and would

1. *What is to be done?* (1902); S.W. I, p. 151.
2. Pierre Chasles, *Vie de Lénine* (Paris, 1929), p. 39.
3. Gaëtan Pirou, pp. 19–22.

thus effect a synthesis between the individualism of Proudhon and the communism of Marx. At the Party Congress of 1902 he refused to remove the word 'revolutionary' from the programme. Yet he conceived of the advent of socialism in evolutionary terms, and of reforms as constituting those quantitative changes which would precede what he admitted would be a qualitative change. Only this last might well come imperceptibly, just as, he says, a ship may cross the equator and enter another hemisphere without anyone being aware of it.[1] Even Guesde, unbending as he was on all matters of principle, became unexpectedly conciliatory when any such practical question arose as that of nationalizing the holdings of the peasants.

Lenz holds that the Second International reached its zenith at the Amsterdam Congress, but that from then onwards it began to decline.[2] In the German Social Democratic Party the 1905 revolution in Russia was the parting of the ways. The leader of the marxist faction was then Karl Kautsky, within a few years to be branded by Lenin as the arch-renegade; and in January 1906 he published an article in *Vorwärts* suggesting that the Russian barricades pointed to the necessity of a change of tactics within the party. This raised the whole question of the nature and purpose of the 'general strike'; and here Bebel took the view that it was a defensive weapon only, that there was no reason why it should provoke a collision with the State and that it would be undesirable if it did so. 'It is,' he said, 'of course an error to say that the Social Democrats are working to bring about a revolution. That is not at all the case. What interest have we in producing catastrophes in which the workers will be the first to suffer?' Thereafter the Party split into three groups – the reformist right-wing, whose doctrine every congress condemned in theory but increasingly applied in practice; the centre, led by Bebel and later joined by Kautsky; and the marxist left-wing under Rosa Luxemburg and Karl Liebknecht, who were to be the founders of the German Communist Party.

Lenin's case against the Second International is set out in numerous writings and particularly in his *The Second Inter-*

1. ibid. pp. 56–9.   2. ibid. p. 75.

national and the War (1915).[1] He admitted that it had rendered useful service by assisting the formation of a number of working-class parties; but this was all he would concede, as it had been neither marxist nor revolutionary and had become finally discredited by the attitude it had adopted in 1914. The Stuttgart Congress of 1907 had committed it to instructing all social-democrats in the event of war to 'utilize the economic and political crisis caused by the war to ... hasten the destruction of the domination of the capitalist class'. Yet when war came every socialist party had supported its government, the majority of members coming out as 'social patriots' and the minority as 'social pacifists', from neither of which element was it possible to create a party pledged to the cause of international revolution. Hence his decision to replace it by a genuinely revolutionary body at the earliest opportunity, with the result that the Third International (or Comintern) was founded in March 1919, and the world labour movement was sharply divided into marxists and social-democrats, a division which has never been more acute than it is today.

Lenin's strictures were not altogether unjustified. The Second International had been no more successful than its predecessor in achieving a united policy, let alone one of pure marxism. Each affiliated body had tended to approach every problem from the point of view of its particular interests; the divergencies thus created had been glossed over at congresses by resolutions so loosely drafted that they could be interpreted in any sense, thus creating the illusion of a solidarity which did not, in fact, exist; while the speakers had commonly employed language which suggested that they were far more revolutionary than they were. Thus, right up to August 1914 a man of the ability and integrity of Jaurès firmly believed, in the face of all evidence to the contrary, that there was no danger of war with Germany, because the French and German workers would combine to prevent it; and in the elections of May 1914 over a hundred French deputies were returned on this platform. It is in the light of the above that Lenin's insistence that the parties

1. *See* also *The Third International and its Place in History* in the *Communist International*, No. 1 (May, 1919).

which affiliated to the Comintern should submit to rigid discipline becomes intelligible.

Again, the former German communist, Arthur Rosenberg, points out that in so far as the Second International did accept marxist principles it failed to interpret them in a marxist sense. Its suspicion of the capitalist State led it to refuse to allow its members to collaborate with bourgeois governments, which Marx would certainly have held to be permissible, provided that it served the cause of revolution. It accepted free trade as a dogma because it made the workers' food cheaper; whereas Marx had held the question of free trade versus protection to be one of expediency only, since each was equally a form of capitalist exploitation. Further, Marx had always regarded war as an instrument of policy; but the Second International made no distinction between wars of capitalist aggression and wars of national liberation, and at one congress after another passed resolutions advocating peace under all circumstances.[1] Yet the fundamental divergence was that the Second International was reformist and not revolutionary; and it was the heresy of reformism that eventually destroyed it, just as the heresy of anarchism had destroyed the First International.

It only remains to add that after the founding of the Third International, those parties which would not affiliate with it but had withdrawn from the Second International in disgust formed themselves into the 'Two-and-a-half' or Vienna International. Efforts to bring about an inclusive organization were made during 1921 and 1922; and in the latter year representatives of all three bodies met at Berlin. The attempt failed on account of the objections raised by the Third International. But in December 1922 representatives of the Second and Vienna Internationals met at The Hague, and it was resolved to issue invitations to a conference to be held in Hamburg in May 1923. At this conference, attended by 620 delegates from thirty countries, it was decided to dissolve the Second and Vienna Internationals, and to form in their place the Labour and Socialist International (L.S.I.). This body continued in existence until 1945, when its place was taken by the International Social-

1. Rosenberg, pp. 293 ff.

ist Conference, which established a Consultative Committee, replaced in 1947 by the committee of the International Socialist Conference (Comisco), consisting of one representative of each member party. At a conference held in Copenhagen in 1950 Comisco proposed that the International Socialist Conference should change its name to the Socialist International, and this was approved in the following year.[1]

1. *See* Saul Rose, *The Socialist International* (1955), pp. 6–9.

PART THREE

LENINISM AND STALINISM

*

14. The Background of Leninism

WE have now to turn to Russia. Here revolutionary ideology developed along lines which were in part influenced by western thought, and in part independent of it. This ideology culminated in marxism, to which Lenin gave a specific direction. But Lenin himself was the heir to a movement that had been going on for three-quarters of a century; and we cannot appreciate the problems with which he had to contend and the manner in which he dealt with them without some understanding of it.[1]

From the 'Decembrist' rising in 1825, when a number of Guardist officers demanded some elementary reforms (it was not for nothing that Russian officers had fought in the wars of Napoleon), and thus led Nicholas I to proscribe every form of political, social, and philosophical speculation, Russian thought turned unceasingly round the idea of revolution. But the history of Russia is characterized by a continual oscillation between the extremes of isolation and dependence upon the west – between a jealous pride in the native genius and tradition of Russia and an equally jealous desire to profit by the achievements of the west and to surpass them. During the immediately following decades, when the Russians were taking their first soundings, this ambivalence led to the intellectual debate between the westerners, who demanded, in the name of reason and enlightenment, that Russia should embrace the liberal ideas of Europe, and the Slavophils, who held that she had a tradition and civilization of her own entirely independent of that

1. See T. G. Masaryk, *The Spirit of Russia* (Eng. trans. 1919); Nicolas Berdyaev, *The Origin of Russian Communism* (1937); *The Russian Idea* (1947).

of the west and should follow her own line of development.

In this early stage the predominant influence was the philosophy of Hegel, which Bakunin had been largely responsible for introducing into Russia. The Russians took for granted all that Hegel had to say about the development of nations. But they could not agree that the end of the dialectic had been to make the Germans the leaders of humanity, for if this were so there was no place for the Slavs. Yet they, too, must have their 'idea' which would be realized in history.[1] This led the Slavophils in particular sharply to criticize the civilization of the west and to emphasize the mission of Russia; and from this there developed in turn a strong sense of Slav nationalism. Thus, Bakunin himself was a Pan-Slav nationalist before he became the leader of the international anarchist movement.

The two most prominent thinkers of this first period, Belinsky and Herzen, maintained a foot in both camps. Each had gravitated, like Marx, through hegelianism to the rationalism of Feuerbach. Belinsky, oppressed by the backwardness of Russia, looked for salvation to the west; and his famous letter of protest to Gogol of 1847, which circulated widely in manuscript and was printed abroad by Herzen in 1855, became the testament of the revolutionary youth for two generations. Yet he never lost faith in a specific and triumphant Russian destiny. Herzen had been in Paris at the time of the 1848 revolution, and he drew from it the same conclusions as Proudhon – that political action was worse than useless. Its failure, due as he believed to the refusal of the west to accept the gift of freedom when it was offered, plunged him into a despair from which he confesses that he was saved only by his faith in Russia. Gradually he reached the conclusion that Russia was destined to fill the vacuum created by the breakdown of the decadent civilization of the west, that the Russian peasant was a potential socialist and revolutionary, and that the structure of the new order existed ready to hand in the peasant commune which would appropriate the functions of the State, and discharge them on a

1. P. Milyoukov, *Russia and its Crisis* (1905), pp. 53 ff.

basis of mutual and voluntary agreement. Thus, Russian socialism would regenerate the new world as Christianity had re-
generated the world of antiquity.[1]

In the sixties the reforming movement began to pass from
the sphere of philosophy into that of action, largely under the
influence of Chernyshevsky, the first revolutionary publicist
actively to participate in one of the new secret societies which
were then springing up. The change is depicted in Turgenev's
Fathers and Sons with its hero, Bazarov. The 'men of the
forties' – the 'fathers' – had been aristocrats. The 'sons' – the
'men of the sixties' – were democrats. Characteristic of this
period was 'nihilism', a mental disposition peculiar to Russian
thought. Its creed was derived, like that of anarchism, from
western ideas. Realist, positivist, and concrete, it challenged
every principle, however sacred, and sought to achieve its end
by terrorist methods. Yet it must not be confused with anarchism, though it was to a large extent anarchistic. For anarchism
is a much wider conception. In essence it is individualistic, and
thus, in order to escape from the dangers inherent in individualism, it stresses those impulses which make for harmony among
men as opposed to those which call for restraint. Hence its
rejection of the State, or of any kind of centralized coercive
authority. Masaryk rightly claims that it is not peculiar to
Russia, and points out that its most notable Russian exponents,
Bakunin and Kropotkin, learned their doctrine from the west.[2]
Yet Berdyaev holds it to be endemic in Russian thought. The
Russian has never accepted the State; he had always regarded
it as something foreign and unnatural, and has been far more
conscious than the west of the evil involved in the idea of
authority. Anarchism has thus powerfully influenced Russian
political thinking. It has taken many forms. It has looked to the
establishment of a kingdom of the spirit in which all men will
live together in unity; and it has issued, as it did with Bakunin,
in a creed of destruction which makes violence the creative
principle of life.[3]

The new spirit of the sixties found its expression in the 'Land

1. *See* Carr, *Studies in Revolution*, pp. 56 ff.
2. op. cit. II, pp. 389 ff.   3. *The Russian Idea,* pp. 142 ff.

and Freedom (*Zemlya i Volya*) movement, for his connexion with which Chernyshevsky spent twenty years in a Siberian fortress. Its collapse led to the emergence of the most remarkable figure of the decade – Nechaev, a disciple of Bakunin, whose *Revolutionary Catechism* lays down all the qualifications required by the professional conspirator – the renunciation of every interest, feeling, and attachment for the sake of the single end of revolution, and the assertion that morality is what assists the revolution and immorality what does not. In 1869 he started an organization among the Moscow students; and in order to knit them together, he murdered one of their number, and leaving the rest to their fate, fled to Switzerland, whence he was later extradited. Bakunin, whom he had at first taken in, ended by breaking off all relations with him.

Dostoievsky represents the extreme Slavophil reaction to the above, and his hatred of it finds expression in Prince Myshkin's outburst in *The Idiot*, in which he reveals his horror of the west, especially of catholicism – the source alike of atheism and socialism – and his belief that Russia alone can give to the west 'that Christ whom we have preserved and whom they have never known'. So likewise did Dostoievsky abhor the revolutionary movement precisely because it drew its inspiration from liberal western thought. The younger Verkhovensky of *The Possessed* is Nechaev, and his helpless and ineffective father has been identified with the St Petersburg liberal Professor Granovsky, a close friend of the westerner Belinsky, who had done everything in his power to injure Dostoievsky and disparage his work. The book is a polemic against Turgenev's *Fathers and Sons*; its moral is that liberal parents can only beget monsters. Similarly, Dostoievsky took the Slavophil side at the time of the Polish rising of 1863. Herzen and the European *émigrés* warmly approved it, as they viewed it through western eyes, and their opinion was shared by many high-placed members of the government; but for the Slavophils it was an act of treason against Slavdom, prompted by those western influences which it was Russia's mission to hold in check. Hence, they supported the government's fight against the Poles – the first occasion on which any action it had taken was backed by a more or less organized body of social opinion.[1] The present wave of Russian nationalism has a close affinity with Slavophilism; and it is doubtless for this reason that Dostoievsky's works were so long tolerated, although he stood consistently for a type of theocratic regime as far as possible removed from that which prevails today.

In the seventies there arose the 'Populist' (*Narodnik*) Party which sought to combine the westerner's enthusiasm for science and education with the Slavophils' belief in the genius of Russia. It took over from Herzen the specifically *narodnik* doctrine that the Russian commune (*Mir*), with its communal property, could be made the basis of the future socialist order, and that Russia would thus escape the evils of capitalism which had corrupted the west. It still aimed at an agrarian revolution in accordance with the then accepted belief that a political revolution would only give power to the bourgeoisie, and to this extent is was anarchistic; but it did not agree with Herzen that it would be brought about by peaceful evolution. In the summer of 1874 it staged the celebrated 'Go to the People' movement, when some two thousand young members of the intelligentsia clad themselves in homespun garments and went to live among the peasants – emancipated since 1861 – only to find that they were not at all interested in socialism and only wanted more land. The lesson of the crusade was that the peasants were not only not ripe for revolution, but that they never would be as long as communal property existed.[2] Yet the populists continued to look to the villages; and although there were organizations in the town, they were regarded as secondary and their members as inferior types of peasant.[3]

After the failure of the experiment of 'going to the people', a new revolutionary party was founded, called once again the 'Land and Freedom', which split in 1879 into two groups, the one advocating terrorism and the other the education of the peasants by propaganda. The first of these groups took the name of the 'People's Will' (*Narodnya Volya*), and was responsible, under the leadership of Zhelyabov – whom Lenin called

1. S. Mackiewicz, *Dostoyevsky* (1947), pp. 98–9.
2. Milyoukov, p. 409.   3. ibid. pp. 413–14.

'the perfect conspirator' – for the assassination of Alexander II in 1881.[1] The People's Will represented a decisive breach with anarchist theory – Zhelyabov declared at his trial that he was not an anarchist and was for the State – and it was thus a step in the direction of that political action of which the populists disapproved. Yet it was no more successful than populism. The assassination of the Tsar led to pitiless police repression and to a revulsion of feeling among the public. It became clear that a new start would have to be made.

In 1883 George Plekhanov, with Paul Axelrod and Vera Zasulich, all exiles in Switzerland, started a group, 'the Emancipation of Labour', with a marxist programme. Plekhanov was its leader, and it was under his influence that the transition from populism to marxism was accomplished.[2] The bankruptcy of the policy of terrorism after 1881 led him to re-examine the basic tenet of the populist creed – the belief that the peasantry was the coming revolutionary force in Russia. His outstanding contribution was his perception, remarkable indeed at that early date, that capitalism would eventually evolve a Russian proletariat; and that it was this proletariat, and not the peasantry, which would ultimately lead the revolution.[3] The peasantry was fundamentally unrevolutionary; the peasant commune could only develop into petty-bourgeois capitalism; the revolution would end in the seizure of power by the workers, but the final step could be undertaken only after a bourgeois democratic revolution, the achievement of which was the immediate revolutionary objective. So far removed from reality did these ideas appear that, provided they were not expressed in openly provocative language, they were passed by the censors, who welcome this division of opinion in the revolutionary camp. Plekhanov's writings thus not only converted Lenin but also, as the latter said, 'reared a whole generation of Russian marxists'. For by the middle of the nineties what he

1. The story is told by David Footman in his *Red Prelude* (1944).

2. Milyoukov, p. 419.

3. Carr, *Studies in Revolution* (1950), pp. 105 ff.; for the official Soviet estimate of his work *see* the *Short History of the Communist Party of the Soviet Union*, pp. 14–15 (pre-1956 edition).

had foretold had come to pass. Under the powerful impulse of Witte, capitalism had begun to make rapid strides; and although, even by 1914, there were not more than three million factory workers, Russian industry had been organized on modern lines in large concerns, with the result that the workers provided both the 1905 and 1917 revolutions with a determined 'vanguard of the proletariat'.[1]

*

How Marx and Engels viewed these developments may be seen from the correspondence between them and their Russian contemporaries published in Moscow in 1947.[2] Russian was the first language into which Marx's *Capital* had been translated from the original; and a few years later the censor had passed the second volume, though he had just confiscated the works of Adam Smith. But even before the translation of his book, Marx had received a striking proof of Russian enthusiasm for his ideas, as a group of Russian revolutionaries had asked him in March 1870 to represent them on the General Council of the First International. As we have noted, Marx viewed the situation with a certain irony. Yet he ended by acquiring a deep respect for the intellectual achievements of the Russians, though certain of their eccentricities always amused him, and nothing enraged him more than Slavophilism, with its belief that it was the mission of Russia to regenerate the west.

But the main issue of the correspondence was Russia's road to socialism. The populists declared that the new order would be based on the commune, and that the country need not pass through the fires of capitalism. In 1881 Zasulich, at that time a member of the party, wrote to Marx from Geneva to ask whether he accepted this. She pointed out that his analysis in *Capital* seemed to deny that it was possible, in which case it

1. B. H. Sumner, *Survey of Russian History* (1944), p. 365.
2. *Perepiska K. Marksa i F. Engel'sa s russkimi politicheskimi deyatelyami.* For a criticism of this collection, which is very incomplete, *see* Isaac Deutscher, *Did Marx expect the Russian Revolution?* (*The Listener*, 4 November 1948, pp. 693–4); but cp. W. Weintraub, *Marx and the Russian Revolutionaries*, in the *Cambridge Journal* (May 1950), pp. 497–503, and Buber, pp. 89–94.

only remained for the Russian socialists to calculate how many hundreds of years it would take for Russia to catch up with the west.[1] Her logic was unassailable, and it put Marx in a quandary. The populists were his friends, and had been the first to raise the banner of revolution in Russia, and respond to marxism in their own Slavonic manner. He had no wish to quench their zeal. Yet what he was asked to do was to concede that, of all countries, backward Russia might conceivably establish a socialist society before it had been achieved in the west. Tkachev, to whose revolutionary doctrine Lenin was to owe so much, had already ventured openly to make this claim on the ground that the Russians were 'the chosen people of socialism'; and at Marx's request Engels had attacked him in an article which had appeared in 1875.[2] After drafting four lengthy replies, Marx therefore sent Zasulich a brief and non-committal answer in which, while admitting that his analysis had been based on conditions in the industrial west, he gave way as little as he could.[3] In the introduction he contributed to the Russian edition of the *Communist Manifesto* of 1882, he declared, however, that 'if the Russian revolution sounds the signal for a proletarian revolution in the west so that each complements the other, the prevailing form of land ownership in Russia may form a starting point for a communist course of development'.[4] Further than this he was not prepared to go.

Engels continued the correspondence after Marx's death. But he gradually moved away from the populist position. In 1893 he told the narodnik economist N. F. Danielson that had it been possible to destroy capitalism 'some ten or twenty years ago', Russia might have cut short her evolution towards it, but that in view of the development of large-scale industry, and the continued disintegration of the commune, it was now inevitable that the country should pass through the capitalist phase;[5] and when, in 1894, he reprinted this article of 1875, it was with a

1. For the text *see* Paul W. Blacklock and Bert F. Hoselitz, *The Russian Menace to Europe*, 1952, p. 276.

2. *Russia and the Social Revolution*, ibid. pp. 203 ff.

3. ibid. p. 278.   4. ibid. p. 228.

5. Letters of 24 February and 17 October 1893, *Correspondence*, pp. 508 ff. and 513 ff.

postscript in which he repeated this. Yet he offered this consolation. If backward countries had before them the 'example' of a proletarian revolution and could see 'how the job is done', the process of their development to a socialist society would be appreciably shortened, and they would be spared much of the suffering that Western Europe has undergone. This, he declared, applied particularly to Russia 'because here a part of the indigenous population has already acquired the intellectual achievements of capitalist development, and it will thus be possible there, in a revolutionary period, to accomplish the social transformation almost simultaneously with the west'.[1] This conclusion seems equally inconsistent with the point of view of the populists and of the Russian marxists, but doubtless Engels was anxious to let the former down as gently as he could. He had, in fact, come round to the side of Plekhanov, and in a letter to him of 1895 he confessed that discussion with men of Danielson's generation was impossible, adding that under the conditions prevailing in Russia it was not surprising that 'the most peculiar and extravagant ideas come into being'.[2]

*

In 1893 Lenin came to St Petersburg and made his first appearance on the political scene. In 1895 he succeeded in uniting a number of small marxist groups into a 'League of the Struggle for the Emancipation of the Working Class', but he was arrested in December and sent to Siberia. According to the official *History of the Communist Party of the Soviet Union*, it was this League that organized in 1896 the strikes that took place in St Petersburg textile factories (the men were demanding a $10\frac{1}{2}$-hour day).[3] Meanwhile, similar leagues had been founded in other cities; and in 1898 the representatives of nine of these met at Minsk, issued a famous manifesto (drafted by Struve), and founded the Russian Social Democratic Labour Party (R.S.D.L.P.). Lenin was not present at this congress. But in 1900 he returned from Siberia, and with two young Russian

1. *The Russian Menace to Europe*, pp. 234–5.
2. *Marx-Engels Ausgewählte Briefe* (ed. Dietz Verlag, Berlin, 1953), pp. 578–9.
3. pp. 16–17, 24–5.

marxists, Potresov and Martov, conceived the idea of founding an illegal paper on an all-Russian scale. For this purpose he went to Geneva, where, not without difficulty, he reached agreement with Plekhanov and his group, and started *Iskra* ('The Spark'), the first number of which appeared in December. It had a large clandestine circulation in Russia, and it made Lenin's brand of marxism an effective force.

Although the Manifesto issued by the Minsk Congress had announced the formation of the R.S.D.L.P., no real party yet existed; there were neither rules nor a programme; nor was there a Central Committee, since its members had been at once arrested and had never been replaced. The period immediately following 1898 was therefore one of great confusion. At the time of Lenin's visit to Geneva there existed a rival foreign centre in Paris, the 'League of Russian Social Democrats', which was seeking to make its journal, *Rabocheye Dyelo* ('The Workers' Cause), the official party organ. The Genevan centre was opposed to this, because the journal was used to ventilate ideas of which it disapproved, and particularly those of the so-called 'economists'. This group held that proletarian activity should be restricted to the economic field, that is to attempting to form trade unions and to organizing strikes, its more moderate section arguing that political action would only divide the workers, and its more extreme section that economic activity would by itself create a revolutionary situation. But Lenin was sharply opposed to this, as he held that trade unionism would certainly develop into reformism, as it was doing in every western European country. For trade unionism, he contended, was 'the ideological enslavement of the workers to the bourgeoisie', and the proper role of the unions was to make use of practical economic issues to develop the *political* consciousness of the workers.[1] Alongside the 'economists' were the so-called 'legal marxists' – most of whom later became Mensheviks – who held fast to the marxist dialectical pattern – introduction of capitalism, organization of the proletariat and bourgeois-democratic revolution – and held therefore that no proletarian revolution should be attempted until all these things had been

1. *What is to be done?*, *S.W.* I, p. 175.

fulfilled. This position was strictly orthodox, and, indeed, Lenin himself subscribed to it in principle up to 1917; but it left room for many differences on tactics, and its literal acceptance would have meant an almost indefinite postponement of revolution. Outside the R.S.D.L.P. was the Social Revolutionary Party (founded in 1901), the successor of the *Narodnik* left-wing, a peasant party which advocated an agrarian revolution and practised terrorism.

The real founding congress of the R.S.D.L.P. was the 2nd Congress of 1903. It began in Brussels in a rat-infested flour-mill surrounded by Russian and Belgian detectives, and continued, after two of the delegates had been arrested, in the August heat of the Tottenham Court Road in London. Tempers ran high, and at the twenty-second session the party split into bolsheviks and mensheviks over the question of party membership. Lenin insisted upon a 'narrow' party to be composed as far as possible of trained revolutionaries, as opposed to an 'open' party of mere sympathizers. Both he and Plekhanov wished therefore to restrict membership to those who 'personally participated in one of the organizations of the party', rather than, as Martov had originally proposed, to those who 'work under the control and guidance of one of the party organizations'. On the particular issue Lenin was defeated but he succeeded by a narrow majority of two votes in securing the election of a Central Committee made up of his supporters. Yet, what seemed at the time a minor disagreement concealed two distinct conceptions of the role of the party in action, and fundamental differences of temperament.

Many of those who supported Lenin on the above issue ended in the menshevik camp, and in the years which followed it was they who tended to take Marx's principles literally, as opposed to Lenin, who held that they must be subordinated to the primary task of carrying out a revolution. None the less, the two groups worked side by side, and they did not separate until the secret Conference of Prague (1912), which Lenin persuaded to assume the rights and functions of a congress, and elect a new Central Committee to replace the properly constituted body.[1] Still a third marxist tendency within the party was represented by Trotsky, who stood apart from both bolsheviks and mensheviks and had a small group of followers. As against the mensheviks, he was in favour of the seizure of power by the working-class, and was opposed to collaboration with the bourgeoisie. But the numerical weakness of the proletariat and the conservatism of the peasants (a class which he deeply distrusted) led him to reject that alliance between the two that Lenin later proposed, and to hold that revolution in Russia would only succeed if it kindled revolutions in other more economically advanced countries. This view was the basis of his celebrated theory of 'permanent revolution'.

1. Wolfe, *Three who made a Revolution* (ed. London, 1956), p. 530.

15. Lenin's Contribution to Marxist Theory

IN Stalin's classical definition, 'Leninism is marxism of the era of imperialism and of the proletarian revolution'. Lenin had to guide his followers in a situation that had at last become a revolutionary one. His interminable polemical writings, most of which make such heavy reading today, give the impression of a man who has, as Edmund Wilson puts it, become 'the victim of a theological obsession with doctrine', though we are continually struck with the inconsistencies of his course. Yet, as Wilson says, to approach him through his writings is to fail to understand him, because, although he thinks they are, the issues are not being fought out in terms of ideas but invariably in terms of practical policy, and his real aim is not to justify theoretically what he wants done but to make men do it. The theoretical side of Lenin is in a sense not serious. It is in the sure instinct with which he grasps the reality of a given situation that his genius lies, though the tactics then adopted are always justified with marxist texts.[1]

Yet we must not underestimate the influence of Marx's ideas on Lenin, and fall into the error of supposing that he simply made use of them to cloak his power complex. In fact, he firmly believed in Marx, and above all in the most fundamental of the marxist principles that 'if a workers' movement is not revolutionary, it is nothing'. Only while marxism acted as a powerful solvent for discrediting liberalism, it offered, as Lenin was to discover, no clear guidance as to what was to replace it. Marx never explained how his revolutionary objectives would be actualized, and seems to have supposed that this was a matter for which the revolution itself would provide the solution. That Lenin, faced with practical problems of administration which had never entered into Marx's orbit, should have found himself obliged to adapt the classic theory accordingly was natural enough; and whether we regard this as a distortion

1. op. cit. pp. 388–9.

of it will depend upon how far we regard marxism as providing the basis of a genuinely democratic society, which it is very doubtful that it does.

Lenin's main contribution to marxist theory can best be considered under the following heads:

1. His theory of the strategy and tactics of revolution as shown (i) in 1905, and (ii) in 1917. The revolution of October 1917 is particularly important, as all subsequent communist revolutions have been modelled on it, and the leaders of national communist parties were to be constantly upbraided for their inability to apply the tactics which Lenin successfully adopted, though under wholly different conditions.

2. His version of the theory of the dictatorship of the proletariat, with which are connected the views which he held immediately before the October Revolution as to how the socialist State should be administered.

3. His theory of the party as 'the vanguard of the proletariat' which guides the masses both before and after the revolution. This was carried even further by Stalin.

4. His theory of the strategy and tactics to be adopted by communist parties with a view to bringing about world revolution. This still constitutes the basis of communist party action in all countries.

5. His theory of capitalist imperialism, which he held to constitute 'the final stage of capitalism' and thus to have created a new revolutionary situation.

6. His restatement of the philosophy of dialectical materialism, which is still accepted as authoritative.

1. THE STRATEGY AND TACTICS OF REVOLUTION

a. *The Revolution of 1905*

The disasters which befell Russia in the Russo-Japanese War led to the abortive revolution of 1905. It started with the massacre of 'Bloody Sunday' (22 January), when a peaceful demonstration before the Tsar's palace was fired on by the police; and this was followed by a wave of strikes, and by the mutiny in June on the battleship *Potëmkin*. In August the Tsar,

Nicholas II, announced the creation of a parliament (the Duma), and later in the year he promised to grant a constitution. But in October the first Workers' Soviet was formed in St Petersburg, a second being soon after set up in Moscow – not, indeed, with the object of taking power, but only of preparing for a Constituent Assembly to be elected on the widest possible franchise. Lenin did not get back to Russia until November, and this was too late to enable him to influence the course of events. For in December the Moscow workers came out on the streets. The garrison troops were unreliable; but a regiment was dispatched from St Petersburg, and the revolution was soon crushed. When therefore the Duma met in April 1906 the powers granted it by the government were very limited, and in 1907 it was dissolved. A large loan from France assisted the Tsar to rule without it; while Stolypin's law of 2 November 1907 giving every peasant the right to demand his land in a single consolidated holding, contributed to staving off revolution for the time being. In the following December, Lenin was obliged to leave Russia, and he remained in exile until his return in April 1917.

The 1905 revolution was a spontaneous rising of the masses, who acted without any directives from above; but it also affected all strata of society and compelled each class to define its point of view.[1] The bolsheviks and the mensheviks considered their own separate congresses held in the spring of 1905, and at a 'unity' congress held at Stockholm in April 1906. At the first of these the issue was the character of the government which would be set up after the downfall of Nicholas II; at the Stockholm conference, in which the mensheviks were in the majority, it was the attitude to be adopted towards participation in the Duma.

The *History of the Communist Party of the Soviet Union* is at pains to represent the bolsheviks and mensheviks as fundamentally divided, from the 1903 congress onwards, and to show that Lenin always took the correct line and that his opponents

1. On the political thought and action of the Russian intelligentsia in the decade up to and including the revolution of 1905, *see* Donald W. Treadgold, *Lenin and His Rivals* (1955).

were invariably in the wrong. In fact, however, the differences between the two were not so much differences of principle as of tactics, and there were few bolsheviks who did not at one time or another side with the mensheviks and vice versa. Thus, both held that the 1905 revolution should be not a socialist but a bourgeois-democratic revolution which would carry forward that industrial development which was the precondition of a proletarian revolution. But the mensheviks believed that for some time to come there could be no question of a proletarian dictatorship, and that the bourgeoisie should therefore be allowed to take power, with the socialists forming an opposition on the western model. Direct participation in such a government they held to be out of the question, since, apart from the question of principle, it would expose the party to a double danger. If it supported the measures of the bourgeois government, it would be discredited with the masses. If it tried to force the government to adopt socialism against its will, it would alarm the middle-class and thus prepare the way for reaction.[1]

Lenin agreed with the mensheviks that, given the existing level of capitalist development, only a bourgeois-democratic revolution was possible. But such a revolution demanded that the bourgeoisie was liberal, and he held that in Russia it was not. Hence the proletariat must 'lead the revolution', and set up what he called in his *Two Tactics* 'a revolutionary-democratic dictatorship of the proletariat and the peasantry'. This regime, which would, of course, be provisional only, would conform to the normal democratic pattern, since, as he put it: 'Whoever approaches socialism by any other path than that of political democracy will inevitably arrive at absurd and reactionary conclusions'. It would seek, however, at the earliest opportunity to convert the revolution from the bourgeois-democratic to the final proletarian stage, a transition which he conceived as being in some sort a continuous process.[2]

Trotsky added a third theory, later to be used against him. The revolution had come too late to be a bourgeois-democratic revolution of the approved marxist type, and the proletariat

1. A. Rosenberg, *A History of Bolshevism* (Eng. trans. 1939), pp. 34 ff.
2. Carr, *The Bolshevik Revolution* (1950) I, pp. 54–8.

would therefore have to carry out that which the bourgeoisie could not perform. A bourgeois-democratic revolution made by the proletariat would tend, however, to become a proletarian revolution, since political power would inevitably gravitate to the class which had played the greatest part in promoting it. The peasantry was incapable of rendering much assistance, and the success of the revolution would largely depend upon the support of proletarians in other countries which he held likely to be forthcoming.[1]

The mensheviks rejected both these. Marx, they said, had taught that the bourgeois-democratic revolution must take place first, and that there would then be a proletarian revolution. The two were quite distinct, and there must be what Plekhanov called a 'significant interval' between them. A bourgeois-democratic revolution undertaken, as Lenin recommended, 'under the hegemony of the proletariat' did not make sense, nor could the two revolutions be telescoped into one another as Trotsky seemed to suppose. There was some force in this criticism, and certainly neither Lenin nor Trotsky made altogether clear how the proletariat was to fulfil the role assigned to it. Yet if the mensheviks had their way, it was unlikely that there would ever be a revolution at all. Henceforward, until 1914, the various groups fought side by side in an uneasy alliance, but were in continual disagreement upon tactics, for example, as to participation in the Duma. In his *Three that made a Revolution*, Bertram Wolfe has skilfully disentangled these inner-party dissensions. Yet the period was a barren one, and we take leave of it with relief.

In his *Left-wing Communism* (1920) Lenin declared that 'without the dress rehearsal of 1905 the victory of the October Revolution would have been impossible'. In his *Lessons of the Revolution* (1910) he gave the following analysis of the situation. Only the revolutionary struggle of the masses can achieve anything worth while. It is not enough to undermine Tsarism; it must be destroyed. The action of the proletariat during the revolution was magnificent, but it needed the support of the

1. W. H. Chamberlin, *The Russian Revolution* (1935) I, pp. 39–40; Carr, *The Bolshevik Revolution* (1950) I, pp. 58–62.

less-advanced sections of the workers. The peasantry came in later, but was much weaker. The Liberals kept a foot in both camps, and when it came to fighting they betrayed the workers. But when at last the proletariat rises and is properly supported, no power on earth will be able to resist them.[1]

b. *The Revolution of February and October 1917*

The sequence of events which brought the bolsheviks into power in October 1917 will be described only in so far as this is necessary for an understanding of Lenin's strategy and tactics. These gave to the revolution, when it came, an altogether unexpected form and largely determined its subsequent development.

In February 1917 there began a series of demonstrations which ended with the abdication of the Tsar on 15 March. He had previously prorogued the Duma; but it had set up an Executive Committee to maintain order, and on 14 March a Provisional Government was formed under Kerensky. But on 12 March there came into existence the Petrograd Soviet, the representative of the Soviets which now began to be formed in every town and village, thus creating that dual authority enjoined by Marx in his *Address to the Communist League*.

The town Soviets were controlled by the mensheviks, and the village Soviets by the *narodnik* social revolutionaries. Both these parties, however, came to a working understanding with the Provisional Government; but while the social revolutionaries immediately joined it, the mensheviks, in accordance with their principles, at first refused to do so. The bolshevik party was then extremely weak, and its leaders, including Stalin, Kamenev, and Molotov, were in virtual agreement with the mensheviks. This was the position when Lenin returned to Petrograd on 16 April.

Lenin's first action was to issue his *April Theses*, regarded as madness by many of his followers, calling for 'no support for the Provisional Government', the establishment of a soviet republic which would prepare the way for the transition to a proletarian government, and the nationalization of the land

1. *S.W.* I, pp. 456–60.

which the peasants were already appropriating. The Provisional Government had undertaken to call a constituent assembly, a step to which the bolsheviks were hitherto as much committed as the mensheviks. But in the *April Theses* Lenin turned his back once and for all on parliamentarianism, though, as he was to explain in his *Left-wing Communism*, he did not immediately call for the overthrow of the Government, as 'this was impossible until the mood of the Soviets had changed', and only suggested that a Congress of Soviets might with advantage replace the Constituent Assembly. It was not until the 7th Party Conference of 24 April that he raised the cry of 'all power to the Soviets'. This would, indeed, have meant a coalition of social revolutionaries and mensheviks. But Lenin believed that the alliance between these parties and the government was artificial and would soon break down – as, indeed, it did; while he also realized that the masses were more concerned with revolution than with loyalty to any particular party, and would support whichever offered most. He saw that the government could not give them what they wanted – peace, bread, and land – and that both the social revolutionaries and the mensheviks were compromised by their connexion with it, the latter having reluctantly agreed in May to the participation in it of one of its leaders, Tseretelli.

In all this, Lenin showed himself a true prophet. The bolsheviks continued their policy of promising the people everything they asked for, and thus continually gained in strength. At the 6th Party Congress of July, Lenin felt strong enough to change the party slogan from 'all power to the Soviets' to 'the dictatorship of the proletariat and the poor peasantry'. In September, General Kornilov attempted a counter-revolutionary coup, and it was largely due to the bolsheviks that it did not succeed. The upsurge of the peasants now reached its height; the armed forces mutinied; and the government lost all authority. In his *Left-wing Communism* Lenin declares that revolution becomes possible only 'when the lower classes do not want the old way, and the upper classes cannot continue in the old way. By October this state of affairs had been reached. On 23 October (Old Style) the Central Committee (Kamenev and Zinoviev dissenting) decided to strike without delay; and on 25 October (7 November, New Style) the bolsheviks seized power after an almost bloodless revolution.

Thus, both the social revolutionaries and the mensheviks were out-played by a party far smaller, but better organized, than their own.[1] The former was the party *par excellence* of the peasantry, to whom the government had given a promise of land, which it had then hesitated to redeem. Had they called a constituent assembly in the summer and obtained authority to deal with the agrarian problem, they might have remained in power. But they had tied their hands by joining a bourgeois government at heart opposed to land nationalization.

The case of the mensheviks is of greater interest, as they stood nearer to the bolsheviks, with whom, despite their differences, they had fought side by side over many years; and it is impossible not to feel some sympathy for the predicament into which Lenin's tactics now landed them. They had done as much as any party to foment revolution, and it was they who were responsible for the order establishing soviets in every military unit, thus disintegrating the Army. But having thus carried out Marx's teaching, they now put themselves in an impossible position. As Plamenatz has shown, two courses were open to them. Either they could have jointed the Provisional Government at the beginning, and have given it full support in the hope of inducing it to make peace and of obtaining other concessions – in which event they might have maintained themselves against the irresponsible clamour of the bolsheviks – whereas they only joined it after it had made irreconcilable enemies of both workers and peasants; or they could have kept out of it altogether and have followed the mood of the people. But this they could not do. They knew that the masses wanted peace, but they felt it their duty to resist the invader. They knew that the peasants were seizing the land, but they did not wish them to become individualist farmers. They knew that the workers were taking over the factories, but this was anarcho-syndicalism. They insisted to the last that the country was

1. On the attitude of the various left-wing parties to the revolution *see* L. Schapiro, *The Origin of the Communist Autocracy* (1955).

not ripe for a marxist revolution, since such a revolution pre-supposed a proletariat sufficiently developed to be able to establish a socialist order which would embrace everything of permanent value in the capitalist system, and this condition was not fulfilled.[1]

Lenin, however, was determined to apply what he held, not without justification, to be Marx's fundamental principles, the utter destruction of the existing social and economic order and the establishment of a proletarian dictatorship and a planned economy. It was true that to do this involved a departure from the orthodox marxist analysis of revolution, and here the mensheviks, as text-book marxists, had him at a disadvantage. Yet Lenin could argue that Marx's real objective had been to abolish capitalism and everything connected with it, that his analysis was simply designed to show how this goal could be achieved under the conditions of western industrialism, and that it was not to be interpreted as proscribing any attempt at a revolution which did not accord with it. He was himself pre-pared to take the risk, partly because he entertained at the time extremely naïve ideas about public administration, and thus did not appreciate the practical difficulties that were certain to arise; partly because he believed that Europe was ripe for revolution even if Russia was not – an error of the first magni-tude in what was presumably a dialectical analysis of the situa-tion; and partly because he controlled a well-organized party, and indeed the event was to prove that it was because it was just one degree less inefficient than any other force against which it had to contend that the bolsheviks were able to retain power. But the result of the revolution was what might have been fore-seen. By carrying it out under the conditions he did, Lenin was obliged to hand over its direction to a centralized and undemo-cratic party. This was inconsistent with socialism as it had come to be understood in the west. Yet if Lenin is to be accused of distorting marxism, the same charge must be brought against those leaders of western socialism who had proclaimed them-selves his followers while eliminating from his doctrine its specifically revolutionary elements.

1. op. cit. pp. 90–2.

2. THE DICTATORSHIP OF THE PROLETARIAT

a. *Theory*

Most revolutionary leaders have waited until they have carried out their revolutions before committing to paper what they intended to effect by them. Lenin, however, is an exception; for in August–September 1917 he wrote the most famous of his pamphlets, *The State and Revolution* (it was not published, however, until February 1918), in which he explains in some detail the new order which the proletarian revolution would establish, and it is here that his theory of the State finds its most mature expression. He argues that the revolution will destroy the bourgeois State and replace it by a new form of government – the dictatorship of the proletariat, of which the Paris Commune was the prototype, and that in so doing it will follow the pattern of revolution laid down by Marx and Engels, to whose doctrine of the State the first half of the pamphlet is devoted.

Here he is primarily concerned to make two points. First, that when Engels said that the proletariat in assuming power 'puts an end to the State ... as a State', and that the State will 'wither away', he had two altogether distinct things in mind. By the 'abolition of the State' he meant the destruction of the bourgeois State, and this takes place immediately after the revolution. But the 'withering away' of the State is a very different matter, and it will not be accomplished until a much later stage. It may be noted in passing that if this was Engels's opinion, he does not make it at all clear. Secondly, that Marx's analysis of the State culminates in his *Critique of the Gotha Programme* of 1875, where he lays down that the dictatorship of the proletariat is the political form appropriate to the transitional period which lies between the abolition of the bourgeois State and the communist society when the State will disappear.

Lenin wishes therefore to warn his followers that the revolution will not mean the end of the State, which will continue in the form of the dictatorship of the proletariat. He is at pains to point out that it will be a temporary order only, and that under it the 'exploitation of man by man' will cease. But it will still perform the coercive functions of the old order, though these will now be exercised by the majority and not the minority. 'Differences, and even unjust differences, of wealth will persist', and men will continue to be paid according to their work and not according to their needs. It will be, in fact, as he says, 'the bourgeois state without the bourgeoisie'. And while he is careful not to obtrude unduly its authoritarian character, he regards it as so important that he lays down that 'a marxist is one who *extends* the acceptance of the class struggle to the *dictatorship of the proletariat*', and that on this touchstone it is necessary to test a *real* understanding and acceptance of marxism.

When Lenin had called in his *Two Tactics of Social-Democracy in the Democratic Revolution* (1905) for a revolutionary-democratic dictatorship of the proletariat and the peasantry, he had pointed out that 'of course it will be a democratic, not a socialist dictatorship', and that 'it will not directly overstep the bounds of bourgeois social and economic relationships'. It would be, in other words, an ordinary left-wing government which would prepare the way for socialism.[1] But while he declared in *The State and Revolution* that 'the dictatorship of the proletariat will for the first time create democracy for the people', he made it clear that it would not be a parliamentary form of government, and he openly identified parliamentarianism with bourgeois democracy. This brought him into immediate opposition with the labour leaders of western Europe, and in particularly with Kautsky, for many years the Pope of the German Social Democratic Party, and the leader of its orthodox faction against the heresies of Bernstein. At the end of 1918 Kautsky published a pamphlet, *The Dictatorship of the Proletariat*, in which he criticized *The State and Revolution*, and Lenin at once replied with his vitriolic *Proletarian Revolution and the Renegade Kautsky*, in which he now advanced the theory of the dictatorship in much sharper terms than he had used a few month earlier.

In this pamphlet the angle is shifted. In *The State and Revolution* the issue was whether the dictatorship was necessary.

1. *S.W.* I, p. 373.

Now it becomes 'the relation between proletarian democracy and bourgeois democracy'. Lenin argues that 'everyone knows that the dictatorship of the proletariat is the very essence of Marx's teaching', which is true in so far as Marx had made it the instrument through which the transition from capitalism into communism would be effected; that 'it is power won and maintained by the proletariat against the bourgeoisie, power which is unrestricted by any laws'; that Marx had shown that the Commune, the archetype of the dictatorship, had abolished the bourgeois-democratic parliamentary system; that 'the Soviets are the direct organization of the toiling and exploited masses, enabling them to organize and administer the State themselves in every possible way'; that 'bourgeois democracy is false and hypocritical, a paradise for the rich and a snare and deception for the poor'; and that 'proletarian democracy is a million times more democratic than any bourgeois democracy, and the Soviet Government a million times more democratic than the most democratic bourgeois republic'. This was the first open assertion of the doctrine of 'proletarian democracy'. The 'one-party system', which is certainly alien to western democratic thought, follows from it as a corollary. For marxists argue that opposing political parties derive from the conflict between different economic classes, and that once their cause is removed they will cease to exist. It is no more necessary that there should be two political parties than that a man should have two heads.

b. *The Administration of the State*

Lenin also explains in *The State and Revolution* how the proletarian State will actually be administered; and what he says is particularly significant, because the attempt to run the country in this manner was certainly one of the factors which reduced it within two years to a condition of utter prostration, with the result that the soviets – though still remaining the nominal rulers as they do to this day – were pushed into the background and the party took control. The transfer was accomplished in the course of 1920, both on the political and the economic level. On the first, it was achieved by seeing that party members were returned at elections and were given key posts; and on the second, by an intensification of State control of industry, which again placed its direction in the hands of the party.

It should be noted that in *The Impending Catastrophe and how to Combat It* (September 1917), which contains the economic programme of communism on the eve of its advent to power, Lenin had not committed himself to more than the nationalization of the banks and a few great monopolist industries, and had not challenged the principle of private property. His proposals were radical, but only communist in so far as they provided that the workers should themselves take over those branches of the national economy which had been brought under State control.[1] But his views upon administration were of an extreme naïvety, since he had succeeded in reducing it to what he called 'accounting and control' – 'operations of registering, filing, and checking' – which he held that capitalism had so simplified 'that they can easily be performed by every literate person'. There would thus be no need for any bureaucracy, and it would be possible 'to reduce the remuneration of *all* state servants to the level of "workmen's wages" '. So, again, in his *How to Organize Competition* (January 1918), he declares that 'we must break the old, *absurd*, savage, despicable, and disgusting prejudice that only the rich (*i.e.* the educated) can administer the State' since '*every rank and file worker* who is able to read and write can do *organizational work*'. 'There are', he concluded, 'masses of people like that.'[2]

He was soon to discover his illusion. Already by April 1918 he had to admit in his *Immediate Tasks of the Soviet Government* that the transition to socialism would be impossible without experts, and that 'the specialists are in the main bourgeois'. Something, he said, had gone astray with the system of 'accounting and control', or these specialists would have been integrated into it. As it was, it had been necessary to pay them high salaries which had caused the enemy to rejoice.[3] At the 8th Party Congress, of March 1919, he insisted that the question of the bourgeois specialists be definitely settled, pointing

1. *S.W.* II, pp. 91 ff., *see* Rosenberg, *History of Bolshevism*, pp. 101 ff.
2. *S.W.* II, p. 258.   3. *S.W.* II, pp. 319–20.

out that it was essential to use them on account of services they could render;[1] while at the 9th Congress of April 1920, at which he finally got his way, he declared that 'for the work of organizing the State we need people who have State and business experience, and there is nowhere we can turn to for such people except the old class. ... We have to administer with the help of people belonging to the class we have overthrown'.[2]

Large numbers of these bourgeois specialists – technicians and industrialists – did indeed lend their services to the regime in order to secure a privileged position; and Carr has pointed out that it was they who were largely responsible for the far-reaching policies carried out in the period of 'War Communism'.[3] Yet Lenin did not conceal his belief that their employment was a necessary, and thus a temporary, evil, and that the ultimate goal was a State which the workers would themselves administer. His attitude towards the bourgeoisie was indeed curiously simple. Its members would of course be deprived of their possessions, and their political rights would be severely curtailed. Yet he seems to have supposed that the majority would accept this as the normal consequence of a proletarian victory, and would collaborate with the new order. But the excesses of the early days of the revolution, which he was fully prepared to justify though he may not have been directly responsible for them, had the natural effect of antagonizing a class upon which he found himself dependent, and his complaints that it sabotaged the revolution are unconvincing. Under Stalin the policy was adopted, particularly after the introduction of the first Five-year Plan, of building up a new generation of experts, of whom the majority would be of proletarian or peasant origin; and this has led to the emergence of a technical and managerial *élite*, the existence of which constitutes perhaps the most serious problem with which the party leaders are faced today.

1. *S.W.* II, pp. 447–8.   2. *S.W.* II, p. 565.
3. *The Bolshevik Revolution*, II, pp. 186–7.

3. THE ROLE OF THE PARTY

In his *Foundations of Leninism* (1924) Stalin sets out the full-dress theory of the party as it is held today. It is the vanguard and organized detachment of the working-class, 'the highest form of the class association of the proletariat', the instrument of the dictatorship of the proletariat and the embodiment of its 'unity of will'. It is thus incompatible with the existence of factions, and must be periodically strengthened by purging itself of opportunist elements. In his *Problems of Leninism* (1926) he defines its role in somewhat similar terms, but with an even greater emphasis. He is at pains to point out that he is merely recording Lenin's opinions, but the passages which he cites are almost exclusively taken from Lenin's *Left-wing Communism* of 1920. On the other hand, the *History of the Communist Party of the Soviet Union* describes the role of the party in much the same terms as Stalin, but gives as its authority Lenin's *One Step Forward, Two Steps Back* of 1904, to which Stalin scarcely refers. But it had greatly influenced him in his younger days, and his early writings show that he had accepted, perhaps even with less reservation than Lenin himself, the doctrine that it was for the party to lead, to organize, and to fight.[1]

From the outset it was clear to Lenin that if you wanted to make a revolution you must have something to make it with, and that this could only be a centralized and disciplined party. These ideas, which point to a very un-Russian passion for system and order, he set out in his *What is to be done?* (1902), in which he laid down that 'without a revolutionary theory there can be no revolutionary movement', and added that 'the role of the vanguard can only be fulfilled by a party with an advanced theory' with which it was necessary that the masses should be indoctrinated.[2] When he spoke of 'unification', he meant, as Wolfe points out, 'the uniting of the autonomous local units of the marxist movement into a centrally controlled and ideologically homogeneous All-Russian Party'.[3] As against the populists, he conceived of this party as proletarian; as

1. Carr, *Studies in Revolution*, p. 209.
2. *S.W.* I, pp. 163–4.   3. op. cit. p. 157.

against the 'legal marxists', as a party of action as well as of theory; and as against the 'economists', as a party with a political as well as an economic programme. His *What is to be done?* is directed to combating the twin errors of 'spontaneity' and *khvostism* ('following in the tail'), both of which, in the form in which they were then being sponsored, illustrate the persistence of the earlier near-anarchist ideology. The first asserted that the workers would become revolutionary by virtue of an 'elemental' force in their disposition, to which Lenin replied that 'the spontaneous development of the labour movement leads to its subordination to bourgeois ideology', and urged the necessity of its direction by the party;[1] while the second was a corollary of the first and implied that the party should defer to the wills of the masses, whereas it was its duty to lead them.[2]

It was round this new conception that discussion centred at the 1903 congress. But while Lenin got his way at the time, he soon found himself violently attacked. In his *Our Political Tasks* Trotsky likened him to Robespierre. Rosa Luxemburg complained in *Iskra* that his policy would give such power to the Central Committee as to enable it to select the members of the National Party Congress.[3] She was then beginning her fight against bureaucracy and centralism in the German Party; but her criticism would have carried more weight had she not ruled her own Polish party at the time with a rod of iron.[4] Above all, Lenin was now abandoned by his old master Plekhanov, who joined the Mensheviks, and attacked him in *What is not to be done? A new Attempt to bring to their Senses the Frogs who asked for a King* and other writings.

Lenin defended himself in his *One Step Forward, Two Steps Back* (1904), the writing which most clearly reveals his contempt for democracy in the sense of government by the people. Here he enters in detail into what had taken place at the London Congress, and points out that its object had been 'to create a party on the basis of the principles advanced by *Iskra*'. He

1. *S.W.* I, pp. 170–7.   2. *S.W.* I, pp. 205–6, 294.
3. Her article, entitled *Centralization and Democracy*, is reprinted in *Marxisme contre dictature* (Paris, 1940), pp. 17 ff.   4. Wolfe, p. 383.

had fought therefore for the principle of organization which 'was inconceivable without the subordination of the minority to the majority, of the part to the whole'; and had insisted that the party should be directed by a central organ and a central committee, and that the latter should be free to rid itself of unreliable elements. He contended that, so far from resisting organization, the proletariat would welcome it, and that the opposition to it came from 'opportunist' and non-revolutionary circles.[1]

Lenin's immediate object was to create in the party an efficient instrument for bringing about a revolution, and in view of the conditions in Russia at the time, his demand that it should be small and highly disciplined was intelligible enough. As it was by definition 'the vanguard of the proletariat', it claimed, not altogether unnaturally, the right to exercise control over the revolutionary movement, and it continued to make use of this prerogative after the revolution had taken place. Thus Lenin was responsible for what soon became in practice the dictatorship of the party, which Stalin was later to perfect. It is true that in his *State and Revolution* he has scarcely a word to say about the party, and appears to have absolute faith in the administrative capacity of the workers. But here his object was to demonstrate the desirability of destroying the bourgeois State, and thus he had to show (and doubtless may even have believed) that if it were destroyed, the workers would be able to take charge. The belief that they would do so was not inconsistent with the conception of the 'leading role' of the party which he had never renounced. But the 'War Communism' years disillusioned him, and when he wrote his *Left-wing Communism* – addressed to communist parties which had affiliated to the Third International and needed to be taught their duties – it was to point out that the bolsheviks could not have maintained themselves in power 'without the strictest discipline in our party'; that without an 'iron party' it was impossible to carry out the dictatorship of the proletariat; that it was the 'highest form of proletarian class organization'; and that 'not a single organizational question is decided by any State institu-

1. *S.W.* I, pp. 322–3, 328–9.

tion without the guiding instructions of the Central Committee of the Party'.[1] These principles were adopted in that section of the *Theses of the Communist International* – approved by the 2nd Comintern Congress of July–August 1920 – which deals with the role of the party; and they were embodied in the Statutes of 1924 and in the final Constitution of 1928. At the same time Article 21 of the *Twenty-one Conditions of Admission to the Comintern* of 1920 laid down that the basis of party organization should be 'democratic centralism', that is, the subordination of the lower party organs to the higher, a principle first adopted by the Russian party at the 6th Party Congress of July 1917.[2]

The issue between Lenin and his early critics goes back to the ambivalence which we have already noted in the marxist system. Marx had sought to effect an equilibrium between consciousness and being, that is between the will of man as a determining factor in history and the objective material world against which he has to contend and which is governed by its own laws. As was pointed out above, his anxiety to stress the scientific character of his doctrine led him to over-emphasize the latter, and thus exposed him to the charge of 'fatal determinism'. It was to refute this charge that Plekhanov somewhat shifted the emphasis to the active, voluntarist side of the doctrine, and it was to him that Lenin owed his introduction to marxism. Lenin's attack on 'subservience to spontaneity' was the protest of a practical revolutionary, who was unwilling to wait upon the dialectical process, and believed that, given the necessary organization, he could, as he put it, 'overthrow all Russia'; and it was thus an implicit revolt against the determinist in favour of the voluntarist element in Marx's teaching. Stalin was to carry this still further by representing that the real determinant of socialist development in the Soviet Union is the State (a euphemism for the party), which is no longer, as it was for Marx, an organ of oppression – superstructural and

1. *S.W.* II, pp. 572, 593.

2. *History of the C.P.S.U.*, p. 198. On the theory and practice of democratic centralism *see* Merle Fainsod, *How Russia is Ruled* (Harvard University Press, 1954), pp. 181–4.

expendable – but has been transformed into the instrument for 'building socialism', and for eventually securing the transition into communism. It has always been difficult to reconcile the voluntarist element with the determinist, which insists upon objective economic laws. For the existence of such laws cannot be denied without repudiating marxism, and thus upon occasions it is strongly re-asserted, as it was, for example by Stalin himself in his *Economic Problems of Socialism in the U.S.S.R.* (1952).[1]

None the less, it is upon the voluntarist factor, that is, upon the role of the party and of the citizen in so far as he co-operates with it, that the stress is now laid. The party rules because, as the most highly developed section of the workers, it represents what the more backward elements would desire were they sufficiently mature to discern where their true interests lie. Whether this is Marx's doctrine is a matter of controversy. It is argued that the *Communist Manifesto* declares that 'the communists do not form a separate party opposed to other working class parties', and 'do not set up any sectarian principles of their own, by which to shape and mould the proletarian movement'. Yet the Communist League was certainly a party, and its constitution envisaged one which combined a legal and an illegal organization. Further, the *Manifesto* asserts that the communists are 'the most advanced and resolute section of the working class', and that their grasp of theory gives them 'the advantage of clearly understanding the line of march', which means that their party, once they should decide to form one, constitutes the 'vanguard' of the workers' movement, with all that this 'leading role' implies.[2]

As for 'democratic centralism', everything depends on where the emphasis is laid. When, for example, the question whether the German peace terms should be accepted came up before the Central Committee in February 1918, Lenin was defeated by Bukharin and the Left Communists, and there the matter rested

1. Aspaturian, op. cit. pp. 1032 ff.; *see also* Carr, *Studies in Revolution,* p. 110.
2. *See* Laski, *The Communist Manifesto,* Introduction. pp 40, 67–8, but cp. my *Marxist Past and Present,* pp. 156–8.

until in the end he gained his point.[1] But at the 10th Party Congress of March 1921 the principle was restated. Until a decision had been reached, the criticism of individuals or even groups would be tolerated, but any attempt to organize an opposition was to be condemned as 'fractionalism' – a ruling which Stalin was soon to invoke to crush opposition of any kind. So long therefore as the emphasis was laid on 'democratic', the application of the principle led to a regime no more rigid than that which prevailed in any continental socialist party, with the possible exception of the French. But when it was shifted to 'centralism', it led to the monolith.

Certainly there is nothing democratic in the organization of communist parties today except its outward form. According to the statutes of every party, the National Congress, normally held biennially, is the supreme authority, and elects the Central Committee which is to act as its executant during the intervening periods. The Central Committee is in turn responsible for electing, immediately after the Congress has taken place, the members of the Politburo and the other central party organs. In fact, the Congress does not elect the Central Committee, but simply approves without discussion a list of members submitted to it. Nor does the Central Committee elect the members of the central party organs, but merely ratifies appointments to them which have been made by the Politburo. The Central Committee is far too large to be able to discharge the functions assigned to it, and the tendency over the years has been to increase its membership. Thus it has no powers of initiative whatever, and consists of persons who are nominated either because they are responsible for some important branch of party activity, or as a reward for long service.

The relationship between the party and the soviets was first clearly formulated at the 8th Party Congress of 1919 which laid down that 'the party must win for itself undivided mastery over the soviets, and practical control over their work', though with the reservation that it was 'to lead the activity of the soviets, but not replace them'.[2] In his *Problems of Leninism* Stalin

1. *History of the C.P.S.U.*, p. 207.
2. Carr, *The Bolshevik Revolution* I, p. 219.

quotes Lenin as saying that the dictatorship is exercised by the proletariat, which is organized into soviets and is led by the party. He declares that 'the party exercises the dictatorship of the proletariat', and that 'the dictatorship is *in essence* the dictatorship of its vanguard, the party', though he insists, not without sophistry, that this does not mean that the party *is* the dictatorship, because things which are '*in essence* the same' are not thereby identical. On the other hand, he defines the soviets as 'the direct expression of the dictatorship of the proletariat', though he admits with Lenin that 'not a single important political or organizational question is decided by our soviet without guiding directions from our party'.[1]

To the end of his life Lenin stood for the 'narrow' as opposed to the 'open' party; and during the period which followed the revolution, he resisted anything which threatened its monopoly. Both he and Stalin agree therefore as to its 'leading role' and its relation to the dictatorship of the proletariat. Already by June 1917 Lenin had seen that it would be the party and not the soviets that would make the revolution. This had led to a difference of opinion with Trotsky, who in common with the majority of the leaders regarded the Soviets as the symbols of constitutional authority, and it was in the name of the soviets that the revolution was in fact carried out. Yet, as Deutscher has pointed out, the dispute had to do with tactics rather than principles. Neither saw any divergence between soviet constitutionalism and party dictatorship. It was taken for granted that the soviets would be the organs of the future proletarian government, and equally, at least by Lenin, that they would submit to the direction of the party.[2] With this reservation, which in no way implied the likelihood of a conflict, Lenin seems genuinely to have desired to make the system a success. This is brought out in the Report of the Central Committee to the 11th Party Congress of 1922, when he says that the level of the People's Commissariats must be raised, and there must be an end to the practice of bringing every petty matter before the Central Committee – and this although he

1. *Leninism*, pp. 132, 135.
2. *The Prophet Armed. Trotsky, 1897–1921*, pp. 290–1.

admitted that of the eighteen existing Commissariats at least fifteen were absolutely no good.[1] Again, in his *Better Fewer but Better* (March 1923), almost the last of his writings, he asks whether there is not 'something improper' in the suggestion of 'the flexible amalgamation of a party institution with a soviet institution'; but answers that such an amalgamation had already proved its usefulness, particularly in the case of the Commissariat for Foreign Affairs, and that it was appropriate for the machinery of the State as a whole.[2] The above pamphlet is quite short, and Lenin does not develop what he meant by a 'flexible amalgamation'. Yet while it seems that he did not intend the party to take the place of the soviets but simply to guide them, it had by this time become supreme in every sphere of activity, and this not from any predetermined design but from the force of circumstances.[3]

4. THE STRATEGY AND TACTICS OF COMMUNIST PARTIES

In May 1920 Lenin published his *Left Wing Communism: an Infantile Disorder*, with its sub-title, *A Popular Essay on Marxist Strategy and Tactics*. It is dedicated in irony to Mr Lloyd George, and is a complete manual of communist *raison d'état*.

In *The State and Revolution* and *The Proletariat Revolution* Lenin had been attacking the right wing. He had now to deal with the left. The tenth of his *April Theses* of 1917 had called for a new International, and in March 1919 the Third International had been founded. But Lenin was determined that it should be a genuinely revolutionary body; and at the 2nd Congress of 1920 he split the world labour movement by giving its sections the alternative of affiliating on the terms laid down in the *Twenty-one Conditions of Admission* or of remaining in the now discredited Second International, with the result

1. *S.W.* II, p. 803.   2. *S.W.* II, p. 850.
3. Carr, *The Bolshevik Revolution* I, pp. 222–7; Julian Towster, *Political Power in the U.S.S.R. 1917–1947* (New York, 1948), pp. 119–34, 178–83.

that a number of parties (including the Italian Socialist Party) which had joined in 1919 now seceded.[1]

The Third International had been formed to organize world revolution – which was no academic issue but a matter of life and death, as it was held indisputable that without it the Russian revolution would collapse. But the greatest obstacle to it was now the intransigent temper of the newly formed communist parties, which interpreted Lenin's teaching to mean that their attitude towards all non-communists must be one of uncompromising hostility. Yet how in this case could world revolution be brought about? Lenin's thesis is therefore that communist parties must abandon their sectarianism, and seek by every means to establish contact with the masses and seize power; and that they could only do so by working within governments, trade unions, and the like, which were at present controlled by their opponents. The revolutionary spirit of the younger communists was admirable, but it was 'abstract communism' which had not matured to the stage of practical mass political action. Parliamentarianism was indeed obsolete. But bourgeois governments had to be captured, and this called for proletarian politicians who would beat the bourgeois politicians at their own game.

Hence Lenin lays down that 'to reject compromise on principle is childish', and adds that Lloyd George was right when, in his speech of 18 March 1918 he urged the Liberals to combine with the Conservatives against Labour because both stood for private property, thus showing that he was a 'clever man who had learnt much from the marxists'.[2] Agitation and propaganda were not enough. The masses must acquire political experience, as they had done in Russia. The party, as the vanguard, represented the political consciousness of tens of thousands. But the success of a revolution would depend on that of tens of millions. Communist parties must therefore strive un-

1. For the *Twenty-One Conditions* and the *Statutes and Theses* adopted by the 2nd Congress of 1920, *see The Communist International, 1919–43: Documents,* ed. Jane Degras, vol. I (1956). On the foundation of the Comintern *see* B. Lazitch, *Lénine et la III*e *Internationale* (Neuchâtel, 1951).   2. *S.W.* II, p. 618.

ceasingly for power; and to achieve it they must know 'how to combine the strictest loyalty to the ideas of communism with an ability to make all the necessary practical compromises – to tack, make agreements, zigzags, retreats, and so on'. Revolutionaries who were not prepared for such accommodations were very bad revolutionaries. It was easy enough to be a revolutionary once the revolution had started. It was much more difficult, and more urgent, to be one when the conditions for the direct revolutionary mass struggle had not yet matured.[1]

The above principles were more amply set out in the Theses adopted by the 2nd Comintern Congress of 1920. The duty of communist parties to participate in elections and run their own candidates was fully recognized; and detailed instructions were laid down which subordinated communist parliamentary fractions to their Central Committees (and hence to Moscow), from which they were to receive their instructions. But the question whether communist parties should enter non-communist governments continued for some time to arouse controversy; and the proposal of the German leaders, Brandler and Thalheimer, to enter the social-democratic governments formed in Saxony and Thuringia in 1923 caused serious misgivings. Again, in the presidential elections of 1928, the German communists refused to support Marx, the candidate of the People's Bloc, against Hindenburg, the candidate of the Right, on the ground that the People's Bloc was not genuinely progressive, and ran Thälmann as their own candidate, thus ensuring Hindenburg's victory. It was not until the 7th Congress of 1935 and the establishment of the Front Populaire in France that communist collaboration with anti-fascist governments became the order of the day, as it has been ever since. (It is strange that this should not have been understood by J-P. Sartre, who is always prepared to engage in chop-logic with the communists. In his play *Crime passionnel*, where the action takes place in 1941, he makes the Central Committee of a country adjacent to Russia decide to assassinate the leader of the communist underground movement, because he had entered into a compact with the bourgeois government under which

1. *S.W.* II, p. 617 ff.

active hostilities against Russia would be terminated, and other advantages to the party be secured; and this not because his action was ill-timed, but because it was contrary to communist principles.)

The Theses of the 2nd Congress were reinforced by those adopted at the 3rd Congress of 1921, which broadened the basis of communist action by introducing the so-called 'united front' tactics under which the communists were to establish contact with the masses either by collaborating with the leaders of non-communist organizations ('united front from above'), or by appealing to the rank-and-file members of such organizations over the heads of their leaders ('united front from below'). But while the wisdom of such tactics is indisputable, it is doubtful whether Lenin fully realized how difficult it would be for communist parties to apply them. From the first the communist had been told that they were not as other men are, and that they must jealously guard the purity of their doctrine. Such teaching did not make for joint action with other parties, as this involved entering into personal relations with the enemy and the danger of eventual compromise on matters of principle. Again, if the communist leaders succeeded in reaching an agreement with the social democratic leaders (which was no easy matter) and kept it, it was unlikely that they would convert the masses to communism, and they would then be exposed to the charge of 'opportunism', that is, of postponing revolutionary action on the pretext that conditions were not ripe. If, on the other hand, they showed undue zeal, they would be accused by their partners of having violated the agreement, and by Moscow of having prejudiced the cause by their sectarianism. Most party leaders found themselves sooner or later impaled upon one horn or the other of this dilemma, nor were their difficulties lessened by the continual fluctuations of Comintern policy.

So important is this question of tactics that it must be pursued a little further. The object of all communist parties is to capture the masses; and in this struggle for power their real enemies are not the right-wing parties (with whom they will deal at their leisure after the revolution has been achieved), but the socialists, who are competing with them for the goodwill of the workers. But while the communists thus regard the socialists with an especial bitterness, it is precisely with them, or with their leaders, that the tactics of the united front require them to cooperate, though the ultimate end of this cooperation is to drive them off the field. As the socialists are perfectly aware of this, and have themselves no love for the communists, the employment of united-front tactics in countries not directly threatened by Russia calls for considerable ingenuity. The middle thirties in France provide the most brilliant example of their successful application.

The French Communist Party had been founded in 1920 as a result of a split within the Socialist Party which had left great bitterness behind it. In 1924 there had been formed a left-wing Cartel des Gauches; but in 1926 it had become the Union Nationale, in which the socialists participated with bourgeois parties. Hence, in the elections of 1928, the communists, in obedience to comintern instructions, adopted the slogan of *classe contre classe*. Abandoning their earlier practice of collaborating with the socialists at elections to secure the defeat of right-wing candidates, they now attacked the socialist leaders with no holds barred, and as a result saw their parliamentary strength reduced to fourteen deputies. So serious was the decline of the party that in 1930 its leader, Maurice Thorez, was summoned to Moscow and sharply reprimanded; but in the elections of 1932 the same procedure was adopted, and the number of communist deputies fell to ten.

In 1932 a left wing 'World Congress against War and Fascism', organized by Henri Barbusse and others, was held at Amsterdam; and, according to a statement made by the French communist leader, Marcel Cachin at the 7th Congress of 1935, the change of tactics ultimately adopted dated from this event. Yet for some time the two parties remained sharply divided. The communists periodically approached the socialists with requests for united action; but negotiations always broke down, if only because the communists would not give the elementary undertaking to refrain from attacking their rivals; and their *démarches* were, in fact, solely prompted by tactical motives, since the refusal of the socialists could always be represented as evidence of a desire to keep the workers divided.

Meanwhile the danger of fascism grew. On 6 February 1934 André Marty wrote in *Humanité* that 'it is impossible to struggle against fascism without struggling against social democracy'; but when on 12 February the socialists demonstrated against the Daladier government, the communists ordered their followers to participate – the first example of joint action since 1928. Yet the communist press continued its attacks, and it was not until the Party Congress held in June that collaboration with socialist organizations on all levels was enjoined and was eagerly taken up by the workers. On 14 July the communist and socialist leaders met, and the communists now promised to do everything the socialists required of them. On 27 July an agreement for collaboration was signed, and although there were murmurings in the Central Committee, Thorez insisted on its observance. The communists now turned to the radical socialists. In January 1935, Daladier attended one of their mass meetings, and on 14 July the three parties took part in a joint demonstration. Thorez left for Moscow to attend the 7th Congress, where he received an ovation. It was well deserved, since, despite its infinitesimal parliamentary representation, the French Communist Party could justly claim to have initiated the Popular Front by virtually blackmailing parties larger than itself into undertaking common action or facing the charge of opposing working-class unity against fascism. In the 1936 elections the party returned seventy-two deputies, and was henceforth represented by the Comintern as a model to be followed by all others.

This policy was officially maintained until the setting up of the Cominform, at the Nine-Power Conference held in Warsaw in September 1947, which laid down that 'the communists must close their ranks, unite their efforts on the basis of the common anti-imperialist and democratic platform and rally round them all the democratic and patriotic forces of the people'. At a meeting of the Central Committee of the French Communist Party at the end of October, Thorez furnished the necessary explanations. The Popular Front, he declared, had achieved certain results in 1935. Yet it had been from the first a wrong policy, because it had been based on the 'united front from above' which had involved alliances with elements that could not be trusted. The party had realized its error by 1939, but during the Resistance it had allowed its own movement, the *Front National*, to participate in the *Conseil National de la Résistance*, and had permitted de Gaulle to dissolve the military formation of the latter in 1945 – a course which Thorez omitted to say that he had approved at the time. There were now only two parties in France – the communists and the gaullists – and the former must sever all connexions with other left-wing elements and devote their whole attention to winning the masses. This was, in fact, a return to the *classe contre classe* slogan of 1928 from which the Popular Front, of which Thorez himself had been the main instigator, had represented a reaction.

The sectarianism was somewhat relaxed in 1948 because the industrial disturbances of November–December 1947 made the French Communist Party fear that it would be declared illegal and would thus lose contact with the masses. Early in 1949, however, there took place such a swing to the right as to constitute a definite change of front. For it was now the primary objective of the party, as the principal outpost of Moscow, to mobilize public opinion in support of its 'peace offensive' with a view to the World Congress, held in Paris in March, which represented Marshall Aid and the Atlantic Pact as acts of aggression directed against the Soviet Union; and on this platform the party was once more prepared, as in the days of the Popular Front, to collaborate with any pacifist left-wing element.

Thus, at the present time, the party is throwing all its emphasis upon achieving 'working-class unity' with a view to furthering the objectives of Moscow, among which the weakening of whatever makes for solidarity between the western powers has the priority. The same is true of the Italian Communist Party, and its conference of January 1955 was remarkable both for its overtures to the catholics and for its appeal for unity of action, not against capitalists in general, but against the 'monopolists', who were represented as a danger to the small entrepreneurs, a class not usually regarded with sympathy by communists. In both countries the party has long been in opposition. It participated in the early post-war governments, and proved wholly unreliable. In France, the communist ministers were dismissed by Ramadier in May 1947 because the party deputies had voted against the government's wages policy; while in the same month the Italian communists opposed De Gasperi's anti-inflation measures, upon which he resigned and formed a coalition without them. Both parties have been trying ever since to get back into the government, but have not found any independent political group prepared to enter into an alliance with them.

*

The same principles have governed communist tactics in the economic field. Lenin laid down, and the Theses of the 2nd Congress confirmed, that all communist workers in a position to do so were to join trade unions, albeit in the hands of their opponents, with a view to obtaining control of them; though the force of this order was somewhat weakened by the foundation in the same year of the Red International of Labour Unions (the Profintern), which led to the formation of 'splinter' red trade unions and raised a problem which was not resolved until the 7th Congress of 1935, by which time, however, most of them had already been instructed to return to their parent bodies.

In the French trade union movement the wheel has indeed gone full circle. In December 1921 the extremist wing of the socialist Confédération Générale du Travail (C.G.T.) broke away and founded the communist Confédération Générale des Travailleurs Unitaires (C.G.T.U.), which affiliated with the Profintern. It made little headway, and in March 1936, when its membership was well short of a quarter of a million, it rejoined the C.G.T. in accordance with the new policy. When the war broke out, the C.G.T. expelled the former C.G.T.U. members, but a reunion was effected in May 1943. After the liberation the Unitaires acquired a predominant influence in the

C.G.T., which they now control; and in December 1947 a second schism took place, only this time it was the socialist minority which broke away to form the Force Ouvrière.

In the years following the second world war the communists attempted to gain control over the international trade union movement through the World Federation of Trade Unions (W.F.T.U.). This organization, which originated in a British initiative, was effectively founded at a congress held in Paris in October 1945, and in the spirit of international solidarity then prevailing, almost every trade union movement affiliated with it. As the price of their cooperation, the communists had obtained the appointment as Secretary-General of Louis Saillant, a former Secretary-General of the C.G.T., who, while claiming not to be a communist, had always followed the party line. As a result, the salaried posts were quickly filled with 'reliable assistants, while control over elective offices was facilitated by Russia's domination over the satellite countries, and by the adhesion of China to the Soviet block in 1949.

It soon became apparent that the communists were up to their usual tricks. Thus it was noted that numbers of organizations in backward countries which formerly counted their membership in tens of thousands were announcing figures, which there were no means of checking, in the neighbourhood of a million, thus submerging organizations of longstanding and established reputation. At a meeting of the Executive Bureau of 19 January 1949, the representatives of the British Trade Union Congress (T.U.C.), the American Congress of Industrial Organizations (C.I.O.) and the Confederation of Free Trade Unions of the Netherlands (N.V.V.) therefore withdrew their organizations, and gave their reasons in a pamphlet issued by the T.U.C., *The Free Trade Unions leave the W.F.T.U.* Their example was widely followed, and the non-communist unions founded their own organization, the International Confederation of Free Trade Unions (I.C.F.T.U.).

The W.F.T.U. continued to maintain its headquarters in Paris until January 1951, when the French government ordered their dissolution and they were transferred to Vienna, where they remained until January 1956, when the Austrian Government raised objections and they were moved to Prague. In addition to its headquarters, the W.F.T.U. has regional liaison bureaux in Peking and Mexico, the one being responsible for Asia and Australasia and the other for Latin America. The main function of the organization as a whole is to disrupt the free trade unions, and it is largely under its cover that the communists carry out their anti-imperialist activities in undeveloped countries, where they can most easily foment nationalist feeling by stirring up labour unrest. One of the four departments into which the Secretariat in Prague is divided is in charge of this.

Work in the trade unions has always been regarded as an especially important branch of party activity, and many high-ranking communist leaders graduated through this school. The tactics to be employed with a view to the penetration and ultimate control of the unions are set out in the relevant Theses of the 2nd Congress of 1920 and the 6th Congress of 1928, which were drafted at a time when almost every union was under the social democratic leadership. The basic principle is the exploitation of the 'partial demands' of the workers, that is, of demands which fall short of those which politically developed communists would put forward. The communists are to foment any existing grievances, and, if there are none, create them. In so doing they must seek to outbid the social democrats, and if the latter decline to follow their lead, discredit them as refusing to sponsor 'the just demands of the workers'. They must try to secure election to the various workers' representative bodies, and they should thus be themselves first-class workers, as this will gain them the respect of their fellows. They are explicitly instructed to attach no importance to collective agreements between employers and employed, and it is pointed out that the respect with which such agreements are regarded by the latter only witnesses to the persistence of 'bourgeois conceptions'.

Here again, the application of these tactics required the most skilful handling and was by no means always successful. The social democratic union leaders cannot be acquitted of having been swayed at times by political considerations. Yet their normal practice was to call out their men only when they believed that there was some genuine abuse which it lay within the power of the industry to remove. The communists, however, had no interest in improving the lot of the workers, but only in creating a revolutionary situation. It was good tactics for them to seize upon some grievance and obtain its redress, as they could then represent themselves as the champions of the workers and steal the thunder of their rivals. On the other hand, their policy of *surenchère* was a dangerous one, since if they engineered a strike based on demands which could not reasonably be conceded, it was likely to fail, and they would then be exposed to the reproaches of the workers, who would find themselves worse off than they were before. Nor was this danger removed if they secured control of the trade-union movement, since a wave of strikes promoted for purely political ends might cause such hardships as to alienate the masses, and so assist the social democrats.

*

No account of communist technique would be complete, however, which did not include the various 'front' organizations which are created either to promote some particular object, or to unite a professional group such as writers, lawyers, or scientists, or to mobilize a particular section of the community such as women, youth, or students. Of these, the most notorious at the present time is the 'Partisans of Peace', directed by the World Peace Council, which originated as a result of a congress of intellectuals at Wroclaw, in Poland, just after the setting up of the Cominform, and was founded with the object of diverting attention from the aggressive policy of the latter. As it purports to be a non-party democratic movement in defence of peace, and as peace is an issue which makes the widest possible appeal, it has attracted a large following among persons who do not realize that in communist jargon 'peace' means unquestioning submission to Soviet policy and unyielding opposition to whatever obstructs it. It is thus the most universal of the front organizations, and is linked with and supported by all the others.

The policy of creating organizations which are 'fronts' in the sense that their real purposes are masked behind a non-political façade of social ideals generally acceptable to progressive public opinion goes back to the early years of the Comintern. At the 3rd Comintern Congress of 1921 it was recognized that communism would make no rapid progress if it was to be fostered only by such organizations as were avowedly communist, and that they must therefore be reinforced by others which would attract sympathizers and to provide a screen under cover of which the communists could advance their policy. The most important of these organizations, many of which still continue under other names, were founded or directed by Willi Münzenberg, the patron saint of the 'fellow-traveller', by whom they were called the 'Innocents' Clubs'. They are naturally represented as spontaneous and independent of Moscow, and thus care is taken that they should contain only a leavening of communist members. The most effective arrangement has been to appoint as president a politically colourless but otherwise prominent non-communist, but to have a communist or crypto-communist secretary in the background who exercises control. Such organizations are of the utmost assistance to the communists in their task of manipulating public opinion. For the support which the latter receive from left-wing elements is of incalculable value. A government has only to suppress a communist newspaper for sedition, or to arrest a leader for proved treasonable conspiracy, to arouse an outcry, in the name of the freedom of the press or of political liberty, led by persons who are not communists at all, but whom no amount of experience will convince that the principles for which they stand would count for nothing were the communists themselves to come into power. For the communist principle has always been that which Montalembert accused contemporary catholics of adopting: 'When I am the weaker, I ask you for liberty because it is your principle; but when I am stronger, I take it away from you because it is not my principle.'

5. THE DOCTRINE OF CAPITALIST IMPERIALISM

Lenin's teaching on imperialism is contained in his *Imperialism, The Highest Stage of Capitalism*, written at Zürich in 1916. Its immediate aim was to show that 'the war of 1914 was on both sides imperialist'; but its central thesis is that imperialism is 'a direct continuation of the fundamental properties of capitalism in general'. It is held by the communists to represent a notable advance in marxist economics; but it is not, in fact, a work of any theoretical originality, and is simply a popularization of J. A. Hobson's *Imperialism* (1902) and Rudolf Hilferding's *Finanz-Kapital* (1910), to which Lenin added certain practical political conclusions of his own.

In Volume II of *Capital* Marx had analysed the principles that govern the accumulation of 'total social capital', and the conditions under which consumer goods are realized under 'extended reproduction'. The gist of his argument was that in a society producing in an exclusively capitalist fashion, there would take place a continual accumulation of capital, whatever was produced being duly absorbed by the home market without recourse to external outlets. He did not indeed assert that the conditions he premissed actually existed, as the capitalist system was marked by variations and deviations which exhibited its basic contradiction; and he was aware that one result of them was to create a tendency to economic crises caused by over-production. It should, however, be noted that, according to Engels, he was dissatisfied with this section of his book, which was still in manuscript at the time of his death, and we cannot therefore be certain that he would have approved the form the latter gave it.

Marx's treatment of this subject was later to give rise to much controversy. For his critics maintained that if capital production was capable, even theoretically, of indefinitely assuring the increase of the productive forces, his whole case was undermined and the central pillar of 'scientific socialism' had fallen. The collapse of the capitalist system would not be due to inherent contradictions within it, but to the fact that it somehow failed to work efficiently. The proletarian class struggle would cease to be the reflection of economic phenomena, and socialism to be a historic necessity. The passage from capitalism into socialism would no longer depend on the development of the productive forces, but on the realization of a new ideal of social justice – a return to utopian socialism.[1]

Nor was the controversy a wholly academic one, as the marxist analysis, albeit theoretical, had a bearing on practical issues. In the nineties Lenin found himself confronted with the economic theories of the populists, who held that capitalism was not viable in Russia, as it would be impossible to consume the goods produced on account of the poverty of the country and the fact that Russia had entered the race for markets too late to secure external outlets. This view was challenged by a group of 'legal marxists' – Struve, Bulgakov, and Tugan-Baranovsky. Struve pointed to the existence within every capitalist society of a third category, which included the professional class, which was neither capitalist nor proletarian, but acted as consumers. Bulgakov, strictly following Marx, contended that capitalism could develop on the basis of an internal market only. Tugan-Baranovsky, while so far agreeing, held none the less that Marx's treatment of the matter was incomplete and unsatisfactory. But as Lenin's concern was to show that Russia both could and must pass through the capitalist phase, he felt no inclination to contest Marx's conclusions. He therefore came out strongly on the side of Bulgakov, and refused to admit that the marxist analysis called for any modification or amendment.[2]

In 1913 Rosa Luxemburg published her *Die Akkumulation des Kapitals*, which attempted a technical re-formulation of Marx's analysis in such a way as to relate the accumulation of *industrial capital* to imperialism, which was shown to be its inevitable outcome.[3] Her thesis was attacked by Bukharin in the early twenties, but it was still permissible for marxists to

1. L Laurat, *L'Accumulation de capital d'après Rosa Luxembourg* (Paris, 1936), pp. 142 ff.

2. J. Choron, *La Doctrine bolchéviste* (Paris, 1935), pp. 71 ff.

3. An English translation appeared in 1953 with an introduction by Joan Robinson.

hold it until 1932, when it was specifically condemned by Stalin. Further, in 1914–15, Kautsky contributed to the *Neue Zeit* a series of articles in which he argued that while the attempt of capital (by which he too meant *industrial capital*) to find outlets constituted a danger, it was no more than a natural phase in the development of the capitalist system, and one which a country could control in proportion as its institutions became increasingly democratic. Such an expansion of capital was not, in his view, necessarily connected with imperialism, and could be carried out without territorial aggrandizement.

When, however, Lenin published his *Imperialism* he attacked Kautsky as a 'bourgeois reformist' who believed that the problem could be resolved within the framework of the capitalist system. But he was careful not to refer to Luxemburg. Her thesis was not relevant to his purpose, as he was approaching the problem from the quite different angle, suggested by Hobson and Hilferding, that *finance capital* represented the emergence of a new factor, as it certainly did, and that it was this that was responsible for imperialism, which is much more doubtful seeing that colonial expansion was no new phenomenon, and had, for example, largely accounted for the wars of the seventeenth and eighteenth centuries.[1] According to Lenin, however:

Imperialism is capitalism in that stage of development in which the domination of monopoly and finance capital has taken shape; in which the export of capital has acquired pronounced importance; in which the division of the world by international trusts has begun; and in which the partition of all the territory of the earth by the greatest capitalist countries has been completed.[2]

The first stage of what he calls 'industrial' or 'flourishing' capital had yielded, by reason of its inherent contradictions, to a second 'moribund' stage which had transferred power from the industrialists to the big banks and financial groups. This first stage had been one of free competition; but the second was

1. *See* Joseph A. Schumpeter, 'Zur Soziologie der Imperialismen' (*Archiv für Sozialwissenschaft und Sozialpolitik* 1919), of which there is an English translation in his *Imperialism and Social Classes* (1951).

2. *S.W.* II, p. 709.

characterized by monopoly control in the form of cartels, syndicates, and trusts. These began by dividing the world 'amicably' among themselves; but in the end they would start quarrelling, until war brought about a redistribution. Imperialism, or 'monopoly capitalism', was thus the final stage of capitalism, beyond which it could develop no further. It would therefore yield dialectically to socialism.

But how did this development affect the class struggle? Lenin argues that from the French Revolution to the Commune, capitalism was on an ascending curve, and the bourgeoisie was a progressive class as compared with the *ancien régime* which it had displaced. As this period was marked by an extension of democratic institutions and the liberation of nationalities, the proletariat, then in process of formation, was obliged to support the bourgeoisie which was, to a limited extent, fighting its battles. The period from 1871 to 1914, which George Sabine calls 'the flat top of the curve', was the age of capitalist domination and of imperialist expansion in which the class struggle became confused through the illusion that it was possible to conciliate two irreconcilable systems.[1] The first world war brought this period to an end and signalized the beginning of the fall of the curve of capitalism. The bourgeoisie had now become a decaying and reactionary force, primarily interested not in production but in consumption. Hence there could no longer be any alliance between the proletariat and the bourgeoisie, and the object of the workers must be the overthrow of international finance capital.

That an ever-growing interest was being shown in colonial development was indisputable. By 1900, Great Britain, for example, had about £1,700 million invested overseas, which yielded an annual income of at least £100 million. At first this capital had largely gone to countries like France and Belgium, with whose governments it was impossible to interfere; but by 1875 these countries were beginning to repay their loans, and as the British investor fought shy of Russia and the more backward European countries, most of the investment abroad, if we except the United States, was in undeveloped countries, and

1. *History of Political Theory* (New York, 1937), p. 732.

came increasingly to involve their control or annexation. For during the nineteenth century the attitude towards colonial possessions had changed significantly, as may be illustrated by the case of this country. Apart from the prestige ownership of them conferred, they had long been regarded rather as a burden than a benefit; and Disraeli had expressed a general opinion, when he said in 1852: 'These wretched colonies will all be independent in a few years and are a millstone round our necks.' But by the turn of the century it had become clear that Germany and America were catching up with British exports, and some anxiety was felt as to whether this country was not entering upon a period of stagnation and decline. As it was our invisible imports alone that permitted us to continue to import more than we exported, colonies came to be increasingly regarded as profitable fields of development, a view shared by the principal European countries, which now also had money to lend, and thus there began a race for such colonial markets as were still available.[1] The importance of Lenin's *Imperialism* does not lie, however, in the fact that he had pointed this out, but in the conclusions that he drew from it.

These were the following:

a. Imperialism explained the continued accumulation of capital, since the imperialist countries were able not only to sell their products to backward countries, but to obtain raw materials from them at low prices. It also accounted for the current improvement in the lot of the workers in the metropolitan countries which Marx had declared to be normally impossible under capitalism. By exploiting backward peoples, capitalism had created a new proletariat at the expense of which this improvement had been effected, though in this case it was difficult to explain why the working-class standard of living should be high in countries like Sweden and Denmark, which had no colonies, and low in France and Belgium, which owned great colonial possessions. Lenin contended, further, that the im-

1. Élie Halévy, *History of the English People* (*1895–1905*) (Pelican Books, 1939), pp. 30 ff. *See*, however, Raymond Aron, 'The Leninist Myth of Imperialism' (*Partisan Review*, November–December, 1951, pp. 646 ff.).

provement in conditions did not apply to labour as a whole, but only to one section – the 'labour aristocracy' – which had been bribed by higher wages, paid from the 'super-profits' of imperialism, into renouncing its revolutionary role in favour of collaboration with the bourgeoisie.[1]

b. Imperialism contained internal contradictions which would hasten the collapse of capitalism. It involved a struggle for markets of ever-increasing intensity, and the division of the world into exploiting and exploited countries. The change which it had introduced into the productive forces was naturally reflected in the productive relations, and had given a new form to the proletariat, which now included the 'toiling masses of the backward countries'. Hence the struggle for revolution could no longer be confined to single countries or groups of countries, but demanded a common front of the peoples of the oppressor countries and those of the oppressed. Further, every country which was an object of capitalist exploitation became *ipso facto* a suitable target for revolution irrespective of its stage of industrial development, though not necessarily for an immediate proletarian revolution.

c. Imperialism intensified the operation of the 'law of uneven development'. Under industrial capitalism, concerned with the export of commodities rather than of capital, some countries had developed more rapidly than others, but their relative strength had remained comparatively static. Under finance capitalism, however, this was no longer so, since it was possible for any country which could acquire new markets in undeveloped areas to make rapid progress at the expense of countries unable to do so. In view of this rivalry, there no longer existed any stability within the capitalist camp, and world peace was consequently endangered.

d. Imperialism must therefore lead to war. Hence marxists contend, contrary to all evidence, that both the world wars were due to imperialism in their sense of the struggle for colonial outlets, in accordance with their central thesis that every conflict must have an economic cause.

To the above Stalin added the rider, in his *Foundations of*

1. Borkenau, pp. 78 ff.

Leninism, that the First World War by creating conditions favourable to a proletarian revolution had rendered it inevitable. For Tsarist Russia was an immense reserve of western imperialism, supplying a vast field for investment which required enormous armies to guard. Russia was thus the 'nodal point' of revolution, because the contradictions of imperialism were most clearly revealed there. Further, he used the 'law of uneven development' as one of the two main arguments with which he justified the doctrine of 'socialism in one country' when he advanced it in 1924–5, since he maintained that it rendered capitalism still more assailable by creating a chain of unequally developed countries which could always be attacked at whatever might be its weakest link.[1]

Anti-imperialism henceforth became an important part of the communist programme, and was directed to broadening the basis of the proletarian class-consciousness, and at the same time to weakening the capitalist system by fomenting or supporting liberation movements on the part of backward peoples who were taught to regard themselves as victims of exploitation. For this purpose innumerable organizations were started which either appealed to humanitarian sentiment, or to the fear of the war to which it was represented that imperialism led. Further, Lenin's teaching reinforced the belief, now apparently ineradicable, that the Soviet Union would itself become the victim of imperialist aggression. The Second World War was thus represented as 'imperialist' until Hitler attacked Russia. When it ended, the Russian leaders returned to their old theme, and indeed devoted to it even more attention than before.

6. LENIN'S PHILOSOPHICAL POSITION

At the turn of the century there arose a neo-kantian school, which attacked the materialistic basis of marxism and led a number of marxists, including the Russian humanist, Nicolas Berdyaev, to break with marxism altogether. Lenin had always attached a profound importance to philosophic orthodoxy, and when he had founded his party in 1903 Plekhanov had been

1. *Leninism*, pp. 20. ff.

its ideological censor, until he went over to the mensheviks in the next year. But about this time, when he was in great need of supporters, he was joined by a group of intellectuals who had been influenced by the phenomenalist school of Ernst Mach and Richard Avenarius. Its leader was A. A. Manilovsky, better known by his pseudonym of Bogdanov, who saw that Engels's theory of knowledge would not do, and sought to replace it, though within the bounds of marxism, by one more consistent with recent developments in philosophy.

Lenin was aware that the views of Bogdanov differed from his own, but as the two were agreed on organization and tactics, he entered into a compact with him under which philosophy was to be neutral ground. In 1907, however, an 'inner party' controversy arose as to the attitude to be adopted towards the elections to the third Duma, in which Lenin held that the bolsheviks should take part, but which Bogdanov and his friends wished to boycott. In 1908 they issued a symposium of marxist philosophy which Lenin declared made him 'mad with anger', and in the same year Bogdanov, Lunacharsky, and Gorky set up a bolshevik propaganda centre at Capri. Lenin succeeded in getting the Bogdanov faction condemned; and feeling that he was now released from his compact, he published in 1909 his *Materialism and Empirio-Criticism*. Here he starts as a realist, concerned only to show that matter exists independently of mind, but then passes into materialism by going on to identify reality with matter.[1] Throughout, he attempts to bring Marx and Engels together by arguing that they were always in agreement, though wherever there is a divergence he invariably follows Engels.[2] Engels had taught that matter possessed an objective existence independently of our sense impressions, or of what Lenin calls 'sensations', of which these impressions could be relied upon to give us accurate 'images'; whereas the phenomenalists, while not denying that matter was the ultimate reality, maintained that we cannot assert the existence of any-

1. On this writing and on Lenin's general philosophical position *see* Wolfe, pp. 496 ff.; H. B. Acton, *The Illusion of the Epoch* (1955), pp. 18 ff.; Anton Pannekoek, *Lenin as a Philosopher* (New York, 1943), pp. 47 ff.; Wetter, pp. 102 ff., 124 ff., 515 ff.   2. Bochenski, p. 40.

thing beyond what we experience through the senses, as this would be to refer it to something which we have not experienced. Lenin held, however, (1) that no philosophy which did not insist upon the objective existence of matter was completely materialist; (2) that to deny its existence led to solipsism; and (3) that to regard phenomena as complexes of sensations coordinated by mind was to admit that mind entered as an active factor into knowing, and that this was to assign to it a dangerous prominence which opened a loophole to idealism, and through idealism to belief in religion and in God.[1] This work was the main contribution which Lenin made to marxist philosophy in his lifetime, as his *Philosophic Notebooks* only appeared posthumously in 1929. After the October Revolution it became, however, the standard of intellectual orthodoxy, any departure from which could be represented as being as much an act of treachery to the revolutionary movement as were divergencies on questions of party strategy and tactics.[2]

As for Bogdanov, who had originated the dispute, he withdrew from political life, and played no part in the October Revolution, though he was prominent in the Proletarian Culture movement of 1920. A doctor by profession, he interested himself in his later years in blood transfusion, and organized the Moscow Institute set up to study the matter, of which he became the Director. He died in 1928, as a result of an unsuccessful experiment performed on his own person.

1. Hook, *Towards an Understanding of Karl Marx*, pp. 61–2.
2. Laski, *The Communist Manifesto*, Introd., pp. 64–5.

16. Stalin's Contribution to Marxist–Leninist Theory

MARXISM, if it is anything, is the product of western thought; and indeed the main charge that can be brought against Marx as an international revolutionary is that he conceived of revolution too closely in terms of western conditions. The Russians took to it with enthusiasm, and it gave them the two things they most needed – confidence and discipline. Unfortunately they have always been lacking in a sense of the relative, and they thus embraced it with an uncompromising dogmatism, so that, with the passage of time, they have converted it into an ossified and inflexible code of which they now claim to be alone the true interpreters. This process was accelerated by Lenin because of the need he felt to provide a marxist justification for whatever was done in the name of the revolution. The goal of the western marxists had been a proletarian state in which men, freed from the fetters of capitalism, would learn how to organize production for the common good. The October Revolution failed to achieve this because it was only 'proletarian' in the new sense Lenin had given to the term, which identified the proletariat with the party as the vanguard of the masses and their most conscious section, with the result that the leadership of the party came to imply its domination, the more so as the country soon became involved in all sorts of difficulties. Lenin seems indeed to have struggled against this inevitable outcome, and the bitterness of his writings against Kautsky may conceal a certain uneasiness of conscience which did not trouble his successor. But the forces he had set in motion did not become immediately apparent, and the obloquy for 'betraying the revolution' has thus fallen upon Stalin, under whom marxism became grafted on to the Asiatic-Byzantine tradition, with a consequent return to autocracy – the only form of government the Russians have ever known.

What has been said of Lenin as a theoretician applies even

more to Stalin. Both were driven to give a new direction to marxist theory, and just as Lenin appealed to Marx, so Stalin was careful wherever possible to invoke the authority of Lenin, so that it was no accident that he gave the title of *Leninism* to the volume which contained his more important writings and public pronouncements. Yet there is a difference between the two men. When Lenin had been obliged, under pressure of unforeseen circumstances, to adopt policies which he would not otherwise have advocated, he had represented them as temporary accommodations, and had sheltered behind the plea of 'cruel necessity', whereas Stalin dragged these policies nakedly into the light of day, and compelled the party to accept them as orthodox applications of the official creed. Yet it is hard to say whether, had he lived, Lenin would not have been obliged to do the same. For the theory upon which the October Revolution was carried out was a compound of political idealism and political realism, and as soon as the new leaders found themselves confronted with the situation they had created, the latter was bound to prevail. But this inevitably involved a re-adjustment of the doctrinal basis. A new turn was given to the theory of revolution; the party was converted into a centralized and all-powerful bureaucracy; the classic theory of the State was reversed, though lip-service continued to be paid to it; an agrarian policy was adopted which was contrary to the teaching of Marx and Engels, and even to that of Lenin himself; and the growth of national sentiment was encouraged. The policy of 'socialism in one country' gave an added impetus to such developments. In a sense it contained nothing controversial, as everyone was agreed that socialism must be built up in Russia. Its importance lay in its implications, and particularly the effect that its application would have upon world revolution.

It was this last issue that led to the great controversy between Stalin and Trotsky, which later became extended to every aspect of stalinist policy. It was the most embittered conflict that has ever taken place between two rival party leaders, and one in which a number of the most prominent 'old guard' bolshevik leaders were to become involved to their ultimate undoing. Its history lies outside the scope of this review. It is impossible to deny the force of much of Trotsky's criticism of stalinism, and had he succeeded Lenin, his conduct of affairs would doubtless have differed in certain respects from Stalin's. Yet what the difference would have been is a matter of pure speculation. Those who contend that his regime would have been less illiberal base their opinion on the supposition that his preference for the 'open' party, which he is known to have favoured since the split in 1903, would have led him to cooperate with the mensheviks and other political groups which had supported the revolution, and point to the plea made in his *New Course* (1923) for the legalization of factions within the party and for allowing the younger generation to have a greater influence. But his theory of revolution in 1905 was certainly more radical than Lenin's; the proposals which he put forward during the period after the October Revolution when he still aspired to power were markedly authoritarian; while had he encountered serious opposition on any issue which he held fundamental, there are small grounds for believing that his imperious temperament would not have led him to crush it, and none for supposing that he would have been withheld by any humanitarian scruple. This last he was at pains to make clear. 'As for us,' he declared, 'we were never concerned with the kantian–priestly and vegetarian–quaker prattle about the sanctity of human life.'[1]

1. *Dictatorship versus Democracy* (ed. New York, 1922), p. 63.

17. The Doctrines of 'Socialism in One Country' and of 'Permanent Revolution'

THE October Revolution was followed by the three terrible years of 'War Communism', which reduced the country to destitution and culminated in the Kronstadt mutiny of January 1921. The official Russian thesis is that the sufferings of this period were due to foreign intervention and internal treachery; but the introduction of large-scale schemes of nationalization, which Lenin later admitted to have been an error, combined with the inefficiency of those responsible for carrying them out, were at least as important contributory factors. Hence, there was introduced in March 1921 the New Economic Policy (N.E.P.), a return to limited private enterprise, under which the country began to recover.

As Bernard Shaw has pointed out, the N.E.P. was, in fact, the policy of the Fabians, for which they had coined the term 'permeation', and it has been argued that had the revolution stopped there, as Bukharin and Rykov wished, it might have been possible to have set up a genuine socialist order. Yet Lenin himself had held it to be no more than a tactical retreat which necessity alone justified, and it is unlikely that the party as a whole would have long acquiesced in an economy so divergent from its principles, and one which was incompatible with the policy of building up the strength of Russia by intensified industrialization. It was therefore brought to an end in 1928–9, when Stalin went sharply into reverse with the first of his Five-year Plans and the collectivization of agriculture.

If there was one point upon which all the Russian leaders were agreed in October 1917 it was that the revolution would collapse unless supported by revolutions outside Russia. Thus, on 7 March 1918 Lenin said with reference to the Brest-Litovsk treaty: 'This is a lesson to us, because the absolute truth is that without a revolution in Germany we shall perish'; and on 23 April of the same year: 'Our backwardness has thrust us forward, and we shall perish if we are unable to hold out until we meet with the mighty support of other countries.' The reason for this belief was the conviction that the socialist and non-socialist orders could not coexist for long in the same world. 'World imperialism', said Lenin on 14 April 1919, 'cannot live side by side with a victorious soviet revolution'; and again on 27 November 1920: 'As long as capitalism and socialism remain side by side we cannot live peacefully – the one or the other will be the victor in the end.' Hence the enormous importance attached at that time to the revolutionary activity of the Comintern.

It was possible to argue in 1917 that revolutionary prospects in the west were favourable, since the later stage of the war had led to disaffection among the workers in many of the belligerent countries. In fact, however, the revolutionary wave which swept over Europe in the wake of the Russian revolution ended in a series of defeats – in Germany, Italy, Hungary, and the Baltic States; and the 5th Comintern Congress of 1924 was obliged to recognize that the tide had ebbed and that capitalism had even achieved a temporary restabilization. Yet in spite of Lenin's predictions, the Russian revolution had not been overthrown. This combination of circumstances led Stalin to advance the policy of 'socialism for one country' which was finally adopted at the 14th Party Conference on April 1925.

The main count in Trotsky's indictment of Stalin is that he gave up world revolution for 'Socialism in one country'. Yet this is not so. Stalin did not renounce world revolution. Trotsky did not reject the chance of building socialism in Russia. There were times when Stalin attempted to further revolution by method, which Trotsky denounced as reckless and adventurist. and there were times when Trotsky pressed for the building of socialism in Russia at a pace which Stalin regarded as rash and disastrous. But as the controversy widened, the two viewpoints became more and more rigidly fixed. In the stalinist scheme the establishment of socialism in Russia came first and world revolution second; in the trotskyist conception, this order was reversed.

Yet, fundamentally, the difference between the two men was

one of temperament and not of theory. Trotsky believed that Europe was 'ripe for revolution'; and from this standpoint the Russian revolution was only the prelude to a much wider upheaval, since the achievement of socialist construction in Russia alone ranked little in comparison with what might be effected by a socialist economy planned on a European scale. But Stalin never shared Trotsky's optimism as to Europe's 'ripeness' for socialism, and estimated the power of resistance in the capital order as still very formidable. To Stalin, his peculiar brand of socialism was of incomparably greater importance than the possibility of socialism in the west. He declined to regard Russia as existing on the periphery of western civilization, and was confident that she was destined to become the citadel of the new Socialist order. It was the old controversy between the Slavophils, with their belief in the specific genius of Russia, and the westerners, with their belief in what Europe has to offer, fought out on the post-revolutionary stage.[1]

Stripped of polemical distortion, the controversy over 'socialism in one country' was not whether it was possible to *build* socialism in a particular country, but whether it was possible to *complete* it, this being in turn obscured by differences of opinion as to what 'building' and 'completion' exactly meant. You could build the walls of the house, but could you put on the roof? And without the roof would it be a house at all?[2] Yet none of the disputants are quite sure of their terms. In the years after the revolution Lenin had never lost sight of the weakness of Russia and of the need for overcoming it. In his *Second International and its Place in History* (May 1919) he declared that 'the proletarian peasant soviet republic was the first stable socialist republic in the world'.[3] But in *The Tax in Kind* (April 1921) he said that he did not think that 'any communist would deny that the term 'socialist soviet republic' implies the determination of the Soviet Government to achieve the transition to

1. See *Trotsky on Stalin* (*Times Literary Supplement*, 17 July 1948, pp. 393–4); E. H. Carr, *World Revolution and Soviet Foreign Policy* (*The Listener*, 3 February 1949, p. 172).

2. Isaac Deutscher, *Stalin* (1949), pp. 281 ff.

3. *S.W.* II, p. 475.

socialism and not that the present order is a socialist order'.[1]
In his *On Cooperation* (January 1923) he argued, however, that
now that the State power was in the hands of the proletariat in
alliance with the mass of the peasantry, and that the State
owned all the means of production, 'the only task that remains
for us to perform is to organize the people into cooperative
societies'; and he concluded that 'although this is not the building of the socialist society, it is all that is necessary and sufficient for this building'.[2] But in his *Better Fewer but Better*
(March 1923) he declared that the 'worst of all assumptions' is
'that we possess to any degree the elements necessary for
building a really new state machine that would really deserve
to be called socialist, soviet, etc'.[3] Lenin's thought is thus by no
means clear. But he seems to have held that while the regime
introduced by the revolution did not yet constitute socialism, it
might be possible to achieve it provided that Russia could
catch up with the west. Yet always at the back of his mind was
the fear that she would not be given the respite necessary to do
so unless the proletarians of the west came to her rescue.

Stalin first advanced the arguments which he was later to
use in support of 'socialism in one country' in his *Foundations
of Leninism* (1924) in what he was to call two 'formulations'.
The first of these, which was based on his interpretation of
Lenin's 'law of uneven development', was that, as a result
of capitalist imperialism, any country could become ripe for
socialism regardless of the degree to which it had become industrialized. The second, which was suppressed in all subsequent editions, but which is given in full in his *Problems of
Leninism* (1926) amounted to a categorical denial that it was
possible to 'organize socialist production' and so achieve 'the
final victory of socialism' without revolutions 'in several advanced countries'.[4] But Stalin then realized that he had gone
too far, and he substituted for this formulation a second in
which he declared that 'the proletariat can and must build up
a socialist society', but that this did not mean that it could
achieve 'the complete and final victory of socialism' in the sense

1. *S.W.* II, p. 702. 2. *S.W.* II, p. 811.
3. *S.W.* II, p. 845. 4. *Leninism*, pp. 152–3.

that it would be guaranteed against the danger of counter-revolution. It was this amended formulation that he used in his *October Revolution and the Tactics of Russian Communists* (December 1924) in which for the first time he urged the adoption of the new policy. He now launched his attack on Trotsky, and selected as his target the latter's doctrine of 'permanent revolution'.

'Permanent revolution' was no new idea. The classic formulation of it is to be found in Marx's *Address to the Communist League*, where he argued that while the bourgeoisie would always want to end its revolution as soon as possible, 'it is our interest to make it permanent ... until the proletariat has conquered state power in all the dominant countries of the world'. Yet the expression is not an altogether happy one. As Carr has pointed out, Russian writers had previously used 'permanent' and 'uninterrupted' indifferently, and it was not until later that an attempt was made to distinguish between them, and to argue that Trotsky had advocated the former and Lenin the latter.[1] That revolution should be 'uninterrupted' in the sense that it should be pursued without relaxation was not, however, in dispute. But 'permanent revolution' came to acquire a quite different meaning. It implied that the various phases of the revolution passed imperceptibly from one into another, as opposed to the view that it developed in clearly defined stages, each of which was valid for a particular period. If therefore the doctrine of 'socialism in one country' signified that socialism must be built up in Russia before there could be any question of world revolution, it would have been contrary to this conception of 'permanence', and although this may not have been what Stalin meant by it, lent itself to this interpretation.

What gives an air of unreality to the controversy is that Stalin and Trotsky seem to be saying the same thing. But Trotsky had given his opponent two weapons. In a preface added in 1922 to his *The Year 1905* he had explained that the idea of 'permanent revolution' had come to him in 1905 because he had been unable to accept Lenin's theory that the proletariat should lead the revolution in alliance with the peasantry, since, if the

1. *The Bolshevik Revolution* I, p. 56n.

revolution came off, the two would soon be involved in a violent collision. Thus it could only succeed if it was accompanied by other revolutions elsewhere. Further, he had added in 1924 a postscript to his *Programme of Peace* (1917) in which he had stated that the Russians 'had not yet undertaken, or even approached, the task of creating a socialist society'; and that although certain steps forward might be taken as a result of agreements with the capitalist world, 'a genuine advance of socialist economy in Russia will become possible only after the victory of the proletariat in the most advanced countries of Europe.'

Stalin contrived to represent these statements as proof that Trotsky was opposed to the alliance between the proletariat and the peasantry upon which the whole concept of the revolution rested, which was quite untrue, because Lenin and Trotsky were in entire agreement on this matter in 1917, whatever may have been their differences in earlier years;[1] that he thus lacked faith in the power of the dictatorship of the proletariat to save Russia, and looked to external revolutions as the only hope of pulling the chestnuts out of the fire, and that he held the doctrine (which was now imputed to the mensheviks) that it was useless to attempt a revolution in any country unless there was a reasonable chance that it would be supported by other revolutions. And in giving this turn to Trotsky's ideas he judged wisely. For, while many of the leaders were suspicious of what 'socialism in one country' might involve, the doctrine came to the masses as a profound relief. They had been taught that unless world revolution occurred their own revolution would fail and conditions of civil war would return. What Stalin asserted amounted to the admission that the Soviet Union was now strong enough to stand on its own feet whatever the outside world might decide to do. Further, it did something to soften the asperities of international relations by suggesting that 'socialism was not for export' – to use a phrase which he was later to employ.

In his *Problems of Leninism* (1926) Stalin discussed the formulation he had earlier discarded. He explained that it had

1. cp. Chamberlin I, p. 157.

been of use at the time, but that he had abandoned it because it had confused two issues which were quite separate – 'the possibility of building up socialism by the efforts of one country', and the question whether any single country would consider itself 'fully guaranteed against counter-revolution without a victorious revolution in a number of other countries'.[1] The answer to the first question was 'Yes', and to the second 'No'. And thus matters stood when, in 1938, a young instructor in the Kursk region, Ivanov, fell foul of his regional secretary and wrote to Stalin asking him to adjudicate between them. He explained that, according to his understanding, 'socialism in one country' involved a two-fold conception – internal and external. He had taught that the first of these had now triumphed, so that, as far as Russia was concerned, it was true to say that 'socialism in one country' had been achieved; but that the second, which was 'the final victory', was only capable of accomplishment on the international scale. But his superior had declared that 'we now have the final victory of socialism and complete security from intervention and the restoration of capitalism'; and Ivanov had been dismissed as a Trotskyist, which was 'a great insult and injury'.

Stalin's reply, of which eight and a half million copies were published in forty-seven languages, was a complete vindication of Ivanov, whose superior was called 'a conceited young official'.[2] He pointed out that the building of socialism in one country was not only possible but had been achieved, despite the protests of Trotsky, Zinoviev, Kamenev, and others 'who afterwards became the agents of fascism', and who had used the doctrine of 'permanent revolution' to conceal their counter-revolutionary designs. On the other hand, the victory of socialism was not yet complete, nor could it be as long as Russia was surrounded by hostile capitalist States. Hence it was necessary to combine the activity of the international proletariat with the rearmament of the Soviet Union. This has since remained the official doctrine, nor was it seriously modified by

1. *Leninism*, p. 151.
2. For the text *see The Strategy and Tactics of World Communism; Supplement I* (Washington, 1948), pp. 148 ff.

Stalin's statement in September 1946 to the *Sunday Times* correspondent, Alexander Werth, in which, while refusing to grant that the capitalist world might not have designs on the Soviet Union, he admitted the possibility of the co-existence of the two world camps, and went on to advance the doctrine that it was possible to achieve 'communism in one country'.

On more than one subsequent occasion Stalin made similar statements. Yet they failed to inspire conviction, as they were belied by his aggressive and uncompromising policy, and by the stream of vituperation directed by official Soviet propaganda against the west. In part they were intended to confuse public opinion, and in part they were motivated by the belief that the Soviet Union needed time in which to build up its strength. In any case, such co-existence as was envisaged was of a purely passive character, and was no more than the recognition of what was the actual situation. It was left to the Yugoslavs after Stalin's death to advance an active theory of co-existence based upon friendly collaboration alike with the communist and the non-communist blocs, though as they wished to be independent of both, and had nothing to gain by the victory of either, their version of co-existence was as much inspired by tactical considerations as that of Stalin. Nor is it easy to reconcile it with the revolutionary dialectic of history, at least as this was understood by Lenin, which denies the possibility of permanent co-existence between two mutually antagonistic systems, and assumes an eventual conflict from which the 'progressive' Soviet Union must emerge victorious. Whether this conflict is precipitated by the imperialist powers attacking Russia, as the doctrine of capitalist encirclement asserts, or by these powers devouring one another, as Stalin in his *Economic Problems of Socialism in the U.S.S.R.* held to be more probable, is irrelevant in this connexion.

18. The Effect of 'Socialism in One Country' upon Marxist Theory

WE have now to see how the above doctrine, in the form in which Stalin applied it, affected certain aspects of marxist theory.

1. WORLD REVOLUTION

After 1921 Russia was obliged to pursue a dual policy. On the one hand, her internal reconstruction necessitated agreements with capitalist countries, while on the other, she was committed, as the leading member of the Comintern, to seeking to overthrow their governments. As long as Lenin lived, he contrived to hold the balance. But in the spring of 1923 ill-health compelled him to retire from active control, and in January 1924 he died. His mantle fell on Zinoviev and Kamenev, both of whom had opposed the October Revolution; and as they wanted a practical organizer they brought in Stalin as the third member of the *Troika*.

In 1923 Trotsky, who, as a newcomer into the party, was not regarded by the bolshevik leaders of the first rank as quite one of themselves, came out in opposition, contending that the country was being run by men whose records, as the opponents of the revolution, were sufficient to account for the failure of the revolution in Germany and elsewhere. For this he was deprived of his post as Commissar for War in 1925; but in 1927 he returned to the attack, in which he was now supported by other party leaders, and challenged Stalin's foreign policy on the ground that he had substituted for marxism the 'petty-bourgeois doctrine' of 'socialism in one country'.

There is no reason at all to believe that Trotsky would have been any more successful than Stalin in bringing about revolution; for the plain fact was that no western European country wanted one, as was shown when the Germans (who were the most likely to have done so) in the first post-war election returned a moderate Social Democratic government by an over-whelming majority. Nor was Trotsky justified, as we have seen, in accusing Stalin of abandoning the cause of world revolution. Yet Stalin's policy undoubtedly affected it. Up to 1924 the Russian Communist Party played an important but not a dominant role within the Comintern. From 1924 to 1929 Comintern policy reflected a series of 'inner-party' controversies, first against Trotsky, then against Zinoviev and Kamenev, and then against Bukharin and Rykov. The 6th Congress of 1928 was the last at which any variety of opinion was permitted. In 1929 Stalin's nominees, Molotov, Manuilsky, and Kuusinen, assumed control of the Comintern apparatus, and its policy was henceforth dictated by Russian interests, on the advancement of which it could be represented, not altogether without reason, that the future of world revolution depended. Public discussion played no part in the formulation of the policy of the 7th and last Congress of 1935, which was called to explain and publicize a change of policy which had already been decided by Moscow, and in certain cases put into operation. Revolutionary move-ments in foreign countries were staged or called off in accord-ance with whether they furthered Soviet policy, and with little regard to the fate of those responsible for them; while almost the whole generation of 'old revolutionaries' was summoned to Moscow and liquidated when Stalin, faced with the growing power of Germany, decided in 1935 to call a halt to revolution in favour of the policy of the Popular Front.

The line of the 20th Congress was maintained until the sign-ing of the Stalin–Hitler Pact of August 1939, when the Com-intern abandoned its anti-fascist crusade, so that the war, when it came, was declared to be an imperialist one. Hitler's attack on the Soviet Union changed the situation by bringing Russia into alliance with the western democracies. Hence the Com-intern, in which Stalin had never reposed any great confidence, became increasingly an embarrassment, and in June 1943 it was formally dissolved by a decree which stated that it had fulfilled its purpose by bringing into existence a world prole-tarian movement which had now come of age. The decree made no mention of the revolutionary policy the Comintern had been formed to promote, which remains unchanged; while the abolition of a central organization which determined what was, at least in theory, a common policy, left the Soviet Union more free than ever to prescribe the line which any particular communist party was to follow.

2. THE STATE

It must always be remembered that in Russia industrialization followed the revolution, instead of preceding it as Marx had said that it should do. Marx had early recognized that it was the factory worker – the real proletarian living in a congested urban area – who was likely to be most receptive to socialist ideas and amenable to organization, and he had seen in the factory an important formative influence. Lenin agreed with this. Industrialization was necessary if Russia was to sustain the revolution. But it also offered the collateral advantage of creating a proletariat which would actively support the regime; and thus, when he launched his scheme of developing electric power, he used the slogan 'communism is soviet power plus the electrification of the whole country'. The French historian of the revolution, Henri Rollin, is perfectly right in saying that one important reason for industrialization was to counter the native hostility of the Russians to any form of organized control.[1]

Stalin carried Lenin's idea a stage further. 'Socialism in one country' was a long-term policy of building up the resources of Russia so that she would eventually be strong enough to direct world revolution instead of being dependent upon it. But to carry out such a policy it would be necessary greatly to accelerate the pace at which industrialization was proceeding; and this, in turn, would call for a tightening of government control (to be represented to the masses as the essence of socialism), and thus for an intensification of the power of the State.

Hence a revaluation of the classic theory of the State became necessary. Both Marx and Lenin had taught that it would still persist during the transition from capitalism to socialism, but they had regarded it as a temporary phenomenon, and the only

1. *La Révolution russe* (Paris, 1931) I, p. 202.

question was how long it would be necessary to endure it. In the years immediately preceding the 16th Congress of 1930, Bukharin had been the leader of a group which held not only that the State should 'wither away', but that the Russian workers should be taught to regard all States, including their own, as evil. But when he introduced the new Constitution in 1936, Stalin attacked this thesis, insisting that the Soviet State was of a special type which neither Marx, Engels, nor Lenin had foreseen. The earlier conception remained valid for the non-communist world, but was inapplicable to a State which was no longer the servant of a particular section of society, but of society as a whole, protecting it from capitalist encirclement, and guiding it into the 'higher phase' of communism.[1] Hence the assurance that he gave that the 'victory of socialism' within the Soviet Union had been won did not lead to any relaxation even of the internal powers of the State, nor indeed could it do so if he was to succeed in his objective, and build up Russia within the shortest possible time into a great industrial country. For as soon as the first Five-year Plan was introduced, the need for increased labour discipline became apparent, and was met by such measures as the decree of the Council of People's Commissars of 7 March 1929 and the circular issued by the Commissariat for Justice on 17 March following.[2]

The necessity for the continued existence of the State has not, however, been fully apparent even to party members. At the 16th Congress of June 1930, Stalin was driven to explain that, according to the dialectic, it cannot 'wither away' until its power has first been developed to the uttermost.

We are, [he said,] for the withering away of the state. And yet we also believe in the proletarian dictatorship, which represents the strongest and mightiest form of state power that has existed up to now. To keep on developing state power in order to prepare the conditions *for* the withering away of state power – that is the marxist formula. Is it 'contradictory'? Yes 'contradictory'. But the contradiction is vital, and wholly reflects the marxist dialectic. ... Whoever has not understood this feature of the contradictions be-

1. Aspaturian, op. cit. pp. 1032–3, 1047n.   2. Rollin II, pp. 245–6.

longing to our transitional time, whoever has not understood this dialectic of historical processes, that person is dead to marxism.[1]

Again, at the 17th Congress of 1934, Stalin dealt with the problem of building a classless socialist society and said that this could only be achieved by strengthening the organs of the dictatorship of the proletariat. He pointed out that this 'elementary thesis of leninism had given rise to not a little confusion among a section of party members' who had argued that, as the country was advancing towards a classless economy, it should be possible 'to relax the dictatorship of the proletariat and get rid of the State altogether as it is fated to die out in any case'.[2] This opinion he condemned. Yet it persisted; and at the 18th Congress of 1939 he was obliged to devote a whole section of his report to the question as to why the State should continue, if, as he maintained, 'the exploiting classes have been abolished and there are no more bourgeois classes'. But now he said that when Engels spoke of the 'withering away of the state', it was on the assumption 'that socialism had already been victorious in all countries or the majority of them'; and that as long as Russia was surrounded by hostile countries, the State would not only have to continue but be made stronger. The upshot of the matter was, therefore, that the State would continue until 'capitalist encirclement is liquidated and the danger of foreign military attack has disappeared'; and this would be so even if Russia passed from the socialist to the communist stage, as he pointed out that she was in the process of doing. It was upon this occasion that we warned his hearers not to look to the classic marxist writings for 'ready-made solutions' of their problems, or suppose that they understood 'the essence of marxism' because they had learnt 'by rote' a few of its general tenets.[3]

The above ideological changes were reflected in the Constitution of 3 December 1936; and a comparison between this and the Leninist constitution of 1923, based upon the 'Declaration of Rights of the Toiling and Exploited People' of January 1918, reveals some significant divergencies. Lenin's constitution

1. Shirokov, p. 304.   2. *Leninism*, p. 518.
3. *Leninism*, pp. 656 ff.

was an attempt to apply marxist principles. The conception of
the State disappeared as a bourgeois invention, and was replaced by the soviets, that is, the workers organized in groups.
For the equally bourgeois conception of the citizen there was
substituted the worker, and only proletarians, peasants, and
soldiers were accorded political rights. The whole machinery
of parliamentary representative government was superseded by
the pyramidal structure of the soviets.

On the other hand, the stalinist constitution brought back
the State and re-affirmed its sovereign powers. It returned to
the conception of the citizen, and conferred political rights
upon every inhabitant of the Soviet Union without respect of
nationality. It set up a bi-cameral parliament on the nineteenth-
century model, the members of which were to be elected by
universal suffrage and secret ballot, and to be subject to the
right of recall by those who had appointed them. It was, in fact,
such a constitution as the mensheviks might well have sponsored, and the only matter for surprise is that the term 'soviet'
should have been applied to it, since its effect was to deprive
the soviets of the constitutional position which they originally
held, at least in theory.

3. THE DICTATORSHIP OF THE PROLETARIAT AND THE ROLE OF THE PARTY

We have seen that in his *Foundations of Leninism* (1924) and
Problems of Leninism (1926) Stalin stated that 'the fundamental
thing in leninism is the dictatorship of the proletariat' of which
the party is 'the main guiding force', but that he insisted that
the two were not identical. He pointed out that Lenin had laid
down that the dictatorship 'has to be realized through the
soviet apparatus', but that 'Lenin never said that the party is
the state power'. When, however, Stalin introduced the 1936
Constitution, he attributed the 'victory of socialism' within the
Soviet Union to the elimination of the capitalists as a class. But
if there were no more capitalists, there could no longer be a
proletariat, seeing that by definition the latter was the class
which the former exploited, and in this event it was impermis-

sible to speak of its dictatorship. For this there was therefore substituted the 'dictatorship of the workers', that is, of the new class into which, according to Stalin, the proletariat had now been transformed. Yet the change had no practical significance, as the dictatorship of the proletariat had never been more than a cant phrase used to conceal the dictatorship of the party, the soviets providing the formal structure behind which it bore rule.[1]

Further, this party, as Ruth Fischer has pointed out, has never become a workers' mass party of the western type. Stalin clung tenaciously to the leninist conception of the 'narrow' party. But while there was some justification for this when its primary role was to prepare the way for revolution, or even during the difficult years of 'War Communism', such a party was none the less undemocratic, and it was against it, as the main instrument of Stalin's domination, that criticism was most sharply directed. At the 14th Congress of December 1925, when the party membership was just over a million, the opposition proposed the cooption of 90 per cent of the industrial workers, then numbering about seven millions, with the object of breaking the bolshevik *élite* and of checking the growing tendency to *embourgeoisement*. The demand was not conceded, and Stalin characterized it as 'idiotic'.[2]

And not only did the party remain 'narrow', but the character of its membership changed.[3] At the 14th Congress of 1925 56·8 per cent of the delegates were classified as workers. At the 17th Congress of 1934, 'workers from production', that is actual as opposed to former workers, had fallen to 9·3 per cent. At the 18th Congress of 1939 these percentages were for the first time not given, the reason being that the new statutes adopted by that congress omitted those clauses which had been originally introduced to safeguard the proletarian character of the Party. Further, the 17th Congress laid down that the Central Committee should be elected not less than once every

1. *Leninism*, pp. 565–6.

2. *Stalin and German Communism* (1948), pp. 482–3.

3. *See* Merle Fainsod, *How Russia is Ruled* (Harvard University Press, 1954), pp. 209–39.

three years, which meant at least triennial congresses. But the 18th Congress did not meet until 1939, and the summoning of the 19th Congress was deferred until 1952. In the interval between congresses party conferences were to be held annually, but after 1934 none was held until 1941, nor have there been any since. The result has been to give unlimited power to the central party organs, of which the Politburo (after the 19th Congress, the Presidium) and the Secretariat are the most important. Thus the tendency, at least from the thirties, has been to make the party less proletarian and less democratic, and to convert it into a centralized bureaucracy – the form of government to which Lenin had been most opposed, though he had been more than anyone responsible for creating it.[1]

The 19th Congress, announced without warning in *Pravda* of 20 August 1952, met on the following 5 October. The main report was delivered by G. M. Malenkov, who thus seemed clearly marked out for the succession. Stalin kept himself in the background, and only pronounced a brief valedictory address. He had, however, already stolen the thunder with his *Economic Problems of Socialism in the U.S.S.R.*, issued just before the Congress met. Its blunt reminder of the existence of economic laws operating 'independently of the will of men', to which even Soviet planners must conform, was doubtless intended to convey a warning to the general public that although the 'construction of communism' would be achieved in the not too distant future, too much was not to be expected in the immediate present. To the preconditions for effecting the transition into communism, which had hitherto been defined as an immense increase in productivity to be brought about by a more advanced technology. Stalin now added the nationalization of the collective farms (*kolkhozy*), which would remove the existing anomaly under which the land and the machines belong to the State, but the produce to the kolkhozy themselves.

The Congress changed the title of the party from the 'All-Union Communist Party (Bolsheviks)' to the 'Communist Party

1. Max Eastman, *Stalin's Russia and the Crisis of Socialism* (1940).

of the Soviet Union', Nitika Khrushchev explaining that its double definition as 'communist' and 'bolshevik' had been originally adopted to distinguish the bolsheviks from the mensheviks, and that with the disappearance of the latter the tautology had lost its meaning. Article 1 of the new statutes redefined the party. It was no longer 'the organized vanguard of the working class and the highest form of their class association', but a ' voluntary association of like-minded communists' which included workers, peasants, and members of the intelligentsia. The term 'dictatorship of the workers' was replaced by 'the socialist order', thus signifying that the party's objective was no longer to struggle to establish a dictatorship, but to consolidate the socialist economy, and so prepare the way for the transition into communism. The articles in the earlier statutes defining the rights of members were left unchanged, but those dealing with their duties were so drafted as to emphasize that the Party was not a 'mass party' but a 'cadre party', that is, a party of fighters for the realization of the ultimate goal of a communist society.

Some important organizational changes were made. The Politburo of 11 full and 4 candidate members was replaced by a Presidium of 25 full members and 11 candidates. No reason was given for this, Khrushchev merely remarking that the Presidium 'corresponded better to the functions hitherto carried out by the Politburo'. The Secretariat was increased from 5 members to 10. The Orgburo, which had for some time ceased to function, was abolished. The Central Committee was increased from 139 (71 full members and 68 candidates) to 236 (125 full members and 111 candidates). Immediately after the death of Stalin [1953] the Presidium was reduced to 10 full members and 4 candidates, and the Secretariat returned to its earlier complement of 5 members. No change was made in the membership of the Central Committee.[1] The 20th Congress

1. On the Congress see Merle Fainsod, *How Russia is Ruled* (Harvard University Press, 1954), pp. 186–9; Boris Meissner, *Die Kommunistische Partei der Sowjetunion vor und nach dem Tode Stalins* (Frankfurt a/M, 1954), pp. 7 ff.; Philip Moseley, 'The Nineteenth Party Congress' (*Foreign Affairs*, January, 1955), pp. 23 ff.

[1956] re-elected the existing Presidium, and raised the number of the candidate members to 6. Membership of the Central Committee was slightly increased.

4. THE BOLSHEVIZATION OF NATIONAL COMMUNIST PARTIES

Having established the predominance of the party within Russia itself, Stalin next subordinated to it every national communist party. In an article published in 1924 in *Bolshevik* he announced that 'the process of crystallization of the true bolshevik parties of the west, which constitutes the basis of the future revolution, has begun'. We may perhaps date this process from a resolution of the Executive Committee of the Comintern of 21 January 1924 (significantly the date of Lenin's death) that 'the centre of gravity of political organization be transferred to the cell [i.e. branch]. It is this that will put the worker in the way to the revolutionary solution of all questions.' The new organization was approved by the 5th Comintern Congress of June 1924. Article 5 of the Statutes of that year laid down that 'the basic party organization (its unit) is the cell at the place of employment (factory, mine, workshop, etc.) to which the member of the Party employed in the given enterprise must be attached'; and the same provision was included in the final Constitution of 1928.

Up to that time communist parties had been organized, like others, on the regional basis of the ward, commune, etc.; and the workers were jealous of their right to hold their local meetings at which they discussed political and organizational issues and elected their own leaders. In their view, it was for them to lay down the policy and for the central organs to carry it out. These democratic notions were dispelled, as it was intended that they should be, by the decision to make the factory cell the basis. The official justification was the primary role that the factories would play in the day of revolution, for as the German leader Walter Ulbricht, who made his career out of the cell (his *nome de plume* was *Zelle*), put it: 'One worker in a big plant is worth ten barbers.' In fact, however, the factory cell depended for its efficiency on its leader, and when the cell was limited to groups of fifteen to twenty men, such persons were seldom forthcoming. Again, the outlook of the members tended to be parochial, and to be limited by their particular grievances. Moreover, meetings were difficult to arrange, as the workers often worked at long distances from their homes, to which they hastened to return as soon as their day's work was done. And finally, the cells offered an easy target to the employers, so that communists who would have welcomed participation in district groups were loath to join them. The non-industrial worker was virtually excluded, since although he was allowed to join a street cell, such cells possessed a lower status. The reorganization was thus bitterly resented, and led to the loss of many valued militants. Nor did it bring about a closer relation with the masses, but rather the contrary.

Yet these disadvantages counted for nothing in the eyes of Moscow. The object of the reorganization was to weaken the power of the rank-and-file in favour of that of the central party organs, and this was achieved. The lower bodies lost the right to choose their leaders, who were now appointed by the higher party organs, while the members of the Central Committee and Politburo were the nominees of Moscow. Thus, as in the Soviet Union, the party apparatus became increasingly hierarchical and bureaucratic, and was made up of paid officials whose jobs depended upon a strict observance of the party line.

5. THE COLLECTIVIZATION OF AGRICULTURE

In his *Eighteenth Brumaire* (1852) Marx argues that Napoleon's land reforms had freed the peasants from feudal exactions but only to subject them to the worse oppression of the usurious bourgeoisie with whom they had therefore no longer a common interest so that they now 'find their natural ally and leader in the urban proletariat, whose task is the overthrow of the bourgeois order'. Again, when discussing with Engels the prospect of a revolution in Germany he says that 'the whole thing will depend on covering the rear of the proletarian revolution by a second edition of the Peasants War', his reference being to the *Beurnkrieg* of 1525.[1] Yet despite the above, neither he nor Engels developed, as Lenin was to do, the theory of alliance between the proletariat and the peasantry in the revolution, as their normal attitude towards peasants was one of contempt and distrust. Engels had once described them in a letter as 'the barbarians of civilization', a phrase which caught Marx's fancy, and which he uses in his *Class Struggles in France* (1850). In his *Eighteenth Brumaire* he explains that they form a class in so far as their economic life, interests and culture are distinct from and antagonistic to those of the bourgeoisie and the proletariat, but that they lack the unity of a class and are rather an agglomeration of individuals, which he compares to a sack of potatoes. In Russia, however, they could not be disregarded, as they accounted for 90 per cent of the population, and no revolution could hope for success without their support. Marx had held their mentality to be essentially bourgeois-capitalist. In *The Agrarian Programme of Russian Social Democracy* (1902) Lenin, however, drew a sharp distinction between the 'working class' which he extended to include hired agricultural labourers, and the peasantry proper, by which he meant the small landowners. These last constituted a reactionary class, but their development, through the abolition of feudal survivals, had to be encouraged as it would create an agricultural proletariat which would eventually destroy them. But it was in his *Agrarian Question* (1908) that he made his classic analysis of the peasantry by dividing them into the rich peasants (*kulaks*) who employed hired labour, the poor peasants or agricultural labourers who owned no land and were 'semi-proletarians', and an intermediate class of middle peasants who farmed their own small holdings, but did not normally employ labour or have any surplus produce to sell.[2] This last group was steadily diminishing, a number working their way up into the kulak class, but many more being thrust down into the poor peasantry. Lenin therefore concluded that the poor peasantry at least had a common interest with the proletariat in the revo-

1. Letter of 16 April 1856, *Correspondence*, p. 87.
2. David Mitrany, *Marx against the Peasant* (1952), p. 61.

lution, and set up that alliance between them upon which the October Revolution was carried out and maintained.

Yet Lenin never believed that the peasantry was the equal of the proletariat, and it was in strict accordance with this view that the final statutes of the Comintern of 1928, based upon Stalin's analysis in *Problems of Leninism* of the 'special form of alliance' existing between the two classes, laid down that while the proletariat should enter into an alliance with the peasantry, it must never share its power with them, since 'the dictatorship of the proletariat implies that the industrial workers alone are capable of leading the entire mass of the toilers'.[1] Behind his teaching were two convictions; first, that it was the task of the proletariat to win the confidence of the peasants with the ultimate object of converting them to large-scale collective agriculture; but secondly, that this must be a gradual process, and that the peasants were not to be coerced. In this he followed Engels, who had declared that the collectivization of the peasants would be the work of generations. Such was the essence of what came to be called 'Lenin's Cooperative Plan'.

The policy of collectivization on which Stalin embarked in April 1929, in spite of considerable opposition within the Politburo, and which ended with the expropriation of the kulaks, is thus a clear departure from Lenin's teaching. Once again it followed from the application of the policy of 'socialism in one country'. The intensification of industry had brought into being a large proletarian class which had to be fed. But this proletariat was producing goods for export, in order to enable the machinery required to carry out the Five-year Plan to be purchased. Hence, there was (and still is) an extreme shortage of consumer goods, and a consequent reluctance on the part of the peasants to sell their produce for money with which they could buy nothing. Stalin got his way and forced the peasants into collective farming. But the ruthless measures adopted by the party to carry out his policy were a landmark in its degeneration.

A similar policy is being gradually carried out in the satellite countries. The first step has been to break up the large estates

1. *S.W.* II, pp. 732, 791.

– a long overdue measure of social justice with which the left-wing parties have always been in agreement – and to distribute the land to the peasants in dwarf holdings generally not exceeding fifty hectares and often much smaller. For the first two years after the war the communists did not seek to go further than this; and, indeed, in Hungary they were so anxious to allay the peasants' suspicion that they were going to be forced into collective farms (*kolkhozy*) that they even broke up model farms and sugar-beet plantations which it would have been economically sounder to have preserved as units, possibly under State management. In fact, one of the charges brought against the Yugoslav Communist Party in the Cominform *communiqué* of 28 June 1948 was that its policy of 'liquidating capitalist elements' was 'adventurist and non-marxist', since conditions for the large-scale collectivization of agriculture do not exist 'as long as the majority of the working peasantry is not convinced of the advantages of collective farming', though it can scarcely be said that Stalin had allowed himself to be influenced by these considerations in earlier years.

Nor was it the policy which the communists pursued in the satellite states as soon as they were in control. That policy, broadly speaking the same as has been adopted in the Soviet Union itself and in China, has been determined by three considerations. First, all these areas suffer from chronic rural over-population, for which the obvious remedy is industrialization which will drain the surplus manpower off the land into the factories. In so far as the rapid industrialization of the satellites was inspired by this motive, and not, as it certainly also was, by the desire to use them to produce goods for Russia, it was a sound policy, though it was not accompanied, as it should have been by a proper regard for the welfare of agriculture, with the result that the economies of the countries concerned became seriously unbalanced. Secondly, if large numbers of persons who have hitherto gained a living from the soil are drafted into industry, increased agricultural production becomes imperative. But here communist thinking was dominated by the view, which Marx and Engels had held strongly, that peasant farming was inefficient, and that the future lay with large-scale agriculture in the form of collective or State farms.[1] This assumed, however, that agriculture lent itself equally with industry to centralized planning, which it does not, as the Russian leaders, after more than a quarter of a century of 'socialist farming', have been obliged recently to acknowledge; and, further, that the peasants will acquiesce in the loss of their land and make a success of a system which experience has shown they bitterly resent. Thirdly, and perhaps most important of all, there is the ideological factor. Peasants are strongly individualistic, and thus unamenable to communist influence. Hence they must be liquidated by giving them uneconomic holdings, and then forcing them, under pressure of starvation, to join collective farms. As the peasants then retaliate by producing less than they did before, this policy defeats its purpose, and communist governments find themselves confronted with recurrent agricultural crises which compel them to make such temporary concessions to peasant initiative as it is hoped will stimulate production. None the less, they have not abandoned collectivization as their ultimate goal, nor can they do so as long as they hold their present political and economic doctrines. What holds them back is their inability to produce the machinery which collectivized agriculture requires, and the fact that experience has taught them that if they press the peasants too hard it will have an unfavourable reaction upon industry. The only hope of making the system work is to pay the peasants appropriate prices for the produce taken over from them, and to make available consumer goods for them to buy with their money.

6. EQUALITARIANISM

Neither Marx nor Engels were equalitarians, and the most complete expression of their views on the matter are to be found in the latter's *Anti-Dühring*. Here Engels shows that every stage of human development had been accompanied by a demand for the removal of inequalities; and that when the bourgeoisie raised this cry against feudalism the proletariat

1. Mitrany, op. cit. p. 27.

joined in, though, while the bourgeoisie demanded only the abolition of class privilege, the proletariat, with its deeper vision, demanded the abolition of *classes themselves*. It is in this that lies 'the real content of the proletarian demand for equality ... and any demand which goes beyond that passes into absurdity'.[1]

None the less, in his *Civil War in France*, Marx had commended the decision of the Commune that 'public service should be done at workmen's wages', and both in his *April Theses* and in *The State and Revolution* Lenin laid down the principle of the 'maximum income', that is, that no State official should receive higher remuneration than 'the average wage of a competent worker'. This was one of the fundamental principles whereby he sought to prevent the dictatorship of the proletariat from degenerating into that bureaucracy which he so much feared, the other two being the unification of the legislative and executive, and the right of recall which enabled the electorate at any time to remove any official from his post. Indeed, as Koestler has pointed out, equalitarianism was taken so literally in the first revolutionary period that, during the Civil War, Lenin himself had to insist upon certain modifications.[2] None the less, the 'maximum income' (about 400 roubles) remained in force for party members, and N.E.P. men and non-party specialists who earned more were regarded with contempt. During the first Five-year Plan, contrasts in earnings became more marked, until the radical change came with Stalin's six-point speech of 25 June 1931, in which he said that *uravnilovka*, or equality in wages, was to cease once and for all, as it was 'alien and detrimental to Socialist production'. Equalitarianism was declared 'a petty-bourgeois deviation' and a crime against the State; and the new doctrine was proclaimed with such force that the masses were eventually persuaded that inequality of wages was a fundamental socialist principle.[3]

1. *Anti-Dühring*, pp. 119 ff.; cp. Engels to Bebel, 8 March 1875, *Correspondence*, p. 337.

2. *The Yogi and the Commissar* (1945), pp. 159–60.

3. *Leninism*, pp. 371–3; cp. I. Deutscher, *Soviet Trade Unions* (1950), pp. 103 ff.

In his Report to the 17th Congress of 1934 Stalin denounced equalitarianism in the name of Engels. It had, he said, nothing to do with marxism or leninism. 'By equality marxism means not the equalization of individual requirements and individual lives, but the abolition of classes', that is, emancipation from exploitation and the State control of production. Under socialism men would be paid according to their work, and only under communism would it be possible to give every man according to his needs. He appealed equally to the authority of Lenin, who had declared that 'equality is an empty phrase unless by equality is meant the abolition of classes'.[1]

The general teaching of Marx, Engels, and Lenin is thus consistent enough. They recognized that men had not been created equal, and in the *Communist Manifesto* one of the charges brought against the utopian socialists was that they preached 'universal asceticism and social levelling in the crudest form'. Yet Lenin so far recognized equality to be a part of the socialist dispensation as to have applied what was virtually the principle of equal pay to all engaged in State administration; and it can scarcely be supposed that Marx and Engels would have agreed that under socialism inequalities of remuneration should become even more glaring than under capitalism. Yet Max Eastman was able to show in 1937 that the gulf between the remuneration of the lowest-paid labour and that of the highest-paid executives was far greater in the Soviet Union than in the United States.[2] Stalin, indeed, maintained that when the transition to communism has been effected men will be paid according to their needs; but this offers no guarantee of equality, seeing that it will be for the State to determine what these needs are.

7. NATIONALISM

If the *Communist Manifesto* is not a genuinely international appeal, it is difficult to know how to describe it. This did not mean that Marx and Engels were free from these prejudices which were common to Germans of their time, and of which

1. *Leninism*, pp. 521–2.
2. *The End of Socialism in Russia* (1937), p. 22.

the most pronounced was a contempt for the Slavs. That Bakunin, once so enthusiastic about everything German, should have taken up with the idea of forming a Slavonic Federation was beyond their understanding; and when he abandoned the project after the Polish insurrection of 1863, they did not conceal their relief. Yet such national preferences are not to be taken too seriously, since both men were primarily concerned with the grand strategy of revolution and with determining the 'historic role' which particular countries were destined to play in it.

Up to 1914 Lenin had been almost entirely concerned with directing the revolutionary movement in Russia, and he had cut no figure in international circles, where he was regarded as an unimportant but potentially dangerous fanatic. But he had spent the most formative years of his life abroad, he spoke the principal European languages and he was international to the core. It is difficult to find in his writings any trace of national bias. Russia had, indeed, taken the lead in carrying out a revolution; but this was due to the fact that she had proved 'the weakest link in the capitalist chain' rather than to any inherent superiority; and it was greatly to be hoped that the nations of the west, by following her example, would enable her to profit by their more advanced cultures. His advocacy of revolution was not even remotely connected in his mind with the territorial aggrandizement of Russia. Indeed, he thought of Russia as a weak and backward country which would be fortunate enough if she maintained her existing frontiers.

But Stalin's policy of 'socialism in one country' was intended from the first to make Russia the spearhead of world revolution, and the more it prospered the more did it become inevitably fused with the extension of Russian interests, particularly after Stalin became convinced that Germany would sooner or later attack Russia with the encouragement, or at least the connivance, of the capitalist powers. As late as the 17th Congress of January 1934 Stalin had, indeed, condemned as 'a departure from leninist internationalism' any deviation towards nationalism 'irrespective of whether the deviation is towards local nationalism or towards Great-Russian nationalism'.[1] But from the 7th Comintern Congress onwards there began to take place a marked revival of nationalism. As W. N. Ewer puts it, soviet power became not simply a means to a revolutionary end, but an end in itself; and soviet power was very much the same as 'Russian power', so that the 'Soviet State' and the 'Soviet Idea' – nationalism and communism – merged to form an ardently nationalistic communism. The heroes of Tsarist Russia – Peter the Great, and even Ivan the Terrible – became heroes of the Soviet Union; while Tsarist generals like Suvorov and Kutusov found high places in rewritten histories.[2]

It was easy enough for Stalin to effect this transformation, since he had never left Russia, save for occasional conferences. He had no spiritual contact with the west, and had always viewed every problem through Russian eyes. In his broadcast on V-J day in 1945 he declared:

The defeat of the Russian troops in 1904 left a grave imprint on the minds of our people. It was a black stain in the history of our country. Our people were confident and awaited the day when Japan would be routed and this dark blot be wiped out. We men of the older generation have awaited this day for forty years, and now it has come.

As Ewer observes, no bolshevik would have spoken like this in 1917, seeing that the party had always referred to the Japanese victory with approval because it had weakened Tsarism; but by 1945 there seemed nothing unnatural about it.

But while national sentiment, encouraged from the middle-thirties, was given a free rein during the war, the alliances entered into with capitalist allied states from 1941 were regarded as tactical only; and thus, soon after the war was over, there was a return to the traditional attitude of hostility, which is now the deeper as the Soviet Union combines the function of being the prime mover in the international communist movement with seeking to advance Russian interests by an aggressive policy to which nationalism is the stimulus. For the

1. *Leninism*, p. 525.
2. *Two Currents in Soviet Foreign Policy* (*The Listener*, 29 July 1948), p. 153.

moment, however, there is little meaning in the problem which exercises non-marxists, whether Russian policy aims at the extension of soviet power or of revolution, since for marxists trained in the stalinist school there is no conflict between the two. In fact, the promotion of revolution by increasing the power of Russia is the inevitable result of the failure of communist parties to bring it about for themselves. None the less, it may well create a problem in the future, and one which Russia will have to face if she is to retain her position as the ideological leader of world communism.

For national communist parties now find themselves in an awkward predicament. After the 7th Comintern Congress of 1935, they were instructed to collaborate with all anti-fascist elements, including left-wing governments; and they were thus driven to appeal to nationalistic feeling, just as did those groups with which they were seeking to combine. During the war, the communists played a leading part in the resistance movements, and so recovered the position they had lost as a result of their attitude between 1939 and 1941; and after its conclusion the re-organized communist parties found themselves stronger than they had ever been before. But in almost every country the war led to a revival of nationalism to which these parties had to defer, and by which many of their members were themselves not unaffected. Thus the communist party of one country has found itself obliged to support nationalist policies opposed by the communist party of an adjacent country, and this has tended to weaken the movement as an international force. The clash between the communist parties of Greece, Bulgaria, and Yugoslavia over the future of Macedonia is a case in point.

Such divergencies are permitted until one party or another is required to give way and adopt whatever policy the Russian leaders may have decided upon; and that it is their duty to defer to Moscow in this as in every other matter is emphasized by the distinction which communist propaganda is forever drawing between the 'bourgeois nationalism' of the non-communist world, which is condemned, and 'proletarian nationalism', which consists solely in loyalty to the Soviet Union as a socialist fatherland. On the other hand, the nationalism of backward countries is encouraged where it can be used to embarrass a capitalist power. And within the Soviet Union itself it still persists. It was carried to fanatical lengths during the ideological campaign conducted by Zhdanov in the years immediately following the last war, when writers, artists, and musicians whose work was held unduly to reflect western influences were persecuted as 'cosmopolitans', and fantastic claims were made that all the important discoveries of western scientists had been anticipated by the Russians. Since the death of Stalin, this form of lunacy has been abandoned. Cosmopolitanism has been dropped from the party vocabulary, though the theoretical journals defiantly assert that the attacks made upon it in the past were fully justified; while the emphasis is now laid upon the importance of assimilating all that western science and technology has to offer. The Soviet rulers can well dispense with aberrations which only made them appear ridiculous. Yet nationalism still remains a potent force, and is likely to continue to be so.

19. The Development of Communism from 1945 to the Death of Stalin

IN his *Historical Destiny of the Doctrine of Karl Marx*, Lenin distinguishes three main periods of world history since the publication of the *Communist Manifesto*: (*a*) from the 1848 revolution to the Commune of 1871; (*b*) from the Commune to the October Revolution; and (*c*) since the October Revolution. Stalin taught that this third stage was characterized by the sharp division of the world into the two hostile camps of capitalism and socialism, and this was emphasized in the preamble to the 1923 Constitution, though it was dropped from the 1936 Constitution, promulgated during the period when world revolution had been set aside in favour of the Popular Front.[1] The capitalist camp is divided against itself, but is fundamentally opposed to socialism, and hence to the Soviet Union, which it will destroy if it is able. In this conflict, the Soviet Union, as the leading country of world revolution, represents the young, rising, and progressive forces which are emerging and will ultimately prevail over the dying forces of reaction, but only after a revolution which will be a life-and-death struggle. This revolution is inevitable, but the way for it can be prepared by aggravating the contradictions in the capitalist camp. These contradictions are: (*a*) that between capital and labour, (*b*) that between the imperialist powers; and (*c*) that between those powers and their colonial and other dependencies. Ultimately they will bring about the downfall of capitalism, but in the meantime they must be exploited, and social democracy, which tends to gloss over them, must be ceaselessly attacked. The struggle may go on for a whole epoch. Hence the Soviet Union must be strengthened, partly by the development of its internal resources, and partly by securing allies. These allies will be: (*a*) the national communist parties in advanced countries, and (*b*) the liberation movements in

1. Max Beloff, *The Foreign Policy of the Soviet Union* (1949) II, p. 5.

backward countries in so far as these movements are calculated to weaken capitalism and bring the countries concerned into the Soviet orbit. The objective is the establishment of the soviet type of socialism in as many countries as possible. But there must be no playing with revolution; it must not be undertaken until an overwhelming force has been concentrated on the enemy's most vulnerable point; and it will be successful only when the ruling class is divided against itself and discredited in the eyes of the masses. It should then be started, albeit as a minority movement. The local communist party will capture the machinery of government, with the assistance of left-wing elements to be eliminated when they have served their turn, and will set up a Moscow-controlled regime. All traces of bourgeois-capitalist mentality will then be eradicated, an operation likely to continue over years. As soon as the revolution has been brought about successfully in one country, steps will be taken to extend it to others in accordance with the doctrine of 'permanent revolution'.[1]

We have now to see how this policy was implemented during the years following the Second World War in the east European or satellite countries, viz. Romania, Bulgaria, Hungary, Poland, Czechoslovakia, Yugoslavia, and for all practical purposes, the eastern zone of Germany. In all these countries, with the exception of Yugoslavia, the local communist parties were weak – indeed the Romanian party only contained about a thousand members – and there was strong anti-communist, and often anti-Russian feeling, which could not be ignored. Both at Yalta and elsewhere the Russians had given pledges to respect the right of the peoples within their sphere of influence to choose their own forms of government, and in the immediate post-war period it was not to their interest too openly to ignore these obligations. Moreover, the communist parties of western Europe had been instructed to win over the social democrats, and an over-ruthless policy towards the satellites would not have assisted this task.

Thus, in the first stage, Russian policy was one of gradualism.

1. For an interesting treatment of the above *see Stalin on Revolution* by 'Historicus' (*Foreign Affairs*, January 1949), pp. 175, 214.

Individuals and parties known to be openly hostile were eliminated, but the communists participated in genuine coalition governments in the form of 'popular', 'national' or 'democratic fronts' which carried out an agreed programme. The second stage was the bogus coalition in which the real leaders of the non-communist parties were ousted, and 'stooge' parties were formed to double them and draw away their members, thus preserving an outward show of parliamentary democracy, though the communists themselves held the key positions. The third, or monolithic, stage was reached when the 'popular front' became a single-party 'people's front', completely under communist control. By the time this stage was reached the communists had forced a merger with the numerically stronger social-democratic parties which had been weakened by purges, and by internal dissension provoked by a left-wing element led by crypto-communists and fellow-travellers. The new party was then given an innocuous title, such as, in the case of Poland, the 'United Workers' Party' which concealed its true nature. Political leaders who continued in opposition or attempted to maintain an independent line were indicted as 'imperialist agents', and sentenced to death or to long terms of imprisonment.[1]

The rapidity with which this was achieved naturally varied in the different countries. In Bulgaria and Romania the bogus coalition stage was reached within a few months of their 'liberation' by the Red Army. It is also doubtful whether Poland ever went through the first stage, as the Lublin Committee, which constituted itself the Provisional Government on 31 December 1944, was scarcely a genuine coalition, though non-communist parties were represented in it. On the other hand, Czechoslovakia was governed for the first three years by democratically elected coalition governments, and it was because this was holding up the sovietization of the country that the communists seized power in February 1948. In Yugoslavia the monolithic stage had been reached as early as 1945, by

1. See Hugh Seton-Watson, *The East European Revolution* (1950), pp. 167 ff. For a good account of Soviet policy towards these countries, *see* François Fejto, *Histoire des démocraties populaires* (Paris, 1952).

which time the Red Army had withdrawn from the country, after playing only a minor part in its 'liberation'. But by the beginning of 1949 at latest, there was no question of effective opposition to the communists in any east European country.

At first, however, the Russians were careful to keep in the background, and communist parties were permitted to make overtures to all sections of society, including the bourgeoisie, and to offer assurances that they had no intention of introducing the Soviet way of life, and that every country would find its own way to socialism. The change over to the tough line began in the spring of 1947, though it is not easy to say whether the announcement of the Truman Doctrine in March of that year was the cause or the result of it, or what part was played by the Marshall Plan, adumbrated in the following June. For the 'cold war', which dates from this period, had deeper roots. During the war years the Russian people had been sustained by patriotism, but the relaxation of peace disclosed symptoms which the party leaders found disquieting, and led them to launch an ideological offensive on all fronts with a view to re-imposing discipline and orthodoxy. A hardening of attitude towards Russia's former allies was simply one aspect of this campaign. Every totalitarian regime needs an external enemy, and now that the Germans no longer filled this role, their place was taken by the western democracies. Vast numbers of Russians had enjoyed for the first time the experience of discovering how these countries lived, and any illusions they might have formed about them had to be corrected. That the west had achieved a high degree of political stabilization only made it appear the more dangerous to men for whom 'capitalist encirclement' was an article of faith.

As the proponent of the new line both within the Soviet Union and without, Stalin chose Zhdanov, long notorious for his 'Great-Russianism'; and it was he who presided over the conference, held in Poland in September 1947, which set up the Cominform. His speech on this occasion contained all the talking points that communist propaganda has since made only too familiar.[1] The war, he declared, had sharply altered the

1. The text was published in *For a Lasting Peace* (10 November 1947).

alignment of forces between socialism and capitalism in favour of the former. After the First World War Russia had dropped out of the capitalist order. Now a number of east European countries had done the same, and had established 'a new type of State, the People's Republic'. Russia had emerged from the war with increased strength, but all the imperialist powers – victors and vanquished alike – had been weakened, with the exception of the United States, where an economic landslide was shortly to be expected. The war had aggravated the crisis in the colonial system – itself the product of uneven capitalist development – and had given rise to numerous national libera-tion movements, since, as Zhdanov, adapting the words of Lenin, declared: 'The peoples of the colonies no longer wish to live in the old way, and the ruling class of the metropolitan countries can no longer govern on the old lines.' The result had been to divide the world into two camps, the one imperialist and anti-democratic, and the other anti-imperialist and demo-cratic. The United States was the leader of the first, and was seeking, through the Truman Doctrine and Marshall Aid, to enslave Europe, destroy Russia and seize world power; whereas the Soviet Union, 'to which motives of aggression and exploita-tion were utterly alien', was the leader of the second, and stood for a 'lasting democratic peace'. The reactionary policy of America, and of those countries which, like Great Britain, had now become her satellites, was then analysed, and was shown to have operated even during the war, as was evidenced by their 'refusal' to start a second front. It was thus the duty of com-munist parties to unite all democratic, anti-fascist, and peace-loving elements against the new forces of war and aggression. The very title chosen for the cominform journal – 'For a Last-ing Peace' – was intended to imply that the western powers were bent upon a third world war.

This analysis provided the theoretical justification for the new aggressive policy. Everywhere communist parties were to go into action, since, as Zhdanov puts it, 'the main danger for the working class lies in underestimating its own strength and overestimating the strength of the forces of the imperialist camp' – a return, as Franz Borkenau says, to the illusion of

1918–19 and of the late twenties that Europe was ripe for revolution.[1] It is of interest to note that it involved the abandonment of the thesis set out by the most prominent of the Soviet economists, Eugene Vargo, in a book published in October 1946, according to which no major economic crisis in the capitalist world was to be expected for ten years, and that he was condemned in May 1947, about three months before the new line was announced. He did what was expected of a loyal communist and admitted his error. 'Comrade Stalin', he said, 'has given adequate exhaustive proofs of the inevitability of wars between capitalist countries at the present stage.' But Stalin had given no such proofs. He had merely asserted that such a revolutionary situation now existed, because if it did not, it would have made nonsense of Zhdanovism.

In western Europe the new policy found its concrete application in a series of political strikes, particularly in France, which reached their climax in December 1947, just before the London meeting of the Council of Foreign Ministers which they were evidently intended to influence. Their failure weakened the communist parties responsible for them, as the workers became disgusted when they realized that their economic interests were being sacrificed to a purely political objective. In the satellite countries the Peasant Parties were the immediate target. Already in August 1947 the Bulgarian agrarian leader, Nikola Petkov, had been judicially murdered. In October, Maniu, the leader of the Romanian National Peasant Party, was brought to trial, and a pretext was found for implicating Tatarescu, the last non-communist minister of any standing, who was succeeded as Foreign Minister by Ana Pauker. In Poland Mikolajczyk's Peasant Party was declared in the same month to be an opposition movement, and as such unconstitutional, and he was obliged to flee the country. In February 1948 the Czech communists, realizing that they were certain of defeat in the forthcoming March elections, seized power by a *coup d'etat*. In the third week of April, as if by way of a rejoinder to the signing on 3 April of the E.R.P. Agreement, the Russians started the 'little blockade' of Berlin with the object of forcing

1. *European Communism* (1953), p. 525.

the western powers out of the city, and in August converted it into a total blockade. Finally, on 28 June the Yugoslav Communist Party, which had been under pressure from Moscow since February, was expelled from the Cominform. But Zhdanov did not witness the aftermath of the policy associated with his name, for he died, somewhat unexpectedly, on 30 August, 1948.

The condemnation of Tito and his party caused a stir for which we have to go back to the excommunication of Luther to find a parallel. The causes of the dispute are too numerous and complex to be examined here.[1] But in proportion as relations with the west deteriorated, the Soviet Union began to demand from its satellites unswerving obedience, and to insist that their communist parties should adopt its revolutionary experience as their model, and accept Russian military and civil advisers to guide them in their task of 'building socialism'. Moscow's real grievance against Tito was that he had resented this. The ideological charges brought against him, as for example, that of allowing his party to become submerged in the 'People's Front' and of failing to understand the nature of 'inner-party democracy', were secondary, and were made partly to discredit him with his party, and partly to provide a rationalization of the action taken by the Cominform on Moscow's instructions. Nor had they any justification. Up to 1947 the Yugoslav regime had exhibited all the characteristics of stalinism. The party had the 'People's Front' well under control; industrialization and the collectivization of agriculture were proceeding at least as rapidly as in the other satellites; and there existed strong anti-western feeling. But these things counted for nothing, and the country found itself exposed to an economic blockade which forced it to seek assistance from the west.

Stalin believed that the Yugoslav party would be quickly brought to heel; but it stood firm, and thus the danger arose that Tito's example would be followed by the leaders of other satellite communist parties. These men fell into two categories.

1. For the correspondence between the Russian and the Yugoslav Parties, see *The Soviet–Yugoslav Dispute* (Royal Institute of International Affairs, 1949).

In the first were stalinist technicians such as Bierut in Poland, Gottwald in Czechoslovakia, and Rakosi in Hungary who had spent the war years in the Soviet Union, and had returned to their countries in the wake of the Red Army; while in the second, were leaders like Tito himself, who, though equally convinced communists, had been engaged during all or part of these years in clandestine activity. Those who belonged to this second group were always suspected of 'nationalism' by Moscow, and it was now felt desirable to remove them. The first to suffer was the Albanian Minister of the Interior, Koci Xoze, who was arrested in November 1948, and executed as a Titoist in July 1949. An even more prominent victim was the Hungarian Foreign Minister, Lazlo Rajk, who found himself accused of having maintained continuous contact with Tito and of having acted under his orders. After a show trial, in which he pleaded guilty to these and other charges, he was liquidated in October 1949. The next to fall was Wladislaw Gomulka, the former Secretary-General of the Polish United Workers' Party. He had been deprived of his post in September 1948 on the charge of Titoism but at the time no further action had been taken against him. In November 1949, however, he was expelled from the Central Committee, and imprisoned, though he was never brought to trial. In the following December it was the turn of the old Bulgarian communist, Traicho Kostov, who had been arrested in the previous March, and was now tried and executed. As he was notoriously anti-Yugoslav, there could be no question of charging him with Titoism. But he had criticized the recent Soviet–Bulgarian Trade Agreements as unfavourable to his country's interests, and was thus liquidated as a nationalist. In April 1949 the Secretary-General, Georgi Dimitrov, who had openly sided with Tito, with whom he had been associated over the projected Balkan Federation to which Stalin was strongly opposed, had been invited to Moscow and had died there in July. His brother-in-law, Vulko Chervenko, a died-in-the-wool stalinist, soon afterwards succeeded him as party leader.

The above measures were naturally accompanied by a purge of party officials and of the rank-and-file, so that it was announced, for example, by the Central Committee of the Czecho-slovak Party in February 1952 that 25 per cent of the members had either been expelled or reduced to candidate status. In the course of this particular operation, a number of persons were arrested on the charge of conspiring against the State, and among them the former Foreign Minister, Vladimir Clementis, who had been relieved of his post in the previous year. The purge seemed at first to be working in favour of the Party Secretary, Rudolf Slansky. But in September 1952 he was dismissed, and in November was arrested on a charge which linked him with the alleged activities of Clementis, with whom he was tried and executed in December. In the preceding May, the Romanian Foreign Minister, Ana Pauker, was dismissed from the Politburo, and in September was deprived of the post of Deputy Premier. The disgrace of Slansky and Pauker may be attributed in part to anti-semitism, of which there had been a recrudescence during the year, as was attested by the fact that of the nine Kremlin doctors whose arrest was announced in January 1953, seven were Jews. But both were intensely disliked, and their removal may also have been designed to make their parties less unpopular.

Had the Russians honoured their undertaking to respect the democratic rights of their satellites, not one of these countries would have the government that is now in power. Yet today all these governments are communists, and exhibit the features which characterize sovietized regimes. There are the rigged elections, those held in Poland and Romania in January and November 1947 respectively providing an illustration of how the communists, while pretending to carry out an international obligation, misuse a democratic procedure in order to confer upon their governments a semblance of constitutional legality. There is the subordination of the judiciary to the government, as a result of which the constantly staged political trials are travesties of justice, and their results foregone conclusions. There is the new constitution, modelled upon that of the Soviet Union, which is introduced in one country after another as soon as the communists are in control, and which vests all power in the central party organs, though a façade of parliamentary government is still maintained. Above all, there is the security police, which performs the same functions as in the Soviet union. Its agents are everywhere, and the terror it inspires ends by paralysing resistance.

At the same time the communists extend their control to every branch of social activity – trade unions, youth movements, the press and radio, education, etc. The unions are remodelled on the Russian pattern; they act as the link between the government and the workers, and are primarily responsible for securing increased production. Control of the press is assured by restricting newsprint, suppressing papers, and arresting members of their editorial staffs. Despite Anglo-American protests, no genuine opposition press has ever been permitted once the communists have been in a position to prevent it.

Education has naturally received considerable attention. The communists aim at creating a new intelligentsia whose members will be discouraged from any mental activity outside their own fields other than that required for indoctrination into marxist-leninist principles. As in the Soviet Union, education is predominantly technical, designed to turn out specialists to assist in the drive towards industrialization which has characterized the planned economies of these countries. Entry into institutions of higher learning is commonly controlled by selection boards, thus making it the reward of political reliability or conditional upon proletarian status – an infringement of the traditional system of university autonomy that has been much resented. In general, the policy has been to sever cultural links with the west, and impose Soviet forms, of which a symbol is the Palace of Culture and Science in Warsaw, an immense 42-storey building in the style of Moscow University which dominates the city, and is described as the gift of the Russian to the Polish nation.

The attempt to impose marxist-leninist ideology has inevitably led to a conflict with the Church. Catholicism, as a rival international organization with its own ideology, is naturally regarded as the greatest danger. Religious freedom is still conceded in theory, but everything has been done to weaken the Church by secularizing education, confiscating ecclesiastical property, placing restrictions upon appointments, and stifling the religious press. The campaign against it has been linked with that against the Vatican, represented by communist propaganda as an agent of western imperialism; and that the hierarchy has obeyed Vatican directives has been used as evidence of its anti-national sentiment, as appeared for example in the trial of the Hungarian Cardinal Mindzenty, who was arrested in December 1948, and sentenced to life imprisonment in February 1949. The death of Stalin did not immediately lead to any relaxation of persecution, and when, in September 1953, the Polish Cardinal Wyszczinski protested against it in a sermon, he was deprived of his functions and incarcerated in a monastery. More recently, however, there have been some indications that the Soviet Government desires a *détente*. In July 1955 Cardinal Mindzenty's sentence was 'provisionally interrupted'; and in the following August the Polish Premier, Cyrankeiwicz, referred to the possible release of Cardinal Wyszczinski, while making it clear that he would not be allowed to resume his former office.

The Orthodox Churches of Romania and Bulgaria have presented an easier problem, as little more has been necessary than to secure their formal allegiance to the Moscow Patriarchate. In Romania, the communists secured control of the Ministry of Cults in October 1947. The 'Church Council' was then packed, and in May 1948 a new Metropolitan, Justinian, was appointed who removed priests 'brought up in the mentality of the past'. Somewhat similar steps were taken in Bulgaria. The Protestant Churches have given even less trouble, and their capitulation has been virtually complete.

The technique as above described is in perfect accordance with Marx's teaching. In all these countries the communists have destroyed the 'bourgeois State' as he said they should do. The only reason why they did not do so immediately was that their parties were at first so small that to have attempted to seize power, even with Soviet military support, would have led to administrative chaos, economic confusion, and the possible intervention of the western powers. The solution was therefore to allow these countries to form left-wing governments in which the communists did not apparently exercise undue influence, and that the latter, through their control of a few key positions, and notably of the security police, should then gradually 'cuckoo' all the non-communist elements out of the nest. Yugoslavia was the only country where these tactics proved unsuccessful, as the Yugoslav Communist Party had made its own revolution with little assistance from the Soviet Army, and was determined to maintain its independence.

*

According to the marxist-leninist doctrine, the revolution would take place in two stages. The first would set up a bourgeois-democratic regime which would stop short of socialism, and the second a dictatorship of the proletariat which would introduce it. Hence it became necessary to explain to which of these categories belonged the new satellite regimes, to which the designation of 'people's democracies' had early been given.[1] This was not altogether easy, because communist theory wished on the one hand to represent them as having arisen as a result of the successful issue of a 'class struggle for national liberation', which was to suggest that the revolutions that had brought them into existence had been proletarian, even if they were not in fact so described; while on the other, it was not thought desirable to define them as dictatorships of the proletariat, partly because this would put the satellites on the same level as the Soviet Union, and partly because it was felt necessary, at least in the early stages, to take into consideration national and non-communist sentiment in the countries concerned. Hence in *World Economy and Politics* of March 1947 Varga defined people's democracies as 'democracies of a new type' which were justified by the existence of 'feudal survivals' in the various countries, though this failed to explain why Lenin had proclaimed the dictatorship of the proletariat in Russia at

---

1. *See* Ruth Amende Rosa, *The Soviet Theory of 'People's Democracy'* in *World Politics*, July 1949, pp. 489 ff : Adam B. Ulam. *The Cominform and the People's Democracies*, ibid. January 1951, pp. 200 ff.; Gordon Skilling, *People's Democracy in Soviet Theory* in *Soviet Studies*, July 1951, pp. 16 ff., September 1951, pp. 131 ff.

a time when that country contained at least as many of them. A somewhat more elaborate description was given in *Soviet State and Law* (Nos. 1 and 3) by I. P. Trainin, who, while preferring the expression 'democracy of a special type', agreed with Varga in regarding people's democracy as belonging to a 'new type', that is, one for which there was no exact analogue in the Russian experience. At the foundation congress of the Cominform, however, Zhdanov described the satellite regimes as 'popular democracies', 'where the leading force is a bloc of the labouring class headed by the working class'. 'As a result', he continued, 'the peoples of these countries have not only delivered themselves from the imperialist grip, but are laying the foundations for a transition to the road of socialist development'.

The quarrel with the Yugoslav Communist Party made it the more necessary to define the relationship between the satellite regimes and the Soviet Union; and on 25 December 1948 the communist press published an important statement made by Dimitrov at the 5th Congress of the Bulgarian Party, in the preparation of which he claimed to have had the personal assistance of Stalin. In it he declared that 'people's democracy was in essence a form of the dictatorship of the proletariat rendered possible by the defeat of the forces of fascism by the Soviet Union', thus stressing, as was now judged desirable, that the satellites had not made their own revolutions as Russia had done, but had owed their 'liberation' to the Soviet Army. In a speech of 21 January 1949 – the twenty-fifth anniversary of Lenin's death – P. N. Pospelov, the then editor-in-chief of *Pravda*, declared that 'the people's democratic regime performs the functions of a dictatorship of the proletariat in suppressing and abolishing capitalist elements, thus solving the problem of the transition from capitalism into socialism'; while in an article of 22 January in the Hungarian party organ, *Szabad Nep*, Rakosi stated that 'the people's democracy, as to its functions, is a proletarian democracy without the Soviet form'. Finally, in an article in *Pravda* of 26 April – the twenty-fifth anniversary of the publication of Stalin's *Leninism* – P. F. Yudin, at that time the editor of the Cominform journal, explained that people's democracy was 'a political form of the dictatorship of the proletariat', but not the 'higher' soviet form, and must pursue a policy of close collaboration with Russia in order to avoid falling into the heresy of Titoism. The Russian workers and peasants had built socialism 'in a capitalist environment, while relentlessly resisting military, economic, political, and ideological attacks by the reactionaries', whereas the peoples of the eastern European countries had been assisted by the defeat of fascism by the Soviet Army, and by the fraternal attitude which the Soviet Union had since displayed towards them.

What emerges from all this theorizing is that people's democracy is not democracy of a 'new' or 'special' type, but is in conformity with the Russian experience. Only whereas Russia had become a socialist country by 1936, the people's democracies are 'building socialism', and are at the stage which the Soviet Union had reached during the N.E.P. period. Hence they are striving, under Russian guidance, to achieve the status that the Soviet Union has by this time attained, since were it to be admitted that they had already done so, the case for such guidance would be seriously weakened. As the Russians have an obvious interest in continuing to exercise it, it is not surprising that the theory does not make clear how these regimes will 'grow into socialism', and thus render it no longer necessary. In fact the main purpose of the theory is to justify their subordination.

There are those who believe that the communism of the satellite countries, and the theory used to sustain it, are specifically Russian; that outside the immediate orbit of Soviet influence the movement might well develop without the concomitants of the secret police, concentration camps, and the like; and that every country gets the form it deserves. There could be no more dangerous illusion. Were a communist party to come into power in any western country, it is certain that the Russians would never be satisfied until communism had been established on 'the best and only pattern' – that of the Soviet Union. In all western countries communist parties are seeking to obtain power by 'Trojan Horse' tactics similar to those employed in countries that the communists now control. There is the same attempt to obtain participation in genuine left-wing coalitions, and then to render them unworkable; and the same readiness to adopt any policy, however prejudicial to their country, provided that it serves the interests of Moscow. If such a party were to come into power, it would not of course mean that the country would immediately become a Romania or Bulgaria. Yet it is certain that the usual methods would be employed to reduce it to that condition. The right-wing leaders would be summarily dispatched. Then would come the turn of the left-wing groups, which would be cut from the tree one by one, until there remained only the extremist faction of the socialist party, whose amalgamation with the communists would early have been secured. The proclamation of a state of people's democracy would follow in due course.

*

In the Far East communism presents a different problem. By far the most important event that has taken place there since the war has been the establishment on 1 October 1949 of the Chinese People's Republic, thus ending the struggle which the communists had carried on intermittently since 1927 against forces incomparably stronger than their own. The nature of Chinese communism and the role which it is likely to play have thus become issues of the first importance.[1]

What must be recognized at the outset is that the victory of communism in China is not to be explained as the unexpected result of the new balance of power which arose as a result of the war, but that it marks a stage in the development of the grand strategy of world revolution as formulated in the first days of the communist movement. This strategy turned upon the central thesis of Lenin's *Imperialism* – the dependence of the imperialist powers upon their colonial possessions for the avoidance of political and economic disaster at home, since it was only by exploiting backward peoples that these powers were able to keep their own proletariat under control. The most

1. For the origin and development of Chinese Communism see Benjamin I. Schwartz, *Chinese Communism and the Rise of Mao* (Harvard University Press, 1951).

effective way of weakening them was therefore to attack them through their colonies and so cut the tap-roots of their prosperity; and this was possible because the very contradiction within the capitalist system which forced the industrialized nations to offload upon backward peoples, in exchange for cheap raw materials, those commodities which their own home markets could not absorb, led to the second contradiction that this policy not only aroused the hostility of its victims, but ended only by providing them with the means of throwing off the imperialist yoke.

Hence as early as 1918 we find Stalin explaining that the east must on no account be forgotten, as it provided 'the inexhaustible reserve and reliable base of world imperialism, a reserve, as he pointed out, not only of material wealth, but also of 'obedient man-power'. This theme was further developed in the *Theses on the National and Colonial Questions*, adopted by the 2nd Comintern Congress of 1920. Communist parties must support national liberation movements, even if these were led by the bourgeoisie, though without forfeiting their independent status, a policy which Stalin adopted in 1923, when he instructed the Chinese Communist Party to enter into an alliance with the Kuomintang, the breakdown of which in 1927 was to lead to a bitter controversy with Trotsky. The final constitution of the Comintern, adopted at the 6th Congress of 1928, emphasized once again the vital role which colonial revolutions were destined to play 'in the struggle for the conquest of power by the working class'. The uneven development of capitalism, accentuated in the period of imperialism, could lead to the 'socialist development' of industrially immature countries, provided that these countries were supported by the Soviet Union and the international proletarian movement. At the same time it was recognized that, in the case of countries like China, 'the transition to the dictatorship of the proletariat will be possible only through a series of preparatory stages', that is that a revolution would not lead to the immediate establishment of socialism; and when Mao Tse-tung laid this down in his *New Democracy* (1940), he was following the orthodox party doctrine.

Stalin's instructions to the Chinese Communist Party in 1945 had been to resume negotiations with Chiang Kai-shek with a view to participating in a nationalist government in which it would then employ its usual tactics. Whether these broke down, or were never seriously entered into, it is hard to say. It is improbable, however, that Mao Tse-tung supposed that the victory of his party would be as rapid and complete as it proved to be, or that Moscow either expected or desired it. In theory it is right and proper that backward countries should throw off the imperialist yoke and set up communist regimes. Yet it is doubtful whether Moscow has ever desired a revolution to succeed which it does not control; and that a vast country with a population of more than twice that of the Soviet Union should become communist almost overnight created an embarrassing situation. Moreover, the fact that the Chinese Communist Party was overwhelmingly composed of peasants occasioned an uneasiness by no means wholly due to scholastic pedantry. That the Russian revolution had been proletarian and was the archetype of all future revolutions was an article of faith, and on it was founded Moscow's claim to direct the world revolutionary movement. To admit that the Chinese revolution had been carried out by peasants, whom marxist-leninist theory relegated to the role of allies of the proletariat, was therefore to concede to it a character of its own, and one to which the principles governing proletarian revolutions would not necessarily apply.

But Mao was careful to preserve appearances, and not to challenge the received doctrine. Thus he represented his movement as proletarian even when it was not, and shifted the centre of gravity of his party back to the cities as soon as this became feasible. He has indeed claimed the right to interpret marxism–leninism in accordance with Chinese conditions. Yet he has accepted it as the official creed, and his theoretical writings are an orthodox interpretation of it. Indeed he has become today its leading exponent, and is the only living communist philosopher to be included in the 1954 edition of the Soviet *Short Philosophical Dictionary*.

As to the character of the Chinese People's Republic, there

appears to be at least a superficial agreement between Peking and Moscow.[1] Its first constitution described it as a 'people's democratic state', and Soviet ideologists almost at once acclaimed it as a 'people's democracy', though they sought to convey the impression that it was a more primitive type than that of the east European countries. Yet there are certain divergencies between the two. First, the Chinese People's Republic maintains that it neither is a dictatorship of the proletariat nor aims at becoming one. It is explicitly defined as a 'government of the four classes' – the proletariat, peasantry, petty bourgeoisie, and national bourgeoisie – 'under the leadership of the proletariat'. Secondly, the Chinese communists hold that it will be possible to 'educate and reform' non-communist and even bourgeois elements into socialism. But this is opposed to what was orthodox doctrine, at least up to the 20th Congress, which not only rejected a peaceful transition from capitalism into socialism, but insisted that during the period of 'building socialism' the class struggle against 'bourgeois survivals' and the kulaks becomes more acute. Thirdly, the Chinese communists have claimed the right to pursue that 'separate path' to socialism which, at least in Stalin's lifetime, was declared inadmissible in the case of the satellite countries. Mao has laid down that certain elements in the official creed are inapplicable to China, and although he has not told us what these are, it is a fair assumption that he is not criticizing its basic premises but the way in which the Russians have interpreted them.

Yet these divergencies may not amount to much in practice. There is no reason to suppose that the non-communist parties in the Chinese government exert any more influence than do their counterparts in the satellite governments. As for the peaceful transition into socialism, it is scarcely borne out by the facts. From all accounts, the land reform has been carried out in as arbitrary a fashion as in the Soviet Union, and it will have been effected even more rapidly if Mao holds to the programme, announced in his speech to the Central Committee of 31 July 1955, of achieving almost complete collectivization by 1960.

1. See B. Schwartz, 'China, and the Soviet Theory of People's Democracy' in *Problems of Communism* (September–October 1954), pp. 3 ff.

The 'four-anti' movement of 1952, directed against the national bourgeoisie under the slogan of 'education and reform', meant in fact the virtual liquidation of the class to which this mode of conversion was applied; while the suppression of everything that makes for a genuinely creative literature has been even more ruthless than in Russia.

The precise relations between the Soviet Union and China are a matter for speculation. The two countries are united by what is fundamentally a common ideology, and by a mutuality of interest, and neither has anything to gain at the moment by a breach with the other. The Chinese communists are well aware of their debt to Russia, and as long as they accept the fundamentals of marxism–leninism, and anti-imperialism with it, they will remain in the Soviet camp. They will only leave it if they become convinced that Russia offers a greater threat to Chinese national interests than does the west, the conclusion which Chiang Kai-shek reached in 1927, when he broke the Kuomintang–Communist alliance, and dismissed his Russian advisers. It is thus to the interest of Russia to encourage Chinese anti-imperialism as long as this embarrasses the western powers and diverts their attention from Europe, but to exert a restraining influence as soon as Chinese intransigence threatens to precipitate a third world war, which Moscow appears anxious, at least for the present, to avoid.

In conclusion, it should be noted that communist theory takes no account of changes in constitutional status, and represents all colonial peoples indifferently as victims of capitalist exploitation, just as it represents the workers in the metropolitan countries as exploited wage-slaves. When, however, communists talk of 'liberating' a backward country, they mean subjecting it to their control, and if a nationalist movement leads to the establishment of a non-communist government, that government will be opposed, however much it may correspond to the constitutionally expressed wishes of the population. Burma provides a good example of this. In that country the movement for national independence was led by the Anti-Fascist People's Freedom League, made up of a number of left-wing political groups, only one of which was marxist.

Under the Anglo-Burmese Treaty of 17 October 1947, Burma was recognized as an independent sovereign republic, and left the Commonwealth. The communists at once attacked the new government as the 'hireling of capitalists and imperialists', and although they had little popular support, they sought to overthrow it by force, only desisting when the Cominform changed its line and ceased to advocate armed insurrections in areas where their prospect of success was negligible.

At the same time, the Soviet Union justifies its own colonial dependencies by the fiction that they are 'Soviet republics', and that their membership of the U.S.S.R. is a 'voluntary association'. Their right 'freely to secede' is formally recognized under Article 17 of the 1936 Constitution, but any movement in favour of it is immediately suppressed. For as it is *ex hypothesei* inconceivable that the 'toiling masses' should desire to be severed from the Soviet Union, any demand for it must come from reactionary circles, and thus be counter-revolutionary.

20. The Post-Stalinist Situation

ON 4 March 1953 it was announced that Stalin was suffering from a stroke which had affected his brain, and on the day following that he was dead. As was expected, Malenkov was recognized as his successor, but on 14 March he exchanged his post as Party Secretary for that of Chairman of the Committee of Ministers (i.e. Premier), with Molotov, Beria, Bulganin, and Kaganovitch as Vice-Chairmen. He retained this office until 8 February 1955, when he resigned and became Minister of Electrical Power Stations, but continued to be a member of the Party Presidium and was re-elected to that body at the 20th Congress of February 1956. Bulganin succeeded him as Premier, with Khrushchev as Party Secretary, to which post he had been appointed in September 1953. The Ministry of Defence was taken over by Marshal Zhukov, hitherto, with Marshal Vasilievsky, Bulganin's deputy. He was made a candidate member of the Presidium at the 20th Congress.

The passing of a dictator who has wielded absolute power for over a generation is bound to be followed by a period of uncertainty during which his successors will review the policy they have inherited. In the present instance, this was very necessary as Stalin's policy had been to meet every situation with increased repression and terrorism; and as this had caused widespread disaffection, it was clearly to the advantage of the new leaders to modify it, or at least allow it to be supposed that they intended to do so. In fact some positive action on their part had become imperative, for the economy of the country was being slowly strangled by excessive over-centralization and bureaucratism which paralysed administration and deprived the lower levels of all initiative and responsibility. At the time of the 19th Congress the leaders had been well aware of this state of affairs. Yet as long the Stalin lived, nothing could be done to remedy it. His death forced them to make at least some attempt to do so, though how far they will be successful remains to be seen.

The above considerations led the Presidium to embark upon the policy which became known as the 'new course'. In the domestic field its principal features were the following: (a) the abandonment of 'one-man leadership' for 'collective leadership'; (b) a reduction of the powers of the State security police and an assurance that the rule of law would henceforth be respected; (c) an undertaking to make available more consumer goods by a shift of emphasis from heavy to light industry; (d) concessions to the collective farm workers (*kolkhozniki*) with the object of increasing the supply of agricultural produce upon which industrial development depended; and (e) the granting of greater freedom to the intellectuals.

As Carr has pointed out, the principle of 'collective leadership' or 'collegiality' was not a new one, for although never written into the party status, it had been accepted in the early days as according with the spirit of democratic socialism that decisions should be made by the collective group rather than by individuals.[1] It was natural enough that it should now be re-affirmed by a group of leaders no one of whom had any compelling reason to trust his colleagues. Thus in an article in *Pravda* of 16 April 1953, and in the May issue of *Kommunist*, L. Slepov sharply attacked the 'cult of personality' as a 'survival of idealism', and this thesis was immediately taken up by the press, which now sought to explain the important role that collective leadership had always played in the life of the party. After 7 June 1954 the names of the leaders were printed in alphabetical order, and not in that in which they stood in the hierarchy. In accordance with the same principle, ministers were instructed to make use of the 'Collegia' of leading officials, which had been abolished in 1934 and re-established in 1938. Acceptance of 'collective leadership' was made mandatory, and if a party official was disgraced, he was now said to have offended against it.

The first top-level leader to be accused of a breach of it was Beria. On 13 January 1953 the press had announced the arrest of the nine Kremlin doctors on the charge of having murdered or attempted to murder a number of prominent persons, and

1. *The Bolshevik Revolution* II, pp. 187–8.

had accompanied this by criticism of the State Security Service, over which Beria, who had been its head up to 1946, still exercised an over-all control. From 1943 the functions of the State Security Service and those of the Ministry of the Interior proper had been carried out by separate departments, but immediately after Stalin's death they were united under the Ministry of the Interior, and Beria became responsible for both. On 3 April 1953 the Ministry announced the release of the doctors, and declared that they had been arrested 'wrongly and without legal grounds'; and on 6 April *Pravda* accused the then Minister of State Security, S. D. Ignatiev, of having displayed 'political blindness and gullibility', and assured the public that the inviolability of the person, guaranteed under Artcle 127 of the Constitution, would be respected in the future. On the following day, Ignatiev was removed from his post as one of the secretaries of the Central Committee, to which he had been appointed when Beria assumed charge of the two departments, and *Pravda* accused his former deputy and head of the Ministry's Investigations Section, Ryumin, of being a 'culpable adventurer'.

The release of the doctors may have been a move by Beria to acquire popularity, but on or about 26 June he was arrested, and on 10 July Moscow Radio announced that he had been dismissed by the Party as 'a foul enemy of the Soviet people'. On 23 December it was officially stated that he had been shot with six of his accomplices, who included V. N. Merkulov, a former Minister of State Security, and V. G. Dekanozov, formerly Soviet Ambassador in Berlin and at the time of his arrest Minister of the Interior in Georgia. In July 1954 Ryumin was liquidated, and in the following December the same fate befell V. S. Abakumov, who had been Minister of State Security from 1946 until replaced by Ignatiev in 1952. For reasons regarding which it is only possible to speculate, Ignatiev escaped. On 28 February 1954 it was announced that he had been appointed First Secretary of the Communist Party in the Bashkir Republic, with which he had had some connexion in the past.

That so many accusations were levelled against Beria was

doubtless intended to obscure the real reason for his fall. There are indications that in the months following Stalin's death he had been attempting to build up his position in a manner inconsistent with the principle of 'collective leadership'. The charge that he had been an imperialist agent for years and was seeking to restore the capitalist system may mean in communist jargon that he was in favour, as was widely believed at the time, of a more conciliatory approach to the German question, or at least of imposing a brake on Ulbricht, the head of the puppet East German government; and this last is not impossible, as he was ultimately responsible for security in Soviet-controlled territories. It is significant that his arrest took place shortly after the Berlin rising of 17 June. The police had been unable to deal with it, and the Army had to be brought in. Its chiefs had always believed that the police were no good, and this confirmation may well have brought them out against him. As for his colleagues in the Presidium, it is readily intelligible that they should have desired to be rid of a man who knew too much about them, and if there is any single explanation of his fate, this is the most probable one. They seem also to have been resolved that his ministry should not be allowed to wield the power it had done in the past, and the charge, whether true or not, that he had sought to place it 'above the government and the party' was the expression of this determination.

The next step was to announce the 'new course' in its application to industry and agriculture; and Malenkov, as Premier, did this in his speech on the budget of 8 August 1953. After recording with satisfaction the expansion of heavy industry under the successive Five-year Plans, he declared that the progress achieved now made it possible to increase the supply of consumer goods and the allocation of further capital to this branch of industry. This, it should be noted, was the most popular feature of the new policy, as the chronic shortage of consumer goods hit every section of society with the exception of a small group of privileged persons, to whom the slogan of 'to each according to his needs' might be said already to apply. More capital would also be devoted to developing the *kolkhozy*, as Malenkov admitted that they had not been receiving sufficient support. Higher prices would be paid for deliveries of meat, milk, wool, and vegetables, and the tax paid by the *kolkhozniki* for their private allotments, against which Stalin had long been waging a war of attrition, would be halved, thus rendering these small holdings more remunerative.

On 13 September 1953 the Central Committee issued a directive for improving agriculture, based on a report by Krushchev, published in the press on 15 September. This report left no doubt that 'socialized farming' had failed to fulfil the expectations formed of it. In 1952 the number of cattle had fallen by 2 million, and there were nearly 9 million fewer than in 1928, that is, before Stalin started his collectivization drive. The position with regard to other livestock was little better. A number of concessions were made to the *kolkhozniki*, and others were announced later, as for example the decision of 1954 greatly to increase the price paid for grain, and that of 1955 to distribute 15 per cent of the maize crop. At the same time, the management of the *kolkhozy* was transferred to the Machine Tractor Stations (M.T.S.) to which in the course of the winter $1\frac{1}{2}$ million part-time and underpaid *kolkhozniki* were drafted. For this management the Second Party Secretary of the district (*rayon*) was made responsible jointly with the technical head of the M.T.S., but these secretaries, now reinforced by 50,000 reliable party workers, were required to live at the M.T.S. headquarters, instead of, as hitherto, in the principal town of the district. The decree of the Supreme Soviet of 9 March 1955, giving each *kolkhoz* the right to plan its own production, was at least a belated recognition of the importance of local conditions. But it did little to affect their control by the M.T.S., since a *kolkhoz* chairman was still obliged to obtain its approval for any plan he had worked out in consultation with his own committee. Thus the effect of the 'new course' on agriculture was that the *kolkhozy* and their members gained materially from higher prices and other concessions, but were more closely integrated into the party machinery of control.

The 'new course' led to a certain improvement in the quantity of consumer goods, particularly of such luxury articles as refrigerators and television sets, designed to absorb the earnings of the higher-income groups but this was not achieved as a result of any considerable allocation of capital to light industry, but by requiring heavy industry firms to manufacture such products out of spare parts in addition to fulfilling their norms. It is not surprising that confusion resulted, and this was doubt-less one of the factors that led the Presidium to reconsider its policy. For from the autumn of 1954 the slogan 'To achieve within two or three years a steady increase in the living stan-dards of the people' disappeared from the press, and was re-placed by others calling for increased production, especially of grain and livestock.

An indication that a change of policy was impending was the renewed emphasis upon the importance of heavy industry. In a conversation with J. D. Bernal of 25 September 1954 (the text of which was not published, however, until 24 December), Khrushchev said that 'heavy industry will have priority in the future'; and on 28 December a leading article in *Pravda* de-clared it to be 'the foundation of the foundations of the soviet economy'. On 24 January 1955 *Pravda* carried a 12-column article by its editor-in-chief, D. T. Shepilov, entitled 'The General Line of the Party and the Vulgar-Marxists', sharply criticizing a number of economists as 'half-baked critics of the marxist theory of capital reproduction', their 'crime' being to have argued that although it was necessary in the first phase of socialist society to give priority to heavy industry, it was now possible to transfer it to light industry, and thus satisfy the needs of the workers.

That in a socialist country heavy industry has priority over light industry is a principle of soviet economic theory. In capi-talist countries, so the argument runs, the form which industry takes is determined by profitability, and thus the development of heavy industry is retarded because the products of light in-dustry have a more rapid turnover and yield higher profits. As, however, the soviet economy is not governed by the profit motive, it has been possible to proceed immediately to build up heavy industry, which will eventually render available a far larger supply of consumer goods than capitalist countries can produce. The flaw in this argument is that once profitability is ignored, there is no criterion of efficiency; and thus what those economists who have ventured to advocate an increase in consumer goods are in fact demanding is that industry should no longer be bulldozed now in this direction and now in that, but should be governed by the law of value, which means in this context profitability.

It was clear, however, that Shepilov's target was not the economists, but the policy proclaimed by Malenkov on 8 August 1953 and vigorously defended by the Minister of Internal Trade, Mikoyan, in a speech of 17 October following. On the day after the appearance of the article, Khrushchev, addressing the Central Committee, declared: 'Lenin taught that *only the heavy machinery industry can serve as the material basis of Socialism.* Developing Lenin's instructions, Stalin emphasized that to slacken the speed of development of heavy industry *would be suicide.* Under Stalin's leadership, the Party steadfastly implemented this only correct policy. It is consistently carrying it out at present, and will continue to do so without wavering.' The view that at a certain stage of socialist development priority of heavy industry yields to that of light industry was condemned as a right-wing deviation similar to that of Rykov and Bukharin, who paid for it in the purge of 1938. It was true that Malenkov had acknowledged that 'heavy industry is the very foundation of our economy', and had merely said that its success had now made it 'essential to increase investment for the development of light industry'. Yet even in this he was now held to have gone too far. Thus on the same day as that of Khrushchev's speech, Mikoyan resigned 'at his own request'; and on 8 February 1955 Malenkov also resigned, after admitting to 'lack of experience in local work', and assuming responsibility for 'the unsatisfactory state of affairs in agriculture'.

The fall of Malenkov has given rise to much speculation, and has been generally represented as the outcome of a struggle for power on the part of Khruschev. Malenkov, it is alleged, was in favour of stimulating efficiency by concessions, whereas Khrushchev stood for maintaining at all costs the supremacy of the Party which any such indulgences might well weaken. Hence Malenkov was responsible for the policy of 1953, of which the main plank was to make more consumer goods available, while Khrushchev opposed this, and eventually succeeded in securing Malenkov's removal and his replacement by Bulganin, presumably a fellow-conspirator. It may be so. Yet there is little firm evidence to support it. If it was felt that the hour called for a realistic policy of concessions, Khrushchev is as likely to have sponsored it as Malenkov, for not only was he more adventurist by temperament, but his long period of administration in the Ukraine would have given him a clearer insight into the state of public feeling than his colleague, whose background was that of controlling the central party organs from the Kremlin, which may well have accounted for his admission that he lacked 'experience of local work'. As no reports of the deliberations of the Presidium are made public, it is imprudent to attribute the collective decisions of that body to individual members of it. On this particular aspect of the 'new course', something like a reversal of policy certainly took place between the summer of 1953 and the beginning of 1955. But at least a possible explanation of this is that the line at first adopted was dictated by a mood of wavering and hesitation, readily intelligible under the circumstances, and revealed for a brief period even in the field of foreign relations; and that a year later the leaders had not only gained in assurance, but found themselves confronted with a number of circumstances which led them to reconsider their earlier and by no means orthodox proposal.

For what priority of heavy industry stands for in the Soviet Union is the sacrifice of present enjoyment in order to build up productive capital for the future, that is, that the community should save and not spend. This is what the country has done through the biggest and quickest economic effort known to history, and to it is attached an almost religious value. The pace may have been too fast, and the methods employed intolerable. Yet it is the mark of the dynamic society that it places the creation of wealth above its consumption – a policy which will never be popular, and is certain to be reversed in the name of 'social justice' as soon as the masses are in a position to do so, as it has been in this country, with consequent inflation and other evils.[1]

Indeed the view that at a given stage of socialism priority of heavy over light industry should be reversed is not far removed from the twin deviations, both sharply attacked by Lenin, of 'economism' and 'tailism' – the first implying in this context an undue preoccupation on the part of the workers with material benefits, and a consequent weakening of their revolutionary zeal, and the second, the tendency of the party to follow the masses instead of leading them, thus subordinating the primary consideration of building up the national economy to the secondary one of providing better working conditions and other amenities. What it would seem that the leaders now wished to make clear was that there would be no such subordination. But this did not prejudge the supply of more consumer goods as and when this might be thought desirable; and much of the so-called Malenkovite policy found its way into Khrushchev's speech at the 20th Congress, in which he promised to make more of them available, besides undertaking to raise wages, shorten working hours, improve housing, and increase pensions.

Whether there was a conflict of opinion within the Presidium when the original line was adopted we have no means of knowing. Yet there is at least indirect evidence that the leaders were agreed at the time, and it is supplied by what took place in the satellite countries, which are microcosms of the Soviet Union, whose policy their own reflects. The case of the Hungarian Workers' Party may serve as an example. In June 1953 the office of Party Secretary was abolished and was replaced by a secretariat of three, this being a concession to 'collective leadership'. In July Rakosi resigned the premiership in favour of Imre Nagy, who at once confessed that the most serious mistakes had been committed both in industry and agriculture, and proceeded to such sweeping reforms that Rakosi had to intervene a week later to restrain him. Yet the latter's report to the

1. For the above see 'The Dynamic Society' (*Times Literary Supplement*, 24 February 1956).

3rd Party Congress of May 1954 still envisaged a 'considerably slower rate of development of heavy industry', and the gearing of the national economy to meet consumer demands. But on 4 March 1955 the Central Committee passed a resolution stating that although the measures taken in July 1953 had 'proved absolutely correct and continued to be valid', they had been seriously distorted by the 'rightist, deviationist, anti-marxist and opportunist' attitude of Nagy, who was criticized for leniency towards the kulaks, for failure to increase the number of collective farms, and for 'denying the leading role of the party'. He refused to recant, and on 3 April was expelled from the Politburo and Central Committee. His successor, Andreas Hegedus, now declared that the principal task of the government would be to eliminate right deviationism, and that priority would henceforth be given to heavy industry. The same sequence can be traced in all the other satellites, and it is hard to believe that the leaders would have carried out the earlier policy so wholeheartedly if any considerable section of the Presidium in Moscow had been opposed to it, of which they would certainly have been aware.

It is possible that the decision which led to the change may have dated from the Plenum of the Central Committee of February 1954. In his report of September 1953, Khrushchev had drawn attention to the parlous state of livestock, but had declared the grain position to be satisfactory; but by the time the Plenum met it was causing grave anxiety, and he now launched his ambitious project of opening up 30 million hectares of virgin land in Siberia and Kazakhstan, whither large numbers of farm workers now proceeded, either under pressure of the party or komsomol [communist youth organization] authorities, or because they were attracted by the higher rates of pay offered.

The ultimate cause of the grain crisis is to be found in Stalin's agricultural policy. But that it came to a head when it did may be attributed to two causes. The liquidation of Beria and the down-grading of his formidable organization had weakened the principal instrument through which the Party had maintained discipline. The effect of this was particularly noticeable among the *kolkhozniki*, who were further encouraged by tax concessions to put in less work on their collectives, and to devote more time to their private plots on which they grew tomatoes, cucumbers and other non-essential produce for sale on the free market. It is significant that soon after the February Plenum – on 13 March – it was decided to create a 'Committee of State Security', separated once again from the Ministry of the Interior, then under Sergei Kruglov. Its head, I. A. Serov, was not a member at the time of his appointment either of the presidium of the party or of that of the government, but his promotion has since been rapid, and presumably also the growth of his influence. Of Kruglov, little had been heard for some time. On 1 February 1956 he was removed from his office and replaced by Nikolai Dudorov, for many years connected with the Moscow City Soviet, and later with the Central Committee. Kruglov was dropped from the Central Committee at the 20th Congress.

The new agricultural policy created economic priorities detrimental to the stepping up of light industry, and to these others were now added. Under its agreement with the Chinese Government of October 1954, the Soviet Government had undertaken substantially to increase the aid it was already giving to the establishment of Chinese heavy industry, and it was now becoming its policy to offer technical equipment to such countries as India and Burma. The satellites were also receiving further assistance of the same nature. Expenditure on the Soviet war machine and on atomic energy was rising. Further, the demand for more consumer goods was largely one for more clothes and boots, the raw materials for which come from the land and are not likely to be forthcoming when agriculture is in decline. There was thus at least a case for reviewing the earlier policy, and when it was decided to change it, it was not unnatural that Malenkov, with whom it was associated in the mind of the public, should have resigned, and have accompanied this, as Soviet practice requires, with a *mea culpa*. Nor in this instance was his self-criticism simply a ritual formality, for it was he who had been responsible for agriculture in the later years of Stalin's lifetime, and who had declared at the 19th Congress that 'the grain problem is now solved, solved successfully, solved definitely and irrevocably'.

Insistence upon discipline and united action is a characteristic of all left-wing parties, and reaches its highest expression in the Soviet Union, where the party leaders are obliged to operate as a monolithic group whose decisions must be represented as having been unanimously agreed. Under such a system, those leaders who in fact disapprove a given policy are not permitted openly to organize opposition to it, and will thus be encouraged to resort to intrigue to get it changed. This may well have occurred in the present instance, though what form it took and who sided with whom are questions which cannot be answered. The resignation of Malenkov is not, however, in itself a proof that 'collective leadership' had broken down, but rather an indication that the Russian leaders were making use of a procedure which has some analogy with the constitutional practice of the west. Malenkov retained his position on the presidium, while Mikoyan, who resigned when the policy with which he had openly identified himself was condemned, suffered no apparent loss of prestige, and is understood to have acted for Khrushchev and Bulganin during their Asian tour.

Nor did the modification of one element of the 1953 policy signify the abandonment of the 'new course'. There is in fact proceeding within the Soviet Union something which may develop into a genuine reforming movement if it is not frustrated by an ideology of which a fundamental principle is that the Party may never share its power. The amnesties of 17 March 1953 and 17 September 1955 were inspired in part at least by humanitarian motives, and were a step in the direction of 'socialist legality'. Indeed the first amnesty decree instructed the jurists to produce a new criminal code within a month, though it has not been forthcoming, nor is it likely to be for many a day. A number of 'Old Bolsheviks' who had passed into obscurity under Stalin have been decorated on their birthdays or on some other suitable occasion; and on 24 February 1956 *Pravda* actually published an article in praise of Bela Kun 'whose memory will be forever preserved', the first instance of the rehabilitation of an important political figure who was liquidated in the Great Purge as an 'enemy of the people'.

Attempts have also been made to simplify the machinery of administration by abolishing ministries, cutting down the number of officials and reducing accounting and other forms of paper work which absorb disproportionate man-power. Measures have been taken to decentralize authority and encourage local initiative. Factory managers have been given wider powers under the slogan of 'planning from below'. Large numbers of enterprises have been down-graded from Category A, of dependence upon Moscow, to Category B, which makes them the responsibility of the districts in which they are located. Republican governments have recovered many of the functions originally assigned to them under their constitutions, but later transferred to All-Union ministries. Where these measures have affected the administrative apparatus, they have, however, been resisted, and in many case nullified, by the bureaucracy which has an interest in maintaining the *status quo*, and the situation is still too fluid to make it possible to say how far they will achieve their purpose.

In the field of literature, and of the arts generally, there has also been a certain improvement. It is true that the articles which Pomarantsev and other authors associated with him published in *Novy Mir* at the end of 1953 and early in 1954 calling for greater 'sincerity' were denounced as 'attempts to revise the fundamental principles of Soviet literature'. Yet a good deal of plain speaking was permitted at the 2nd Congress of Soviet Writers, which convened in Moscow in December 1954, the last having met in August 1934; and although members were reminded in a message from the Central Committee that it was their duty to 'combat relapses into nationalism, cosmopolitanism, and other manifestations of bourgeois ideology', and the editors of the *Literaturnaya Gazeta* and the Secretariat of the Writers' Union were sharply attacked, no one was deprived of his post, which was at least an advance upon Zhdanov's inquisitorial methods. It is also significant that in 1955 official approval was secured of the publication of a complete edition of the works of Dostoyevsky.

In the field of foreign relations the 'new course' has operated in very much the same way as in that of domestic politics. Provided no matter of principle or of essential interest has been involved, the Soviet Government has shown itself prepared for a *détente* which will enable it to consolidate its gains and deal with its internal problems. Its first actions were indeed in the nature of gestures, as for example its decision to permit certain Russian wives to join their American husbands, and to recommend the Chinese communist and North Korean governments to agree to the exchange of disabled prisoners. But in June 1953 it dropped the claims it had been advancing since 1945 to certain purely Turkish territories; in the following July it agreed to the Korean armistice, negotiations for which had been hanging fire since Malik's proposal to United Nations in June 1951; in July 1954 it assisted to end the war in Indo-China, where the danger of American intervention seemed to be growing, and later in the year it used its influence to stop the Chinese communists from starting a war over Formosa. In April 1955, the Austrian Chancellor, Raab, was invited to Moscow, and within four days all the obstacles that 250 meetings of the Council of Foreign Ministers had failed to remove were swept away, so that in May a treaty was concluded under which Austria pledged herself to neutrality. At the end of that month Khrushchev and Bulganin visited Belgrade, and on 2 June they signed a declaration of friendship and cooperation with the Yugoslav Government.

The *rapprochement* with the Yugoslavs was an attempt to rectify one of the most glaring mistakes of Stalin's policy. Doubtless the violence of his onslaught made it impossible for him to retreat without loss of face, but it was certainly to the interests of his successors to come to terms with a country which had not only maintained its position in spite of every form of Soviet pressure, but was adopting towards the west an attitude that Moscow could not but regard as an ambiguous one. At the same time, it was of equal interest to Tito that the world should witness the spectacle of the two heads of an immensely powerful State visiting Belgrade and acknowledging their error, seeing that Khrushchev's attempt to throw the blame for what had passed upon Beria was too ridiculous to be taken seriously. Two points in the agreement should however be noted. First, that for all Khrushchev's efforts, it was one between governments only. Yugoslavia did not return to the Cominform, and the relations between the Yugoslav and the Russian parties remain undefined. Secondly, the agreement recognized what Stalin's intransigence had refused to concede – that the Yugoslav party was 'building socialism', though in its own way. But if this was true of the Yugoslav party, it was equally true of the parties of the satellite countries, many of whose leaders had suffered for 'nationalist deviationism'; and it will be more difficult to justify the treatment of such men as Gomulka now that the 20th Congress has laid down officially that the transition into socialism takes place in different countries in different ways.

The expectation that the 'new course' would at last render possible a settlement of the problem of Germany – the principal cause of international tension – was, however, to be disappointed. At the Berlin Council of Foreign Ministers of January 1954 the views of the western powers were set out in the 'Eden Plan'. This provided for the reunification of the country in five stages – the holding of free All-German elections, the convening of a National Assembly, the drafting of a Constitution, the formation of an All-German government and the negotiation of a peace treaty. But Molotov rejected this *in toto*. Both then and since the Russians have maintained that Western Germany is being rearmed contrary to the Potsdam Agreement, that the North Atlantic Treaty Organization (NATO) is an 'aggressive military grouping' directed against the Soviet Union; that the future of Germany must be decided by negotiations between the Federal Government and the East German Government at Pankow, which the former refuses to recognize; and that reunification is dependent upon the wider issue of European security. At the Geneva summit conference of July 1955, they appeared to be adopting a more conciliatory attitude, but in his report to the Supreme Soviet immediately after its conclusion Bulganin re-affirmed the old position, from which, when the Council of Foreign Ministers met at Geneva in October, Molotov refused to make any retreat.

Thus where major issues are concerned, the Russians have been as uncompromising in the post-stalinist period as they were before. After years of obstruction, they concluded a peace treaty with Austria because its terms would appeal to that section of German opinion which is in favour of reunification even at the cost of abandoning all ties with the west. At present they may feel that they have nothing to gain by yielding to the western powers. The eastern zone forms part of the cordon they have created to act as a buffer between Russia and the west; and to agree to free elections would be to throw over the East German Communist Party (the S.E.D.) and the Pankow Government, which would not only prejudice their position with the communist parties of the satellite countries, but with such parties everywhere. Yet if they decide that Germany is more important to them than the western Slav nations, they may well offer to make territorial concessions at the expense of Poland and Czechoslovakia; and were the terms offered to be sufficiently attractive, it is unlikely that any West German government would refuse to enter into relations with Pankow, which would certainly be the precondition of any settlement. Such a Russo-German *rapprochement* would confront the west with a most serious danger.

Meanwhile, Russian domination over the satellites has been formalized by the Warsaw Pact of 15 May 1955, which coordinated their armed forces under the command of Marshal Koniev with headquarters in Moscow, and in May 1956, its scope was extended to economic cooperation. The Russians are not prepared to discuss the regimes they have set up in these countries, and have said as much in their note to the Western Powers of 27 May 1955; for as *Pravda* announced on 14 June following: 'It must be obvious to anyone that there exists no "problem of eastern Europe" since the peoples of these countries, having thrown off the rule of the exploiters, have set up people's democracies, and will tolerate no interference in their internal affairs by anyone.'

The present policy of the Soviet Union is, however, that laid down by the 20th Congress of February 1956. The main report was delivered by Khrushchev in a speech which, while exhibiting personal authority of a high order, bore indications of having been the outcome of considerable discussion and debate. Certain elements in the official stalinist creed were toned down, either because they were outmoded, or because they were calculated to alienate circles otherwise not unsympathetic to communist objectives. Thus while imperialism and the 'bourgeois ideology' which supports it were attacked, the doctrine that wars are inevitable as long as imperialism exists was abandoned – an intelligible concession seeing that it was useless for the Russians to go to Geneva and elsewhere talking about peace if wars could not be prevented. Yet to admit that they could became dangerously near to repudiating Lenin's teaching. He had maintained that capitalist countries could not exist without colonies, and that as there were no more of them to be had, they could only satisfy their needs by seizing each other's. But the events of the last decade had confounded this thesis, since the major part of the colonial world had recovered its independence and the metropolitan countries had not collapsed as they should have done. The 19th Congress had indeed chosen to ignore this, and to represent such new countries as India and Burma as colonial dependencies and their leaders as 'agents of imperialism'. However, the Kremlin had since revised this opinion, and now found it convenient to recognize their independence, and to court their still uncommitted rulers instead of attacking them.

At the same time, the conflict between the capitalist and the socialist camps was reaffirmed. The contradictions within the former were stated to have become accentuated, with the result that the 'forces of reaction' were preparing 'bloody wars' against the Soviet Union and its allies. Yet these are the platitudes of every communist congress, and not only were they proclaimed with less bitterness than is customary on such occasions, but they were held compatible with the expression of a desire for better relations with Britain and America, and indeed with all countries, Israel alone excepted. Moreover, the Congress recognized that there are ways of establishing 'socialism' other than by revolution; that parliaments, which Lenin had taught were only to be made use of for the purpose of destroying them, could serve as organs of 'genuine democracy for the working people'; that 'cooperation with social democrats' was 'possible and essential'; and that 'separate paths to socialism' were permissible. The admission that the transition from capitalism to socialism can be accomplished without a revolution is indeed a significant departure from the traditional marxist-leninist convention which identified revolution with some form of proletarian mass action. But communist techniques have changed with the times, and the purpose of their infiltration tactics is precisely to enable a party to seize power without a popular uprising, as in the case of Czechoslovakia, which was specifically cited as an example of peaceful change. The concessions, if they can be so described, were evidently made with a view to inducing the social democratic parties to form popular-front governments with the communists. It is unlikely that the leaders of such parties will be deceived, but experience has shown that the same cannot be said of their rank and file.

The most spectacular development at the Congress and in the period immediately following it was, however, the repudiation of the stalinist 'cult of personality', of stalinist policies generally, and finally of Stalin himself, which was the more remarkable in view of the adulation heaped upon the dead leader by the men who denounced him, and of the extent to which they had been responsible for carrying out the measures they now denounced, and of which they had been in many cases the beneficiaries. It is as yet too early to say what will be the outcome of this, though the decision to dissolve the Cominform – the symbol of Soviet hostility to the west – must be accounted as one of them. Up to the present, it has been in the satellite countries that the effect of the change of line has been most observable. Kostov and Rajk have been rehabilitated; and the Bulgarian and Hungarian Party leaders Chervenkóv and Rakosi have been dismissed, as has also Gottwald's son-in-law Čepička, the Czechoslovak Deputy Premier and Minister of Defence. In Poland, Jacub Berman and certain other leaders have been removed, and criticism of the Party has been particularly outspoken. That the present party was mainly built up during those very years when stalinist autocracy was absolute is an evident source of weakness to the leadership now that the policies associated with that autocracy are being disavowed by Moscow itself.

Thus the Soviet leaders are now seeking to convince the world that their condemnation of stalinism is sincere, though they have yet to explain what specific elements in current communist theory and practice are assignable to it. Yet to exorcise stalinism will be no easy matter. It has become the expression of the aspirations of a world movement, so that to disown it would be to disown the form that movement has taken and substitute another for it. How far the leadership is willing or able to do this only the future will disclose.

21. Conclusion

THE purpose of government, and the central problem of political philosophy is the adjustment of the claims of the individual and the community. In the last century, the subjective individualism which entered western Europe with the Renaissance and the Reformation issued in liberalism and *laissez-faire* until, in its third quarter, the tide turned in the direction of collectivism, and this has been advancing ever since. The change was primarily due to two causes – on the one hand, the extension of the parliamentary suffrage and the development of organized labour, and on the other, the growing complexity of the international world market which led the workers to believe that political rights were of little account if they failed to secure them a livelihood. Thus there arose the demand, which became intensified in the inter-war years, for such security as logically demands a State-controlled economy. Of this type of economy Russia is the most extreme example, as it is based upon collectivist principles applied with complete ruthlessness.

The ideological foundation upon which the Soviet order is founded has already been considered. We have seen that it is materialist because its fundamental assumption is the primacy of the economic factor, of which whatever else exists is held to be the reflection. It follows therefore that if society is to be reconstituted, the first step must be to change its economic basis by collectivizing the productive forces which capitalism has been hitherto exploiting. These productive forces will now 'belong to the workers'. But the communists are well aware that the workers are powerless to direct them, and under the new order this will become the responsibility of the party, which, by a convenient fiction, is held to represent the single class of 'toilers' to which the community will now be levelled, all of whom are assumed to possess the same class interests. Within such a framework, democracy of the western type is meaningless. One-party government alone makes sense, for there is nothing for a second party to represent; if it agrees with the official party it is superfluous; if it does not, it is counter-revolutionary. Nor can there be any limit to the powers that may be exercised by a regime which represents *ex hypothesei* the will of the single and undivided people. The individual has no status outside the group to which he belongs, and what part he can best play within it is for his leaders to decide. The law becomes an instrument for suppressing whatever they may choose to regard as subversion, as Soviet jurists have not troubled to conceal. Philosophy, literature, art, and science can claim no autonomy under such a system, for their value and justification lie solely in the degrees to which they strengthen it. The family, long ago exposed by Engels as an immature form of association, will only be upheld in so far as the State may decide to make use of it, seeing that it is to society and not to its parents that the child belongs. Religion will certainly not be tolerated for long, since it threatens to create a dual loyalty in a world in which all things have become Caesar's. The engineers of the new society can brook no rival. Yet God is a serious rival; even the very thought that He may exist is unendurable. Thus the individual is completely absorbed into the collective, in which he must live and move and have his being.

To the west, democracy of this totalitarian type will appear a mockery. Yet, as J. L. Talmon has pointed out, it is a part of the European tradition, and coeval with democracy of the liberal type. Both derive from the belief entertained by the eighteenth-century *philosophes* that there existed a natural social order, the counterpart of the cosmic order of Newtonian physics, which everyone, if properly instructed, would accept because it corresponded with what Rousseau called the 'general will'. The jacobins shared this belief, but only to discover that their own particular specific for setting the world to rights not only failed to command universal assent, but excited violent opposition even among those whom it was intended to benefit. Clearly there could be nothing wrong with the specific itself. The fault lay with the people, who were too immature to see what their true interests were, and must therefore be induced to do so, if necessary, by force. Thus the 'general will' becomes transformed into the will of the leaders, and we find such men as Robespierre and Saint-Just using the same arguments to defend their actions as Lenin and Stalin were to employ a century and a quarter later.[1]

The jacobins had believed that they could realize their objectives without interfering with the rights of property. All that was necessary was to rid society of kings, priests, and other obstacles to liberty, substitute good laws for bad, and educate men in the virtues of citizenship. But when Marx revived the revolutionary tradition half a century later, he made the abolition of the existing property system the precondition of the establishment of a just social order. The private ownership of the means of production was the source of all evils, and with its abolition they would disappear. Society could not be restored by constitution-making after the manner of a Siéyès or a Bentham, but only by radically changing the whole complex of productive relations, of which he held the property system to be the most important element. From the revolution that would bring this about there would eventually develop a genuine communist society in which men would agree to abandon their individuality, of which property is an expression, and live solely in and for the collective whole. Yet to believe that they will ever voluntarily do this is the very extreme of utopianism. The tension between the individual and society is a natural one, and it is not resolved by getting rid of one of its elements, any more than is the equilibrium of a pair of scales restored by removing one of its balances.[2] There is nothing in Marx's teaching to show how this transformation of human nature will be brought about; while in *The State and Revolution* Lenin dismisses the question as one to which there can be no answer and which no one has the right to ask.

The truth is that neither Marx nor Lenin ever seriously considered what would be the result of practising the revolutionary

1. *The Origins of Totalitarian Democracy* (1952); *see* especially pp. 1–13, 99–131, 249–55.

2. Pierre Bigo, *Marxisme et humanisme* (Paris, 1953), p. 158.

principles they preached. To have applied them in an advanced industrial country was never feasible. But in backward Russia it proved possible, and thus caused irreparable damage by arresting what should have been a process of genuine democratic development. Revolutions proceed according to a logic and inner necessity of their own by which those responsible for them are bound whether they recognize it or not. It is possible that Lenin continued to believe that his own revolution was 'bringing the masses into active participation in the work of government' long after it had become obvious that it was having precisely the opposite effect. However this may be it was certainly he who laid the foundations of the autocracy of the party, and it was no accident that after his death the prize of the succession went to the man who controlled its machine.

As Talmon says, liberal and totalitarian democracy agree in affirming the supreme value of liberty. Only while for the former liberty lies in reducing coercion to a minimum, for the latter it can only be realized in the collective pursuit of an ideal order – universal, harmonious, and all-solving – which must ultimately come to pass. The Russians are the present-day exponents of this way of thinking, which is bound to issue in totalitarianism, and there is as yet no firm evidence that they have abandoned it. Stalin, it is true, carried his arbitrary rule to such a point that his successors have been obliged to denounce it. Yet given the objective situation, it was inevitable that the Soviet regime should have taken the form it has, and whether it was more or less oppressive than it need have been is simply a matter of degree. By carrying out the revolution under the conditions he did, Lenin plunged the country into chaos, with the result that the party took control, and acquired a vested interest which time has converted into a stranglehold. As he was convinced that the west was ripe for revolution, and equally that unless this occurred the new soviet order would collapse, he set up the Comintern as a rallying point for it, so that from the first Russian policy towards the western powers was interlocked with that of an organization whose object was to subvert them. When these 'scientific predictions', as he once called them, were both falsified, the obvious policy was to build up Russia's internal strength so that she could not only direct the revolutionary movement, but also maintain herself should it continue to tarry; and it was this that Stalin introduced under the slogan of 'socialism in one country'. But to carry it out meant the rapid transformation of what was still an over-whelmingly peasant country into a highly industrialized one, and this in turn involved the regimentation of all sections of the community, and especially the workers. And as it is impossible to industrialize a country unless the greatly increased number of persons now engaged in industry can be fed, agriculture had then to be brought into line, though here the issue was confused by ideological considerations, with the result that so ruthless a policy was pursued that it failed to achieve its purpose. None the less, Russian industry expanded at a prodigious rate, though at a cost in human sacrifice that no democratic regime would have tolerated.

The principles on which the revolution was effected and the form that came to be given to them worked in the same totali-tarian direction. Marxism is nothing if it is not revolutionary. The entire fabric of society is to be turned upside down, and be rebuilt on wholly new foundations. The bolsheviks accepted this as their starting point. They were the more attracted to the marxist dialectic by reason of the native Russian tendency to see everything in terms of absolute opposites, and to refuse to admit the possibility of any intermediate position. Thus, for the party, there is no alternative between total victory and total annihilation; the line it adopts is the only correct one, and any other would lead to catastrophe; and there is nothing between complete loyalty to the communist cause and equally complete hostility.[1] This 'all-or-nothing' way of thinking excludes any sort of compromise, and makes changes of policy impossible, save when they are undertaken for purely tactical reasons. Thus communism is essentially aggressive and intolerant, and its adherents are taught from the first that they are living in a hostile world which is seeking their destruction, and that they

1. See N. Leites, A Study of Bolshevism (1953), pp. 404 ff., and Margaret Mead, Soviet Attitudes Toward Authority (Eng. ed. 1956), pp. 31 ff.

must never relax their 'revolutionary vigilance' against its machinations. For, as Lenin laid down in his *What is to be done?* (1902), there are only two possible world views, the bourgeois and the socialist, and whatever weakens the one must strengthen the other. Hence the importance attached to 'party-mindedness'. The Communist must be governed solely by the ideology of his class as this is interpreted by his party, and any attempt to meet the arguments of a non-communist on their merits, or even to concede that they can have any, is to be guilty of 'bourgeois objectivism'.

It is true that the formalization of this ideology coincided with Stalin's rise to absolute power. None the less, its essential elements were contained in Lenin's belief in revolution as the precursor of an order of absolute social justice, to which was opposed the iniquitous existing order of capitalism – the germ of the doctrine of the 'two camps' – and in his theory of the dominant role of the party both before and after the revolution and of its relation to the masses. Stalin did no more than render these elements more explicit. If therefore the present slogan of 'back to Lenin' is to be taken literally, we cannot expect any greater concessions than those made at the 20th Congress, which, on examination, do not amount to much. If, on the other hand, it means the condemnation of the stalinist ideology (its debt to Lenin's being tacitly passed over), and if this is something more than a tactical device, we may expect to see the gradual disappearance of its more objectionable features. It is significant that a number of prominent ideologists were elected to the Central Committee at the 20th Congress, and that the *History of the Communist Party of the Soviet Union*, attributed to Stalin himself, which sets out the official ideology in its most rampant aspect, was condemned and is, apparently, to be re-written.

Communism is the extreme expression of that view of the self-sufficiency of man which nineteenth-century rationalist materialism took over from eighteenth-century perfectionism. It claims to be able, through science and social action, to create an ideal order in which the needs and desires of mankind will be fully satisfied, and thus it unscrupulously exploits strains, tensions, and anxieties which cannot be completely resolved because they are inherent in the human situation. And this order is held to possess an absolute value, any means are justified which assist its attainment. Such a claim is sufficient to bring it into conflict with Christianity, which can never allow its absolute standard to become identified with the relative historic process – a truth to which no one in our day has drawn attention with greater force than Reinhold Niebuhr. Yet liberalism reaches much the same conclusion as long as it remains faithful to its empiricist premises. Locke, the founder of modern empiricism, is never weary, as Bertrand Russell has pointed out, of emphasizing the uncertainty of our knowledge, nor with any sceptical intention, but to make men aware that they may be mistaken, and that they must take this into account in their dealings with other men.[1]

The example of the Soviet Union should serve therefore as a warning to those who believe that if the community is organized according to some single and exclusive pattern, the result will be a perfect social integration. Berdyaev quoted with approval an observation of the Hungarian Communist Georg Lucàcs that the character of revolutions which make this their aim is not determined by the radical nature of their objectives, nor even by the means used to attain them, but by the total demands that their authors will be driven to make if the life of the community is to be regulated according to an absolute social purpose.[2] This purpose is at first conceived as immanent alike in man's reason and in the laws that govern society. But the attempt to actualize it inevitably leads to the predominance of an *élite*, whose members claim, by virtue of some special illumination, a deeper insight into its nature than their fellows, and thus demand that their will be accepted as that of society as a whole. Unfortunately, revolutions carried out in the name of ideologies invariably lead to consequences that not even their authors had anticipated, and this may certainly be expected when the ideology is of such a nature as to require that every branch of economy and form of social expression be subjected

1. *Philosophy and Politics* (1947), pp. 20–2.
2. *The Origin of Russian Communism* (1937), p. 124.

to centralized direction and control. The wider the gulf between what the revolution sets out to do and what it accomplishes, the more will those responsible for it be compelled to resort to one fiction after another to account for what has taken place, and to apply coercive measures to suppress opposition to it.

Yet in the end these measures will be found self-defeating, as they paralyse those qualities of initiative and independent judgement upon which a society depends if it is to go forward. This raises an awkward problem. If the repressive policy is pursued, the country may fall behind, and crises dangerous to authority arise; whereas to relax it is to start a process of which the outcome cannot be foreseen. It is this dilemma with which the present Russian rulers are confronted, and from which they are seeking to extricate themselves by easing the tensions where they feel they can do so without compromising the principles upon which their system of government rests. How far they will be successful in this, time alone will discover.

Yet we are not entitled to conclude that the attempt will fail, and great disservice is done by those who are for ever dwelling on Russia's internal difficulties, and predicting that they must inevitably lead to the collapse of the regime. The communist party structure is exceedingly strong, and it owes its strength to that very feature that non-communists most dislike – the rigid discipline it imposes. Doubtless it will be found possible to concede more political freedom, though how much any given society can stand without abusing it is hard to say. Russia has made enormous progress, and there is no reason to suppose that she will not continue to do so. The Soviet worker does not suffer from unemployment; but he must work where his services are required, fulfil his allotted norm, and accept what wages the State chooses to pay him. According to the prevailing current of western thinking, this is the negation of democracy, and indeed it is much to be desired that the Soviet rulers should come round to this way of thinking, as their country would soon become less formidable than it is at present. As long as their dispositions remain unchanged, they may be expected to continue to advance their objectives by such methods as experience has shown to be effective. But unless they are prepared to resort to war, which appears improbable, and are victorious, they cannot impose their way of life upon the west, and if western communist parties gain control, it will be because the way has been prepared for them by those who have accepted the more utopian elements in the marxist system, and have then been unwilling or unable to face the consequences.

Bibliography

THE bibliography appended to the fifth edition of this book has been brought up to date by listing some works published in English since 1957 which may be useful to readers. These additional titles will be found in their alphabetical order. Readers are also referred to the late R. N. Carew Hunt's bibliography entitled *Books on Communism* published in 1959. No attempt has been made to modify the author's basis of selection or evaluation and the additional titles, marked with an asterisk, have therefore been left without comment.

L.S.

(NOTE. *All the books listed were published in London unless otherwise stated.*)

ACTON, H. B., *The Illusion of the Epoch* (1955). An important book which contains the best account in English of Lenin's philosophical position, and an admirable criticism of the doctrine of historical materialism.

ANDLER, Charles, *Le Manifeste communiste. Introduction historique et commentaire* (Paris, 1901). The standard critical edition of the *Communist Manifesto*.

ASPATURIAN, Vernon V., *The Contemporary Doctrine of the Soviet State and its Philosophical Foundations*. A valuable essay on the development of the Marxist theory of the State, published in the *American Political Science Review* of December 1954.

BARBU, Zevedei, *Democracy and Dictatorship* (1956). A study of the psychological basis of communism as contrasted with that of fascism.

BARTHOLI, Henri, *La Doctrine sociale et économique de Karl Marx* (Paris, 1950). A well-documented analysis, particularly of Marx's economic theory.

BEER, Max, *Fifty Years of International Socialism* (1935). Interesting for the history of the Second International.

BENDA, Julien, *Trois idoles romantiques* (Paris, 1948). Studies of Dynamism, Existentialism and Dialectical Materialism.

BERACHA, S., *Le Marxisme après Marx* (Paris, 1937). Of interest for its treatment of Bernstein, Kautsky and Sorel.

294 BIBLIOGRAPHY

BERDYAEV, Nicolas, *The Origin of Russian Communism* (1937). *The Russian Idea* (1947). Both are well worth reading, particularly the second.

BERLIN, Isaiah, *Karl Marx* (1939, re-issued 1948). A brilliant short life of Marx.

BIGO, Pierre, *Marxisme et humanisme* (Paris, 1953). An interesting study of the development of Marx's economic doctrine.

BOBER, M. M., *Karl Marx's Interpretation of History* (Harvard University Press, 1927). The most complete discussion of the Marxist doctrine of historical materialism that has appeared in English.

BOCHENSKI, I. M., *Der Sowjetrussische dialektische Materialismus* (Bern, 1950). A valuable introduction. The author, a Polish Dominican, is a professor at Freiburg University.

BOHM-BAWERK, E. V., *Karl Marx and the Close of his System* (Eng. trans. 1898). One of the earliest and most important criticisms of Marx's economic system. The author was a professor at Vienna University and sometime Austrian Minister for Finance.

BORKENAU, Franz, *The Communist International* (1938). *European Communism* (1953). These two books deal with the policy and activities of the Third International and with the history of the more important national Communist Parties. *Socialism, National or International* (1942). Discusses the extent to which nationalism has displaced the older socialist conception of internationalism.

BOTHEREAU, Robert, *Histoire du syndicalisme français* (Paris, 1945). An excellent introduction to the French trade-union movement and to syndicalist ideas generally.

BUBER, Martin, *Paths in Utopia* (1949). A most interesting exposition of the thesis that there were two main trends in nineteenth-century socialist thought, the first, represented by Proudhon, aiming at a decentralized society, and the second, represented by Marx and Lenin, aiming at the establishment by revolution of one that is centralized.

BURNS, Emile, *What is Marxism?* (1939, re-issued 1947). A good, brief introduction by a leading communist. *A Handbook of Marxism* (1935). A most valuable source-book of selections from the writings of Marx, Engels, Lenin, and Stalin.

CAMERON, J. M., *Scrutiny of Marxism* (1948). Especially interesting for its criticism of the Marxist ethic.

CARR, E. H., *Karl Marx. A Study in Fanaticism* (1934). A very good biography.

The Romantic Exiles (1933). Of great interest as a study of the Russian *émigrés* in the middle of the last century.

Bakunin (1937). This is the standard biography.

Studies in Revolution (1950). A series of articles reprinted from *Times Literary Supplement*.

The Bolshevik Revolution, 1917–1923, Vols. I–IV (1950–54). The most complete study of the period from 1917 to 1924.

* Volumes V and VI of this work entitled *Socialism in One Country 1924–1926* appeared in 1958 and 1959 respectively.

CHAMBERLIN, W. H., *The Russian Revolution; 1917–1921* (2 vols., 1935). A standard work.

CHAMBRE, Henri, *Le Marxisme en Union Soviétique* (Paris, 1955). An objective and well-documented study of the application of Marxist–Leninist principles to the various fields of Soviet life, and of special value for its treatment of Stalin's later writings.

COLE, G. D. H., *What Marx Really Meant* (1934). A stimulating exposition of the Marxist system but at times open to the objection that while Marx would have been well advised to have adopted the positions attributed to him, he did not, in fact, do so. A revised edition appeared in 1948 with the title, *The Meaning of Marxism*.

A History of Socialist Thought, Vols. I–IV (1954–1956). This work, which is still in progress, is indispensable for an understanding of the development of the Socialist movement. The fifth volume of this work was published in 1960.

COLE, G. D. H., and POSTGATE, Raymond, *The Common People; 1746–1946* (1938). A most useful account of the development of the Labour Movement.

COLLINET, Michel, *La Tragédie du marxisme* (Paris, 1948). An interesting study, and of especial value for its account of Marx's attitude to the revolutions of 1848 and the Commune.

CONZE, Edward, *An Introduction to Dialectical Materialism* (London, n.d.). A moderate statement by a German Marxist.

COURTADE, Pierre, *Essai sur l' antisoviétisme* (Paris, 1946). A good example of the type of propaganda directed at intellectual circles. The author was formerly the Political Editor of *Humanité*.

CROCE, Benedetto, *Historical Materialism and the Economics of Karl Marx* (1914). The Italian original was first published in 1900.

History of Europe in the Nineteenth Century (1924). This book, which is one of the most stimulating of Croce's writings, was first published in 1931. A great part of it is devoted to the study of liberal and revolutionary movements in Europe up to 1914.

Come il Marx fece passare il communismo dall'utopia alla scienza (1948).

DESROCHES, H. C., *Signification du marxisme* (Paris, 1950). An interesting and well-documented study by a Catholic priest. It is followed by a valuable introduction to the bibliography of Marx and Engels by Ch-F. Hubert.

DEUTSCHER, Isaac, *Stalin: a Political Biography* (1949). An admirable study, and likely to be for many years the standard work upon the subject.

The Prophet Armed. Trotsky 1879–1921 (1954).

DIEHL, Karl, *Über Sozialismus, Kommunismus und Anarchismus* (Jena, 1922). This volume of lectures delivered at Jena University is of great value not only for its criticism of Marxism and Bolshevism, but for the account it gives of the development of Marxism in France and Germany and of the various movements, e.g. anarchism and reformism, which it had to encounter.

DOBB, Maurice, *Marx as an Economist – An Essay* (1946).

Studies in the Development of Capitalism (1947). An important contribution to the subject. Traces the development of the capitalist system in this country, with special reference to Marx's criticisms of it. Written from the communist angle by a Cambridge economist.

DURANTY, Walter, *U.S.S.R. The Story of Soviet Russia* (1944). A readable introduction written from a not over-critical standpoint.

EASTMAN, Max, *Marx, Lenin and the Science of Revolution* (1927).

The Last Stand of Dialectical Materialism (1934).

The End of Socialism in Russia (1937).

Stalin's Russia and the Crisis of Socialism (1940).

Marxism. Is it a Science? (1941). All Eastman's writings are stimulating. *Marxism. Is it a Science?* is the most important of those listed.

ENGELS, Friedrich, *Anti-Dühring* (1877).

The Origin of the Family (1884).

Ludwig Feuerbach (1886). Printed in the 2-volume edition of the *Marx–Engels Selected Works* (1950).

FAINSOD, Merle, *How Russia is Ruled* (Harvard University Press, 1954). A full-dress study of the Communist Party and Soviet Government apparatus.

FEDERN, Karl, *The Materialist Conception of History* (1939). A very interesting study of which considerable use has been made in this book.

FISCHER, Ruth, *Stalin and German Communism* (Harvard University Press, 1948). A detailed history of the German Communist Party during the twenties, when it was the leading Western European Section of the Third International.

FOOTMAN, David, *Red Prelude* (1944). A most interesting study of the revolutionary group which assassinated the Tsar Alexander II in 1881.

FRÖLICH, Paul, *Rosa Luxemburg* (1940). Of value for the light which it throws on the left wing of the German Social Democratic Party.

GARAUDY, Roger, *Le Communisme et la morale* (Paris, 1954). Of value as a statement of the Marxist position. Its author is a member of the Central Committee of the French Communist Party.

GIDE, Charles and RIST, Charles, *A History of Economic Doctrines* (ed. 1948). A standard work first published in France in 1909 and many times reprinted.

GRAY, Alexander, *The Socialist Tradition from Moses to Lenin* (1946). A good review of Socialist thought. Useful in particular for the precursors of Marx.

GRAY, J. L., *Karl Marx and Social Philosophy* in *Social and Political Ideas of the Victorian Age*. Edited by F. J. C. Hearnshaw (1933). A valuable essay.

GRIERSON, Philip, *Books on Soviet Russia, 1917–1942* (1943). An indispensable bibliography.

GURVITCH, Georges, *La Vocation actuelle de la sociologie* (Paris, 1949). The last chapter is a most important contribution to Marxist sociology.

HALÉVY, Élie, *Histoire du socialisme européen* (Paris, 1948). A useful introduction, based on a course which Halévy gave yearly at the École des Sciences Politiques, and put into book form by a group of former pupils after his death in 1947.

HEGEL, G. W. F., *Lectures on the Philosophy of History* (Eng. trans., Bohn Library, 1856). The most easily digested of Hegel's works, and well worth reading as a book which has exercised great influence.

HILL, Christopher, *Lenin and the Russian Revolution* (1947). A short biography. The author is a Marxist.

HOOK, Sidney, *Towards an Understanding with Karl Marx* (1936). *From Hegel to Marx* (1936). Both are excellent studies.

HYDE, Douglas, *The Answer to Communism* (1949). An interesting popular exposure of communist theory and methods by the late News Editor of the London *Daily Worker*.

JOLL, James, *The Second International* (1955). The best account in English.

JOSEPH, H. W. B., *The Labour Theory of Value in Karl Marx*. A very important criticism of Marx's economic theory.

KAUTSKY, Karl, *Terrorism and Communism* (1920). Of interest in connexion with Lenin's *Proletarian Revolution and the Renegade Kautsky*.

KELSEN, Hans, *Sozialismus und Staat* (Leipzig, 1923). Of great interest, particularly for its criticism of Marxist theory of the State.

The Political Theory of Bolshevism (Univ. of California Press, 1949). An extremely able short critical analysis.

KOESTLER, Arthur, *The Yogi and the Commissar* (1945). Contains much stimulating criticism of the Stalinist regime.

* KOLARZ, Walter, *Religion in the Soviet Union* (1961).

LABRIOLA, Antonio, *La concezione materialistica della storia* (1895, ed. Bari, 1947). An important book. Croce holds Labriola to be the only Communist who made any really significant addition to Marx's teaching.

LASKI, H. J., *Communism* (1927). A good introduction, if somewhat out of date. See also the *Communist Manifesto* under MARX.

LAZITCH, Branko, *Lénine et la III⁰ Internationale* (Paris, 1951). Invaluable for the early history of the Comintern.

LEFEBRE, Henri, *Le Matérialisme dialectique* (Paris, 1940; 3rd. ed.

1949). Of special interest for its account of Marx's use of the dialectic.

LEITES, Nathan, *A Study in Bolshevism* (The Free Press, Glencoe, Ill, 1953). A well-documented analysis of the various concepts which make up the operational code of the communist movement.

LENIN, V. I., *Complete Works* (18 vols.; English translation authorized by the Lenin Institute, Moscow. n.d.).
  Selected Works (12 vols., 1936–9).
  The Essentials of Lenin (*Selected Works*, 2 vols., 1947).
  The War and the Second International (1914).
  The State and Revolution (1917).
  The Proletarian Revolution and the Renegade Kautsky (1918).
  Left Wing Communism (1920). The above pamphlets are available in the 'Little Lenin Library' series, published by Messrs Lawrence and Wishart.

LENZ, J., *The Second International* (New York, 1932). A history of the International from the communist angle.

LEONTIEV, A., *Political Economy. A Beginner's Course* (1936). An English translation of an official Russian introduction to Marxist economics.

LEPP, I., *Le Marxisme, philosophie ambigue et efficace* (Paris, 1949). An interesting and stimulating criticism of his Marxist philosophy.

LEWIS, John, and others, *The Communist Answer to the Challenge of our Times* (1947). A collection of essays of a group of British communist intellectuals.

* LICHTHEIM, George, *Marxism. An Historical and Critical Study* (1961).

MACKIEWICZ, Stanislaw, *Dostoyevsky* (1947). Interesting for its comments on the Russian revolutionary movement.

MACMURRAY, John, *The Philosophy of Communism* (1933). A stimulating essay on dialectical materialism.

MARKHAM, S. F., *History of Socialism* (1930). A good general introduction.

MARX, Karl. There is still no complete edition of the works and papers of Marx and Engels in the original languages, as that which was being issued in Berlin under the auspices of the Marx–Engels–Lenin Institute in Moscow was interrupted by the accession of Hitler to power in 1933. The Russian edition, which was appearing simultaneously, is further advanced, but is still not complete. The most serviceable edition is the *Selected Works* (2 vols., 1950).

The Communist Manifesto (1848). This has been many times reprinted. A recent edition, which included the prefaces written by Marx and Engels for the various editions, appeared in 1948 with an interesting introduction by Professor Laski.

Contribution to the Critique of Political Economy (1859). (Eng. trans. Chicago, 1909).

Capital (first published in German, Vol. I, 1867, Vol. II, 1885, Vol. III, 1894). First English translation: Vol. I, London, 1889; Vol. II, London and Chicago, 1907; Vol. III, Chicago, 1909.

The Class Struggles in France (1850).

The Civil War in France (1870–1).

The Critique of the Gotha Programme (1875). All the above are included in the 2-volume edition of the *Selected Works*.)

Der Briefwechsel zwischen Friedrich Engels und Karl Marx (edited by A. Bebel and E. Bernstein, 4 vols., Stuttgart, 1913).

Marx–Engels Selected Correspondence (edited by Dona Torr, 1935).

Economic and Philosophic Manuscripts of 1844 (Moscow, 1959).

MASARYK, T. G., *The Spirit of Russia* (2 vols., 1919. This is the standard work on Russian thought in the nineteenth century and on the various currents of western thought which influenced it.

MAULNIER, Thierry, *La Pensée marxiste* (Paris, 1948). Selections from the writings of Marx, Engels, and Lenin interspersed with some acute criticism.

MAYER, Gustav, *Friedrich Engels* (2 vols., The Hague, 1920; abridged Eng. trans. 1935). The standard biography.

MEHRING, Franz, *Karl Marx* (1920: Eng. trans. 1936, re-issued 1948). The standard life of Marx by a German communist upon which all later biographers have drawn. It includes an excellent bibliography of Marx's writings.

MEYER, Alfred G., *Marxism, The Unity of Theory and Practice* (Harvard University Press, 1954). A critical study of the Marxist philosophy.

* *Leninism* (Harvard University Press, 1957).

MILYOUKOV, Paul, *Russia and its Crisis* (1905). Extremely valuable for its account of the development of the Russian revolutionary movement in the nineteenth century. The author, the leader of the Constitutional Democrats, was for a time Foreign Minister of the Provisional Government set up in March 1917.

MITRANY, David, *Marx against the Peasant* (1951). Essential for an understanding of the communist attitude towards the peasant problem.

MONDOLFO, Rodolfo, *Il materialismo storico in Federico Engels* (ed. Florence, 1952). This book, first published in 1912, is by far the best analysis and defence of historical materialism which has ever been written from the Marxist standpoint.

MONNEROT, Jules, *Sociologie du communisme* (Paris, 1949). A big book and the first to attempt to deal with the subject comprehensively. It contains much that is of interest though its style is by no means an easy one.

MOORE, Jr, Barrington, *Soviet Politics. The Dilemma of Power* (Harvard University Press, 1951). A valuable analysis of the factors which have contributed to create the Soviet regime.

* NOLLAU, Günther, *International Communism and World Revolution. History and Methods* (1961).

PASCAL, Roy, *Karl Marx: Political Foundations* (1943). Interesting as showing how Marx's opinions took form during the 1840s.

PIPES, Richard, *The Foundation of the Soviet Union, 1917–1923* (Harvard University Press, 1954). Deals fully with the attitude adopted by the Bolsheviks towards the non-Russian minorities in the period covered.

PLAMENATZ, John, *What is Communism?* (1947). A most able little book to which the writer of the study is much indebted.
  German Marxism and Russian Communism (1954). An account of Marx's doctrine, and an explanation of how Bolshevism arose out of them.

PLEKHANOV, G. V., *In Defence of Materialism* (1895).
  Fundamental Problems of Marxism (1908). Plekhanov was Lenin's teacher, and his writings are still referred to with respect, since, although he broke with Lenin in 1904, the latter said that no one had the right to call himself a Marxist who had not read him. A new English translation of the first of these books appeared in 1947, with an introduction by Andrew Rothstein. The second has been re-issued in the 'Marxist–Leninist Classics' series.

POLITZER, Georges, *Principes élémentaires de philosophie* (Paris, 1938). A course of lectures on Marxist philosophy given at the Workers' University in Paris.

POPPER, K. R., *The Open Society and its Enemies* (2 vols., 1945–7). The second volume provides a most searching criticism of the philosophical and historical doctrines of Marxism.

POSTGATE, Raymond, *Reflections on May Day* (*Horizon*, May, 1948). An interesting appreciation, written on the occasion of the centenary of the publication of the *Communist Manifesto*, of how far Marx's predictions have been fulfilled and of what Marxism stands for today.

RENNES, Jacques, *Georges Sorel et le syndicalisme révolution-naire* (Paris, 1936).

ROBBINS, L. H., *An Essay on the Nature and Significance of Economic Science* (1934). Valuable for its criticism of the economic interpretation of history.

ROCKER, Rudolf, *Anarcho-Syndicalism* (1938). The best presentation of the anarcho-syndicalist position.

ROLLIN, Henri, *La Révolution russe* (2 vols., Paris, 1931). A most important book.

ROSENBERG, Arthur, *A History of Bolshevism* (1939).
Democracy and Socialism (1939). Both are valuable. The author was sometime professor of history in Berlin University, a Reichstag deputy and a member of the Politburo of the German Communist Party, which he left in 1929.

RUSSELL, Bertrand, *Freedom and Organization, 1814-1914* (1934). The section on Marxism is excellent.
The Practice and Theory of Bolshevism, 1949. First published in 1920 and now re-issued.

SABINE, George H., *A History of Political Theory* (1937). This work, by a professor of Cornell University, contains valuable sections on Hegel, Marx, and Lenin.

SARTRE, J.-P., ROUSSET, David, and ROSENTHAL, Gerard, *Entretiens sur la politique* (Paris, 1949). An interesting symposium which contains an attack on Marxists of the Stalinist obedience by leaders of *soi-disant* Marxist Rassemblement Democratique Révolutionnaire.

SCHAPIRO, Leonard, *The Origin of the Communist Autocracy, 1917–1922* (1955). An important study of the political parties at the time of the October Revolution, and of the means by which Lenin secured the domination of his own.
* *The Communist Party of the Soviet Union* (1960).

SCHLESINGER, Rudolph, *The Spirit of Post-War Russia* (1947).

A cautiously written defence of Stalinism by a former member of the German Communist Party.

Marx. His Time and Ours (1950). An exposition of present-day communist theory, set out in the idiom of the Party and not easy reading.

SCHUMPETER, Joseph, *Capitalism, Socialism and Democracy* (1950). Part I of this volume is an important essay on Marx as an economist.

Imperialism and Social Classes (1951). A translation of two articles, 'The Sociology of Imperialism' and 'Social Classes in an Ethnically Homogeneous Environment', published in German in 1917 and 1927 respectively.

SCHWARTZ, Benjamin I., *Chinese Communism and the Rise of Mao* (Harvard University Press, 1951). The best account of the origin and development of Chinese Communism.

SCHWARZSCHILD, Leopold, *The Red Prussian* (1948). Contains some new material, but should be read with great caution as its central thesis is that Marx was a stupid man who was always wrong.

'SCIENCE AND SOCIETY', an American journal edited from New York. The number issued in 1948 on the occasion of the centenary of the publication of the *Communist Manifesto* (Vol. XII, No. 1) contains interesting articles on various aspects of Marxist theory.

SÉE, Henri, *Le Matérialisme historique et l'interprétation économique de l'histoire* (Paris, 1927). A good essay by the author of the standard works on French seventeenth- and eighteenth-century political thought.

SELIGMAN, E. R. A., *The Economic Interpretation of History* 1902). One of the earliest attempts to deal with this problem. The approach is sympathetic but critical.

SELSAM, Howard, *Socialism and Ethics* (New York, 1943; London, 1947). The most complete Marxist study of this subject.

Handbook of Philosophy (New York, 1949). A dictionary of philosophical terms, and of interest as indicating the sense in which Marxists use them.

SELZNICK, P., *The Organizational Weapon* (New York, 1952). A study of communist objectives and of the means used to attain them.

SPRIGGE, C. J. S., *Karl Marx* (1938). An excellent quite short biography.

STALIN, J., *Leninism* (Eng. trans. 1940).

   Dialectical and Historical Materialism (1938);

   Foundations of Leninism (1924), 'Little Stalin Library'. The last two are printed in *Leninism*. The second is the most authoritative short treatment of this subject, and represents an attempt to simplify Marx's doctrine by abandoning as far as possible its Hegelian terminology.

   History of the Communist Party of the Soviet Union (1938; Eng. trans. 1943). This most tendentious work, ascribed to Stalin, is the official version.

   Concerning Marxism in Linguistics (1950).

   Economic Problems of Socialism in the U.S.S.R. (1952).

STEWART, Niel, *Blanqui* (1939).

STRACHEY, John, *The Theory and Practice of Socialism* (1936). A valuable introduction to Marxist theory. There is a useful appendix which gives a brief account of the principal writings of Marx, Engels, Lenin, and Stalin.

SUMNER, B. H., *Survey of Russian History* (1944). This is a standard work, but is largely concerned with the general history of Russia, as its title indicates.

SWEEZY, Paul M., *The Theory of Capitalist Development* (New York, 1942; London, 1946). The most comprehensive study of Marxist political economy which has appeared in English. The subject is treated from the communist angle.

TALMON, J. L., *The Origins of Totalitarian Democracy* (1952). Of great interest as a study of the relation between Communism and the liberal movement of the eighteenth century.

   * *Political Messianism. The Romantic Phase* (1960).

THOMAS, Ivor, *The Socialist Tragedy* (1949). Argues that there is no essential difference between present-day Socialism and Communism, and that both seek to establish a State monopoly which must involve the ultimate destruction of democratic liberties.

THOMSON, David, *The Conspiracy of Babeuf* (1947).

TIMASHEFF, N. S., *Religion in Soviet Russia* (1943). The best recent account of the Soviet attitude towards religion and the Russian Church, of the various phases of persecution and of the present position of relative reconciliation.

TOWSTER, Julian, *Political Power in the U.S.S.R.: 1917–1947* (New York, 1948). The most complete study that has yet appeared in English on the theory and structure of government in the Soviet State.

TREADGOLD, Donald W., *Lenin and his Rivals* (1955). A study of the emergence of the major political parties in Russia in the early years of the present century.

TROTSKY, Leon, *The New Course* (1923; Eng. trans. New York, 1943).

History of the Russian Revolution (3 vols., 1932–3).

Third International after Lenin (New York, 1936).

Stalin's Falsification of History (1937).

The Revolution Betrayed (1937).

The Living Thoughts of Karl Marx (1940).

Their Morals and Ours (New York, 1942).

Stalin (1947).

Trotsky's selected works in 7 vols. were published in New York in 1936, edited by Max Schachtman. His outstanding book is *The History of the Russian Revolution*. For his indictment of Stalinism *see* particularly *The Revolution Betrayed* and *Stalin's Falsification of History*, to which his recently published *Stalin* adds little.

* TUCKER, Robert C., *Philosophy and Myth in Karl Marx* (Cambridge, 1961).

* ULAM, Adam B., *The Unfinished Revolution. An Essay on the Sources of Influence of Marxism and Communism* (New York, 1960).

VENABLE, Vernon, *Human Nature: The Marxian View* (1946). A scholarly account of the Marxist system written from the communist angle.

VENTURI, Franco, *Il populismo russo* (Turin, 1952). A masterly work, and indispensable to the student of early Russian Socialism.

* An English translation was published in 1960.

WALTER, Gérard, *Histoire du Parti Communiste Français* (Paris, 1948). The best available history of the French Communist Party.

WEBB, Sidney and Beatrice, *Soviet Communism* (1935; latest edition 1947). A comprehensive account of conditions of life within the Soviet Union, though it does not add to the authors' otherwise well-deserved reputation as social observers.

WETTER, Gustav A., *Der dialektische Materialismus* (Vienna, 1952). The most important contribution that has yet appeared to the study of the development of Marxist–Leninist philosophy in Russia.

* An English translation was published in 1959.

WILSON, Edmund, *To the Finland Station* (New York, 1940). A brilliant study of the nineteenth-century revolutionary movement carried up to Lenin's return to Russia in April 1917.

WOLFE, Bertram D., *Three Who Made a Revolution: Lenin, Trotsky, and Stalin* (New York, 1948). By far the most complete account that has yet appeared of Russian revolutionary policy up to 1914, and of the divisions which separated the various groups. An edition was published in this country in 1956.

YAROSLAVSKY, E., *History of Anarchism in Russia* (?1926). Useful as giving the official Bolshevik view.

Index

Some other Penguin books
are described on the
following pages

THE NEW COLD WAR
MOSCOW *v.* PEKIN

Edward Crankshaw

For several years a new Cold War has been simmering, almost unknown to the millions in both the West and East, between the two giants of the Communist world, Russia and China. Although most commentators until some two years ago were dismissing this new Cold War as a mere family squabble, Edward Crankshaw has been studying and writing about it since 1956.

In this Pelican he gives the first popular account of the conflict. He shows that the differences sprang initially from the differences between the Russian and Chinese revolutions – the one made by exiled intellectuals, the other by well-tried generals and administrators. He traces the first signs of open conflict to the famous 20th Party Congress of 1956, and goes on to give the inside story of the two critical conferences of world Communist Parties in Bucharest and Moscow in 1960.

What are the roots of the argument that is threatening to tear the Eastern bloc in two? Why does Albania mean China in Russian mouths, and Yugoslavia mean Russia when used by Chinese? And what is the likely outcome of this battle of giants? It is these questions that this book sets out to answer. The answers will affect the whole world over the next ten years, for even though Khrushchev has gone, the basic cause of the conflict remains.

This book, originally a Penguin Special, has now been brought up to date with a postscript by the author.

'A veritable *tour de force* of condensation' – *Daily Telegraph*

THE MAKING OF MODERN RUSSIA

Lionel Kochan

'This is a history of Russia from the earliest times up to the outbreak of the Second World War. However, in keeping with his choice of title, Mr Kochan has concentrated on the modern period, devoting about as many pages to the eighty years following the Emancipation of the Serfs in 1861 as to the preceding 800-odd years. . . . The result is a straightforward account of a complicated story. A successful balance has been held between such conflicting themes as foreign policy . . . foreign influences and native intellectual trends . . . His book could be a valuable introduction to the general reader in search of guidance . . . a commendable book' – *Sunday Times*

'He handles his material with skill and sympathy. I cannot think of a better short book for acquainting the general reader with the broad outlines of Russian history. I hope many will read it' – Edward Crankshaw in the *Observer*

'Gives proper weight to economic, geographical, and cultural, as well as political and military factors, and which, while giving long-term trends their place, manages very often to convey a sense of real events happening to real people' – Wright Miller in the *Guardian*

'It reads easily, it is the ideal book for the general reader' – *The Economist*